Reap a Destiny

Douglas Swinscow (photograph by Nicholas Toyne, 1988)

DOUGLAS SWINSCOW

Reap a Destiny

Divagations of a Taoist

The
MEMOIR
Club

ISBN 0 7279 0255 5

By the same author:

Statistics at Square One
Macrolichens of East Africa (with Professor H Krog)

Made and printed in Great Britain by
Cambridge University Press

Sow an act, reap a habit.
Sow a habit, reap a character.
Sow a character, reap a destiny. – *Motto inscribed on an old*
Devon jug

To Josephine

Contents

Preface

As my young grandson squeezes a bar of chocolate in his hands it becomes warm, twisted, knobbly, extruded, fragmented. In the pages below I have tried to depict the forces that have moulded me into the person I am. People have turned my thoughts this way or that. Some had high hopes of me, others despaired. But the story told here has a serious theme running through it, for I attempt to answer, if not directly at least by allusion, the question that has always haunted me most: how free is our choice? As I show the kind of person I was born to be, taught to be, and grew up to be, and depict some of the people whom circumstance or friendship cast me among, I hope the reader will recognise a glint here and there of the person I partly chose to be, and will be led to reflect on that mixture of chance and choice we call destiny.

Sudden illuminations have been important in my life. From the first of them that I remember, when I was 18 months old, to my last recorded reflection at the age of 70, I am conscious of sudden changes, psychological mutations, directing the course I have taken. In prospect they took me by surprise, in retrospect seemed inevitable. Both the dark and the light sides of the mountain have drawn my steps. At least two sides of every question have generally appealed to me. I have doubted certitude. So my beliefs instead of becoming settled remain to many people uncomfortably wayward. Like the alpine flowers in spring, life keeps breaking through the crust of snow.

ACKNOWLEDGMENTS

The editor of the *British Medical Journal*, Dr Stephen Lock, kindly invited me to write this autobiography and has allowed me to make use here, by quotation or paraphrase, of passages from several articles that I contributed to that journal. Mrs C Nisbet kindly put at my disposal the diaries (now in Cambridge University Library) of her late husband, my cousin Ulric. I am grateful to my wife for making helpful comments on the text, and to our daughter Katherine for typing the final draft and incorporating while doing so some skilled editing. Ms Ruth Holland, of the BMJ staff, combined discernment with tact in the expert advice she gave me.

I am indebted to the following publishers and agents for permission to reproduce extracts from the publications indicated: Cassell PLC (from Winston S Churchill, *The Second World War*, Vol 4, 1951). Faber and Faber Ltd (from T S Eliot, "East Coker" in *Four Quartets*, 1944; and from W H Auden, "In time of war", parts of sonnets XXI and XXVII, in Auden W H, Isherwood C, *Journey to a War*, 1939 (not as published in Mendelson E, ed, *W H Auden: Collected Poems*, "Sonnets from China", XVI and XVIII, 1976). William Heinemann Ltd and Yale University Press (from James Boswell in: Brady F, Pottle F A, eds, *Boswell in Search of a Wife*, 1957; and in Ryskamp C, Pottle F A, eds, *Boswell: The Ominous Years*, 1963). Martin, Secker and Warburg Ltd (Thomas Mann, *The Magic Mountain*, translated by H T Lowe-Porter, 1928). John Murray (Publishers) Ltd (from John Betjeman, "Hertfordshire", in Earl of Birkenhead, ed, *John Betjeman's Collected Poems*, 1958). Oxford University Press (from J E Lovelock, *Gaia: A New Look at Life on Earth*, 1979). Society of Authors (from James Joyce, *Finnegans Wake*, Faber and Faber, 1939). Unwin Hyman Ltd (from Arthur Waley, *The Way and its Power*, 1934). A P Watt Ltd on behalf of Michael B Yeats and Macmillan London Ltd (from W B Yeats, in Finneran R J, ed, *W B Yeats: The Poems*, 1983).

PART 1

1 Genes and shadows

In a cabinet beside me as I write are two glass goblets of fantastic design. Their tall, hollow stems support coloured bowls such as a fairy godmother might sip moselle from on a summer's afternoon. My mother won them as prizes for revolver shooting during the first world war, for she was a crack pistol shot and proud of it. At school she had been captain of hockey and something of a tomboy. "They used to call me the coal heaver" was one of her favourite recollections of her youth, to which she would sometimes add with a distant smile, "I should have been a boy." Yet despite a few masculine mannerisms she had an entirely feminine personality, with her soft features, pale and slightly freckled complexion and, when she was young, thick auburn hair that hung down below her waist.*

Born in 1889, she had parents who were strangely contrasted with each other, but it was her father who left his mark on her impulses and ultimately on a destiny that reflected both the obverse and reverse of his character. Dominating, energetic, peremptory, irascible, he directed his family this way and that, was impatient of opposition, and did as he pleased. He died before I was born, so that my only knowledge of him came from my mother, and not till I grew up did I learn to distinguish the facts of his life from the powerful emotions they had generated in her.

Percy Alleyne came of an old family of Norman origin who had received a baronetcy in the eighteenth century, when some of them were making fortunes from the sugar trade in

---

* Many years later she remarked to a 4-year-old friend of one of our daughters, "My hair was so long I could sit on it." To which the wondering girl replied, "What – instead of a chair?"

3

the West Indies, and I fear (with the conscience of a later age) they may not have been scrupulous in their employment of slaves. My grandfather served in the Indian Army for the first half of his life, I imagine without great military distinction, since he retired with the rank of captain, but he did see active service in South Africa during the Boer war and was mentioned in dispatches. Though always a hard rider and hard drinker, he was a keen explorer during the long leaves he was permitted from duty in India. He several times went on mapping expeditions – or just for the fun of travel in remote places – over the Himalayan passes and far into Tibet, though without reaching Lhasa. In contrast to family tradition he was probably not the first European to enter Tibet after the expulsion of the Jesuits in the seventeenth century (I raised this question in correspondence with the late Peter Fleming, the writer-explorer, who sought information on it), but he was certainly one of the earlier enthusiasts who went over the top there in the nineteenth century. His expeditions were on a small scale, sometimes only himself and some bearers, and undertaken as much for his own pleasure as for the more serious purpose of acquiring knowledge, so that, alas, he left only scrappy notebooks instead of thorough reports, and brought back a miscellany of cultural artefacts (now in the British Museum) instead of the well labelled collections which would have added so much to the record of a culture now crushed and desecrated by the march of dialectical materialism. Occasionally I am afraid he went too far in obtaining some article of special, even sacred, value to its possessor, and at least one expedition came to an end with his precipitate flight over ridges, through forests, down valleys till he breathlessly reached a haven in the Indian foothills.

My mother's mother, in contrast, had a placid, rather meek demeanour that overlay a nevertheless firm character. She was a first cousin of Douglas (Earl) Haig, of Bemersyde, and together with a handsome face and upright bearing resembled her countrymen in being patient, forthright, and conscientious. How she came to marry her husband is a mystery now buried for ever, so disparate were their temperaments. But this is a question that a glance around the circle of our acquaintance often prompts us to ask about the conjunctions to which our friends and relations yield in their passions. At any rate she stuck to him through a very trying relationship, outlived him by many years, and herself died after several years of invalidism from heart failure.

In middle life my grandfather retired from the Indian Army and took his family to live at Westenhanger Castle, in Kent, where he worked as secretary to the Folkestone race course. My mother enjoyed the rigours of life when she was a child at the castle, always cold and draughty despite its walls three feet thick, many of them crumbling. Servants were not keen on staying there and so were often "troublesome". But, much more to her liking, my mother loved to recall her conflicts with the rats, which were both numerous and importunate. Indeed she became adept at catching them with her bare hands.*

When her family went to Westenhanger my grandfather was still fairly well off, but, as has so often happened, by the time he died in his 60s the fortune had dwindled away sufficiently to cause anxiety to his widow and regret to his children. The last years were a sad decline through the vintage port and brandy that he so much enjoyed together with other delectable drinks on the side.

Of his three children the eldest was a girl christened with the remarkable name of Lilith, who according to early Jewish (but not Biblical) literature was the first wife of Adam before the creation of Eve, a legendary and even a demon lover. His second child, a son, was more conventionally named Victor. In outlook and temperament both these children took after their mother more than their father, leading quiet, un-obtrusive but worthy lives (Victor in the Royal Navy). When the time came to christen their third child, my mother, her parents sank into the comfortable bathos of Nellie, a diminutive of her mother's name Helen. As their later lives were to show, and the reader will discover in due course, the

---

* Later, when I was a boy at Torquay, she was always game to have a rat hunt when one was sighted in the pantry or kitchen, as they too often were, but then she had an Alsatian dog to help her.

names Lilith and Nellie would have been better conferred the other way round.

The Swinscow side of the family can be traced back to the eighteenth century through pedigrees written by hand in a religious book. The name is presumed to have originated in the Viking invasions of the tenth and eleventh centuries, as it is Old Norse for a "swine's wood," and a village with the variant spelling of Swinscoe was early established in what is now Staffordshire and once contained families of the same name. The first eighteenth century reference we have in the family records is the marriage of a Timothy Swinscow to the granddaughter of Bishop Weston of Exeter; her father was a Guards officer, and an uncle was tutor to Horace Walpole before he went to Eton. The record from there is continuous, but I must admit it lacks both the sparkle of historical celebrity and the notoriety of public gossip.

A perceptible decline socially seems to have marked the family since Timothy mingled with the Church and the Guards, for my father's father was a hatter in Bond Street, apparently both fashionable and successful but unquestionably in trade. He lived in style in Streatham (in a large house since used by a gas board for its offices), and was accustomed to drive up to Bond Street daily in his carriage, saluting as he approached his shop in mid-morning the numerous people of quality to whom he was a well known figure. But of course to salute a duke is not to be a duke. At the day's end he was therefore content to return to Streatham well remunerated but not publicly honoured. In this way he amassed a fortune, and when he died his widow and five children were left well off.

My father was born in 1868 and died aged 85 in 1954. He thus lived a span of years that covered the most stupendous technical advances man has ever known. Brought up in a world before the invention of the internal combustion engine, he lived to see the roads gradually fill with motor cars, the towns tremble and stink from the crush of passing lorries, the skies fill with aeroplanes, and finally to read of whole cities burnt up in atomic explosions. From the Maxim gun to the atom bomb, from the hot air balloon to the jet airliner, from leeches to penicillin, his world underwent a transformation unimaginable in prospect to all but visionaries, incomprehensible in retrospect to all but historians of science. In his youth he had been a good-looking man, with clear-cut features, blue eyes, a firm jaw, and fair wavy hair. Driving a pony and trap, and later one of the first steam cars, he had been quite a gay dog in society, popular with women and often dancing into the early hours of the morning. Boxing was a favourite sport, and he was also a sound billiards player. When Parliamentary elections came along, they were rip-roaring affairs in those days of large and boisterous public meetings when hecklers vied with supporters to make the most noise. In the public turmoil my father enjoyed playing the buccaneer. He and his friends, he told me, used to buy a sackful of crowns at the bank on polling day and spend them freely in the pubs buying drinks for possible supporters or even hand out the crowns themselves as bribes. Whether the consistent return of his favoured candidate over the years (a Tory) owed much to the bribes is doubtful, for I believe that equally effectual persuasion was being exerted by the friends of his opponent on what, we need to recall, was a much more restricted electorate than we have today. But when he spoke of those days it was the fun of the thing rather than the result that my father seemed to relish, and that was specially noticeable to me who in my own lifetime saw him only as a distant, dejected monolith on the horizon, on which a glint of sunlight shone too rarely.

Strangely enough, he had been regarded as too delicate to attend a school, so a succession of tutors saw to his education, which must have reached a high standard for at about the age of 20 he went into the brewing industry as a chemist. When he was in his 70s I came upon a nineteenth century textbook of brewing to which he had contributed a chapter on chemical techniques. The discovery of this book was a surprise to me, because he had never mentioned it or even let on that he knew anything about chemistry. But there may have been a special reason for this, for by that time he had long ceased to regard himself as a brewer.

After a few years he became director of the Cheltenham

Original Brewery, then the main employer in the town, and subsequently of various subsidiary breweries, including the Hereford Cider Factory, where glass-lined machinery was used for the first time in this country to make their particularly fine cider.

In 1893, that is, 24 years before I was born, an event took place that indirectly but decisively affected my whole life. At the age of 24 my father married Edith Keswick, a member of the well known Hong Kong banking family. Well off financially, pretty with wavy brown hair, charming and at ease with men, she won my father's entire devotion, was the perfect complement to him in the role he had now assumed of a country gentleman in Gloucestershire, and seemed to him the fulfilment of his youthful dreams. Two children were born – a boy, Alister, and a girl, Daphne.

Living in a beautiful sixteenth to seventeenth century Cotswold stone house at Minchinhampton called The Hermitage, this family must have seemed a paradigm of the Edwardian age, that is, of its prosperous, sunny side with its broad lawns and herbaceous borders, its proprietorial gardeners, and the servants coming and going contentedly and busily, polishing solid furniture, sweeping thick carpets, dusting gently chiming clocks.

Although my father was a sociable and pleasure-loving young man, there was another side to his nature. It was this other side that was turned entirely towards me from the earliest years that I can remember him as an individual, and I have struggled to pass through the looking glass in order to present the glimpses given above of his halcyon youth. By the time I knew him he was strikingly reserved, even secretive, about his real thoughts and feelings. He would always turn a serious question aside and in conversation would aspire positively and with conviction to the most neutral conclusion he could reach. An impermeably conventional outlook seemed to have given him a respect for banality that governed his every thought. Though this trait was obvious to me by the time I grew up, my belief that it was part of his character in the days of his youth, and not simply the result of the

8

disillusion of his later years, is based on its being present also in other members of my family, especially his eldest son Alister. Approach any subject however cautiously, as soon as it became serious my father would edge the conversation back to safe trivialities. But his exaltation of the commonplace would be so swiftly effected that it took the listener by surprise, as when a friendly hand is extended which, when grasped, is unexpectedly limp and cold.

Thus a moment came in 1910 when Edith, perhaps wearied by his reserve and a temperamental meanness over money – over the ordinary daily calls on his pocket as much as on greater expenditure – let her eyes fall with interest on a friend of my father's called Colonel Perkins. They fell in love, if that is the right phrase, and she departed with the colonel.

The blow shattered my father's peace of mind. He had every possession of Edith's cleared out of the house, every trace of her occupation swept away, every photograph of her destroyed – except one that survived among the belongings of their son Alister, and which I now have. Rather unusually for those days, he also promptly instituted proceedings for divorce. Several years later, when accompanied by Alister, he saw Colonel Perkins in the distance unexpectedly and said bitterly, "There is the man who ruined my life." Since Alister told me the story I have wondered whether my father made this remark before or after he married my mother, but I did not like to ask, and now death has borne the evidence away.

My father never spoke a word to me about his first wife, and my mother knew little about her, but I did learn from Alister, who kept in touch with her and the colonel, that Perkins was an outgoing, lively, self-confident man and great fun to meet – qualities which may well have outshone what my father had to offer even before this tragedy crushed so much life out of him. Certainly Edith and the colonel made a more successful marriage. It lasted till his death, and she subsequently married for the third time, winning the heart of a man much younger than herself.

Through all this turmoil my father was doing well in his

business at the Cheltenham and Hereford breweries and continuing to live in the Cotswold house.* My mother had meanwhile moved to Ilminster in Somerset and was doing war work in a hospital there. My father met her while she was there, proposed, and was accepted. They were married in 1915 in a church at Teignmouth in South Devon, where my father's mother was living in widowhood and where a parson had been found, after considerable search, who was willing to carry out the ceremony despite my father's having divorced his first wife.

My mother was 21 years younger than my father and, though possessed of a forceful spirit, had been brought up in a family where, as we have seen, her father commanded respect rather than won affection. She therefore tended to approach men in a mood of challenge under which lay a craving for love, while looking in the first place for someone whose qualities aroused her admiration rather than a warmer passion. My father seemed to supply the needs that had thus grown up in her. From his much greater age and experience of the world he offered her many fatherly qualities, together with some that her own father would have been all the better for possessing but notably lacked. For her new husband-father was fairly well off in contrast to her own relative poverty as a result of her father's having squandered his inheritance. Her new home seemed likely to be well ordered, frugally run though comfortably furnished, and the focus of the local society in which her husband had built an honorable position. She was as it were a daughter transported from one home to another with wider horizons, but a home containing for the first time a fatherly figure at whose steps her heart could beat faster for love rather than fear.

In my mother, with her relative youth and innocence of the world, my father may have seen a wife more malleable, less "flighty", and indeed more financially dependent on him than Edith had been, someone from whom he might expect,

* It had a secret priest's chamber up a stone stairway leading from inside the large fireplace in the hall, the chimney being turned to one side to accommodate it. Unfortunately, later owners destroyed this feature, and only traces of it are now left in a cupboard.

owing to the wide gap in their age, a more docile affection and, owing to her relative youth, a loving ardour such as Edith had long since translated to another's arms. At the same time, as a family friend who knew him well a few years later once told me ("He married her for her aristocratic connections"), he may have taken some pride in the thought that a cousin on her father's side was a baronet and on her mother's side was Sir Douglas Haig, as he then was, commanding great armies on the Western Front. Like most conventional people my father was something of a snob, not cruelly in conversation nor, as professionally ambitious people may be, in tracking down and associating with prominent people, but rather in his private assumptions about his place in Gloucestershire society and what he hoped would be the place of his family in it. In holding these aspirations he did not differ from a great many other people who aim at unobtrusive social advancement either in his day or in our own.

The marriage therefore got off to a good start, as marriages are wont to do, but with turbulence in the depths on both sides, for the shadows of my mother's father and of Edith fell across the wedding ceremony. As well as my father and mother, the church united these two shades. Though I never met either of them, they were present at my birth on 10 July 1917.*

* A question (*koan*) customarily put by a Zen master to a novice is as follows: "When your mind is not dwelling on good or evil, what was your original face before you were born?"

2 Illuminations

It has been observed in all ages, that the advantages of nature or of fortune have contributed very little to the promotion of happiness... – SAMUEL JOHNSON[1]

The search for a nurse to look after me had been completed, and at birth I was entrusted to the care of a West Indian nanny – "coal black and very kind," as my mother told me later. A single snapshot survives testifying to both qualities. She was the first of several nurses who cared for me over the years, and my mother, who never had the slightest trace of racial prejudice, used to say she liked the Barbadian the best. My father did not interfere with what he would have regarded as a matter entirely for his wife's decision.

As well as The Hermitage in which I was born my father at this time owned a larger and grander house down the hill nearer Nailsworth called Holcombe, on to which he had built a "full size" billiard room (the full size was always mentioned when it was spoken of). The house had beautiful grounds, with a fine beech avenue along the drive (cut down by the vandal who bought the house from him), and to light the front staircase there was a large window containing a cockerel in stained glass.*

Some months after I was born we moved down to Holcombe, and the sight of the stained glass window is the earliest sense impression to have been implanted in my memory. As we left the house when I was 18 months old, I can date the operation of my memory from that time. The stained glass took the form in my mind of a mass of bright

* The present owners kindly allowed me to see this house in 1987, when I found that the stained glass had been replaced by clear and the billiard room had been converted into a dwelling.

colour. Though I was far too young to understand then that it represented a cockerel, the vision remained an inchoate but nevertheless luminous certitude captured with wide-eyed wonder. When I was about 5 or 6 I spoke to my mother about it, and she then explained its exact nature. Despite my being unable to understand the pattern and so to "name" it, I retained a clear impression of it that is so far uneffaced. Or is it? There does seem to be continuity between the first imprinting of the colours on my mind and my recollection of them now nearly 70 years later, but since in the intervening years I have often called to mind the original scene I am uncertain of just what I recall when I think of it. Of this and several other early memories I am not sure whether I remember the original impression or recollect a later memory of that impression. For memories live, change, fade, revivify, and imperceptibly direct our steps throughout life.

But why should this gleaming cockerel have so impressed itself on my mind as to have a permanent niche there? For, in contrast, at about the age when the sight of it became embedded I fell down the same staircase and broke my left collar bone, yet I retain no trace of that tumble. The answer to this question is central to my life and is the reason I recall the episode for these pages now. We all of us tend to forget unpleasant incidents, so that the oblivion burying my broken bone is natural enough. But the stained-glass cockerel, even though no more than a gleam of unorganised colours to my uncomprehending mind, has with a half-conscious perception always been a symbol of lucid, glittering beauty at the heart of the universe. The bright colours, penetrated and illuminated by the sunlight outside, shone into the heart of my infant world and gave me the assurance, established there a lifelong perception, of glorious colour, harmony, happiness, infusing from a mysterious, still centre the greater world into which I grew up, with its strife and disappointments, its doubts, bewilderment, and eagerness.

In accordance with a common custom of the time, the names chosen for me at my christening were those of various relations. So I came to be called Thomas after my father's brother, Douglas after cousin Haig, and Victor after my mother's brother. The name by which my parents preferred to call me was my second name, Douglas; or would have been but for a slight complication. Celebrated as Douglas Haig was at that time as the commander of great armies, he was of necessity the originator of decisions that led a few to glory but many, in terrifying numbers, to death. He inspired awe perhaps but anxiety too, and in the minds of sensitive people even revulsion or detestation, if not in person at least through the office he held and the fateful orders that flowed from it. My mother herself felt a certain disquiet mingled with the admiration that was appropriate to our leading soldier, and at heart preferred another cousin, called Dougal, a gentle and brave man in a humbler station who had been killed the previous year on the Western Front. Consequently, she and so the rest of the family and then my intimate friends called me by this name which, though it sounds as though it might be a variant of Douglas, is in fact distinct and in no way derived from it.

Bearing through life these two Christian names (though only from courtesy so termed, for neither has much to do with the Christian religion), I have had to make a decision with everyone I meet who gets on to Christian names terms with me whether they should call me Dougal or Douglas. I have sometimes given a great deal of thought to this, because the difference expresses a degree of intimacy, rather as a French man or woman will be particular about "tutoyer", an Italian about when to drop the third person singular feminine, or a Scandinavian about the transition from surname to forename. This may seem a silly fuss about a triviality, but I cite the Continental parallels to show that it represents something deep in human nature and is in fact very widespread. In practice, it has usually been close friends and colleagues who have been favoured with Dougal and acquaintances, sometimes holding the status of acquaintance for many years, for whom Douglas has been reserved. But not always. When staying in a hotel in Chicago to take part in a conference, I had a name tab on my lapel to tell the members of the conference that I was Douglas Swinscow. Coming down to breakfast in the dining room I waited at a counter to collect a tray of food, and was delighted to be met there by a waitress who, after glancing at my name tab, uttered the cheerful greeting, "Hi, Doug, what can I get ya?"

When I was about 18 months old my father sold The Hermitage and Holcombe and we moved to Looe in Cornwall, leaving the beloved Barbadian in Gloucestershire. Meanwhile, with a second baby on the way, my mother developed appendicitis. This of course was at a time when, apart from the shortages that followed the war, anaesthesia and surgery were primitive by the standards of only 20 years later. To add to her anxieties, she was operated on under chloroform by a doctor who she always declared was drunk. She had little faith in him before the operation and less after it, for when she should have been blissfully unconscious of her surroundings she was distinctly aware of "coming round" and hearing the doctor say to the nurse, "My god! This woman is pregnant." Despite these disturbances, my brother was born when I was 20 months old, was christened Godfrey Alleyne, and remained for several years a rather sickly child. Nor was I altogether robust for, in addition to being born with a slightly deformed left foot, I developed rickets. What were fancied to be bulges in my forehead were attributed to this disease rather than to the shelter they gave to the great brain behind them.

Here at Looe the second of my early memories that were of so much significance to me had its origin. I had just had my second birthday and three of us – my parents and I – were in a rowing boat out in the bay fishing with a couple of lines over the side. In the calm water we drifted lazily along, and my mother, thinking to keep me interested, told me to hold her line for a time. After a few minutes I said I could feel a fish on it. She took it from me, tugged a little, felt no response, and said no, there was nothing there. I took it again and insisted, "Yes, there is." So my mother hauled the line in, and there sure enough was a very small fish on the end of it. It was far too small to eat: we detached it from the hook and threw it back again. But the parental gasps of pleasure at the skill of their son evoked in me a sense of infantile pride – and much more. I felt then incoherently, as later I came to feel mystifyingly, that I had wrested a secret from the depths, whether the depths of the world or myself I am not sure. Certainly what had been inapparent to the grown-ups was to me perceptible, alive, a messenger from somewhere beyond. Thus a world which, as I had learnt on the staircase, already contained beneath its commonplace surface a colourful treasure, would also respond to my exploration by showing me a secret life in its depths, a life that other people would first deny existed and then, as the reality became plain, accept with surprise. So are poems born.

After a year at Looe we moved to Torquay in south Devon, where the remainder of my boyhood was spent. The first of our two houses there has long since been converted into a hotel and the second into four "maisonettes". From the age of $2\frac{1}{2}$ to 6 I lived in that first house and learnt every detail of it so explicitly that on visiting it 50 years later I could describe to its owners how it looked in my day and explain to them the meaning of various alterations that had puzzled them. In front of the house lay a garden alongside which a fuchsia hedge six feet high bordered the drive. At the edge of the lawn was a line of dracaena trees (now called cordyline), lily-scented in summer when they came into flower, and at one side was a eucalyptus that flowered and fruited abundantly, producing its pungently scented top-shaped seed capsules to delight my inquisitive sense of smell. These were happy years for me.

My mother taught me to read and write when I was 4, mainly with the aid of that masterpiece *Reading Without Tears*,[2] which served in their turn for my children too. For some reason, when learning to write numbers I found the figure 8 difficult. I practised with my mother's help but without attaining the proficiency she, and hence I, expected in this simple task. So, knowing that I coveted a tea set of miniature cups, jug, and teapot I had seen in a toy shop, she offered to give me the set when I could write a presentable 8. This put me on my mettle, and in a short time I conceived a solution. When her back was turned I produced a series of 8s by drawing the lower half as a circle and then drawing the upper half as a circle on top of it. The beautiful line of figures that resulted pleased even though it puzzled my mother when she returned, but I had earned the tea set. So off we went, and she kept her side of the bargain.

The prominence of this event in my memory is not so surprising – since I suppose most people must remember learning to read and write – as the choice of that particular present, a dolls' tea set, for I enjoyed ordinary boyish pursuits and indeed later became something of a menace with an airgun. But one reason for my wanting it may be that, although my brother and I still lived in a nursery upstairs with nanny, we were normally brought downstairs for tea.

We had had several nannies since leaving Gloucestershire. One I particularly detested was called Miss Simm. She was only about 18 at the time, as I later learnt, and I can now quite understand that her frequently hitting me with the broken off edge of a tray was no more than an expression of a teenager's impatience with a wilful little boy. At the time it caused me some misery, and so I was pleased to detect hints in my parents' conversation that they were not satisfied with her, though on very different grounds from those presented by her conduct towards me. She powdered her face, even "painted" it, an error of social taste that set my parents slightly aghast. Furthermore, she "permed" her hair, something my mother held in especial contempt because she herself had never needed to resort to any artificial treatment of her thick, naturally wavy tresses. Matters came to a head when it was discovered that Miss Simm had engaged herself to act in the Christmas pantomime at the local theatre, in fact to dance in the front row of the chorus. The end followed swiftly. She departed to perdition. I smiled with relief.

Miss Simm's successor was called Kitty Bigwither; and what a wonderful contrast she was in her kindness to me. With a lean, muscular, energetic figure, a pretty face, brown frizzy hair, and a sporting, no-nonsense manner, she became my heroine for a year or so. But inevitably the day came when my mother decided to do without the help of a nanny. As she sometimes declared with a touch of drama in after years, "I cleared the nurses out and looked after you myself." Not in the least resenting the prospect of my mother's personal attention, I nevertheless wept many tears at the departure of my darling Kitty.

On looking back to those years I am surprised at how much freedom I was allowed to wander the streets when I was no more than 4. Violent crime such as we know in the 1980s must have been rare, and of course traffic was much sparser. One of my cherished toys was a simple trolley on which I could sit and propel myself forwards by hand levers connected to the rear wheels, while with my feet I steered by directing the front wheels this way or that. On this contraption I roamed along the pavements of the neighbouring roads. While so travelling one day I noticed an open door leading into a garden. On peering through it I saw a beautiful lawn with flower beds round its sides except at the far end, where one of Torquay's many cedars had its stately presence. While I was inspecting this peaceful scene, a grey-haired lady with thick spectacles came up to me and asked if I would like some cake. I accepted with a mixture of surprise, gratitude, and trepidation. In other words, I wondered slightly nervously what I was letting myself in for. In the garden we were joined by another elderly lady like the first, with grey hair and glasses. A maid brought tea out on to the lawn, and we sat round a table eating thin cucumber sandwiches and cake. A wooden monkey with a long tail that curved under him and contained a counterweight at its tip perched on a branch of the cedar tree, so that at a touch he could be made to swing for a while on it. When I got home and told my parents about my visit, they were surprised at my temerity and in due course called on my hostesses to find out more about them. They proved to be sisters called the Misses Webb, and thus began a friendship between them and me which led to my receiving invitations from them over the next year or so to have tea in the garden or the house. They were the first friends I ever made outside the family circle.

In these happy years, marred only temporarily by the harshness of Miss Simm, a third illumination joined the glittering window and the captured fish in my imagination. When I was aged about 4 I procured a bowl of warm water from the kitchen together with a piece of soap. These I carried into the garden and set down on the lawn. Then in the warmth of a sunny afternoon I squeezed the soap through my hands in the water, dissolving more and more of it till the water became first cloudy, then opaque, and finally completely permeated with the soap. The thought filled my mind that I was in the act of creating soap, that by working it through my hands and so putting into it part of my spirit, I should actually produce more soap than I had brought out on to the lawn. In these words of course I am interpreting a creative act that then seemed to me instinctive, inexpressible. But the desire to make something more out of something less was clearly felt in my ruminations over the bowl of water and the soap. This was another of those moments of revelation, unexpected, unprepared for, flooding my being yet incomprehensible, still locked there so many years later in the depths, a song without words.*

When I was 6, in 1923, we moved to a larger house up on one of the hills, with an attractive glimpse down into the bay and at the end of the road a view of Dartmoor in the distance.

Torquay in the 1920s was a town of much greater contrasts than might have been expected. We lived in a fine house with two and sometimes three domestic servants. The garden surrounding it was about an acre in extent and presided over by a wholetime gardener, Hext (an old Devon name), a man in his 30s whom we took on with the garden when we moved into the house. Though no scholar, he had received some training at Suttons, the seed firm, and was a wonderful horticulturist, filling the conservatory with flowers summer and winter and bringing to the kitchen perfectly grown salads and vegetables. His skill with cucumbers grown in outdoor frames on beds of manure was unsurpassed. Often I would go up the garden and make a nuisance of myself in his greenhouses and potting shed, the delicious fresh smell of which lingers with me still. Over considerable areas too the

* And I have since come to see that this combination of a mystical sense of creation with elementary chemistry was an alchemical experience.

garden provided those wild shrubberies that boys love to roam and hide in, and a variety of trees in them gave my brother and me practice in climbing their tolerant boughs.

Alongside us in the neighbouring roads were equally fine houses and gardens, mostly dating from the middle of the nineteenth century before the design of even good houses degenerated into the urban and suburban meanness we saw everywhere later. But immediately below us on the hill were streets where exceedingly poor people lived, where the children, though shod, had ragged clothes, and the houses shared or in some cases lacked primitive sanitation. Most of the poorer people in Torquay did in fact have better houses than these, but it so happened that we lived alongside the worst of the slums.

Because of the wild children who lived in these streets and played enviably riotous games there, my brother and I were forbidden to enter them alone when we were young for fear that we might be set upon – and perhaps with good reason. For one day when I was 7 I was out riding my "fairy cycle" near our house when a gang of boys from down the hill formed a line across the road ahead of me with the idea no doubt of pushing me off my cycle. But fortunately for me, as they became increasingly threatening at my approach and eager to make a capture, I was able to ride straight on at them and then a few yards short of their line wheel smartly to the left into the drive of our house. This sportive attack was a rare event, though, and my main feeling for the boys living in their different world and driving their hoops along the street or playing hopscotch was that I was missing exciting diversions in a less restricted world than the one I inhabited. They seemed to me then, and probably were, even less supervised by adults than I was and, just as important, to enjoy the company of numerous friends like themselves, whereas in the large houses spread out over the hills, many with elderly occupants, few children of my age were available to be friendly with except through rather formal expeditions to tea parties or evening parties, which to a shy boy like me were rather daunting.

A surprising number of the occupants of Torquay's large

houses were retired, even at quite a young age, or did little or no work without having entered a status they could call retirement. My father himself was in this category, since his job as director of the breweries at Cheltenham and Hereford required only a two-day visit to Cheltenham once a month (and in the 1930s even less frequently). He had long ceased to regard himself at least publicly as a brewer. In the parlance of a later age I suppose he would have been a "company director", had not this term already begun its downhill slide on to the lips of every confidence trickster describing his occupation to the judge who finally hears his story. So in the 1920s, as indeed for the rest of his life, my father when required to record his occupation on any kind of document would always inscribe the word "gentleman". I have no doubt that almost everyone else we knew did the same. Just as there were gentlemen and players on the cricket field, so there were gentlemen and workers in the office.

A minority did not need to announce themselves as gentlemen because they were manifestly so by virtue of a title of some kind – Sir Jonathan Smith, Admiral Robinson (our neighbour), Dr Stabb (his actual name), or Captain Jones. But the last needed further investigation before one could be certain where this captaincy came from, for of course an army captain was nothing much, perhaps merely the title retained by a "temporary gent" from the first world war, whereas a naval captain was someone of consequence, especially in a county that retained strong links with both the Royal and Merchant Navies. Nor could a doctor necessarily expect all doors to open to him, for his species ranged in social standing from our own Dr Stabb with his education at St Thomas's Hospital, his silver hair, gently whiskered ears, grey Homburg hat, and Rolls-Royce, to scarcely known and certainly unacknowledged doctors who dressed in casual fashion, drove in open Morrises, and practised behind green windows that looked more like shop fronts. That they too were generally doing a fine job caring for the sick I did not learn to appreciate till much later.

Apart from the doctors, who led busy and responsible lives, most of the circle in which we moved – "circle" rather than friends, for my parents made few friends – were energetic but idle, unoccupied but competitive, and so spent many an hour on a tennis or badminton court, a golf course, or, in their spare time from these exertions, trying to outwit each other through clouds of cigarette smoke at the bridge table. Sailing and sea fishing were of course popular pastimes too, but not among my parents' acquaintance, except for one disastrous episode to be recounted later.

Catering for the sporting needs of the town were a tennis club, two golf courses, and several bridge clubs in addition to a variety of public courts on which my parents would not normally have set foot. My father was not really a sporting person at all, though he enjoyed a quiet game of tennis or golf, but for my mother any kind of sport, the more competitive the better, had always been an absorbing occupation, demanding priority among the choices open to her and entire concentration in its performance. If luck went against her, as when a ball just toppled over the net at tennis or the cards gave her a succession of poor hands at bridge, she would complain bitterly about the unfairness of her fate for some hours.

As well as the clubs which my parents frequented and where they would often take me from the age of 8 or so to play golf or tennis, another institution catered for the town's society, and that was Bobby's restaurant on the Strand (now no more). In mid-morning we used to go upstairs for "elevenses," which usually consisted of that favourite eighteenth century drink, hot chocolate. Sitting on wicker chairs round glass topped tables, my parents would enjoy a chat with acquaintances at nearby tables, my brother and I would lap away at the chocolate (cream-covered), and somebody would be nodding in time to the orchestra on its dais – piano, violin, and cello – playing the popular tunes of the day. Often my mother would send me up to the players to request a tune: "Smoke gets in your eyes" was one of her favourites in the 1930s, and I would march to and fro self-consciously between the tables.

But shadows from the past had already begun to fall across these sunny lawns of my youth. I was about 7 when I realised that my parents often quarrelled over things I knew little or nothing about. I would go into the drawing room or study and see them disputing with each other, my father probably seated and my mother standing, and hear them quieten down at least in the early years of their dissension to spare either my feelings or the exposure of their embarrassment. Or hearing them in the distance I would creep along a corridor, sit on the top stair of the staircase, and listen to their disputes with a lump in my throat and tears welling into my eyes. For I was a sensitive boy and readily dissolved into tears when cross words passed between them.

Sitting at his desk looking out of the window, his features bitterly impassive against my mother's more articulate complaints, my father would briefly contradict her assertions. Sometimes the cause of the quarrel was money, for my mother had little of her own and my father was too cautious to spend any without a great deal of carefully balanced thought, which usually came down against any expenditure. Though I have described him above as mean – certainly my mother often so described him to me – he was so not from pleasure at causing discomfiture by this trait, and not from Calvinistic satisfaction in denying a pleasure to others that he felt no need to enjoy himself. Rather, extreme caution was a feature of his character, pervading every judgment he made. Moreover, an equally compelling cause of his avoiding as much expenditure as he could was probably by now beginning to influence him. Having greatly reduced the work he did at the brewery and become a director who lived 150 miles away, he was earning much less than he used to do. At this time he must still have had fairly ample means inherited from his father, but only 10 years later he was complaining he had to spend capital to maintain the family. As was customary in those days, he did not discuss financial details with my mother (and consequently I got to hear nothing of them), so she attributed his reluctance to spend anything to a defect in his regard for her and his sons, though it may have stemmed partly from a necessary financial prudence. But overlying all this was a coldness that had entered his second marriage and left him a prey once again to the memory of his first wife's defection, with its deadening of his capacity to love and its undermining of his self-esteem.

His age too must by now have begun to seem a disadvantage to my father in making contact with his two young sons. When I was 7, for instance, and my brother 5, our father was in his mid-50s and had already brought up one family. We boys must have seemed rather a tiresome distraction to his later years. In addition, therefore, to playing hardly any part in our games and hobbies, he appeared to stand wholly on the sidelines of our education. It was our mother who kicked a ball about on the lawn with my brother and me, taught us how to do everything, and fetched us from school if we did not come home by tram.

A year or two earlier my mother had horrified my father by having her hair bobbed in the fashion of the day – the long, thick tresses he admired so much were cut off partly, as he no doubt recognised, as an assertion of independence from him. Just as Sarah, the first Duchess of Marlborough, cut off part of her hair to pique her husband, so my mother went off to the hairdresser, as she herself was glad to declare in later years, because she could not stand any longer being weighed down with useless hair which took too long to dress each day, hindered her from leading an active life, and (what she did not add but I suspect felt) specially appealed to her husband. There were better things to do in life than spend a lot of time on one's appearance, she would say. Also to emphasise her independence and to declare her allegiance to the masculine (rather than male) society she liked to frequent, she took to smoking. At first it was cigarettes, but in a few years she smoked nothing but small cigars which she bought by the hundred in drums, though she occasionally let herself go on more expensive ones in deliciously scented cedar wood boxes. Later in life she smoked a pipe, at first as an alternative to cigars but then exclusively.

The time now came too when, not content merely to enjoy, even to flaunt, the symbols of independence, she was able actually to establish her freedom decisively. She taught herself to drive. This excursion into man's domain was something my father could not willingly accept for, as well as being in itself unwomanly, he considered it greatly increased the hazards already to be met with on the roads owing to the notorious incompetence of the female sex at the wheel. Furthermore, it could only loosen the bonds of marriage, and therefore of society itself, because women would be going off without a man at their side – or the wrong one. And this is just what happened with my mother.

However, she first had to acquire a car of her own, and this she succeeded in accomplishing by using the family car to hire out her services to her friends and then to their friends, and so on. In a short time she had built up a large clientèle of people who would pay her to drive them out for shopping or for trips to the seaside further along the coast or up on to Dartmoor. With the fees thus earned, together with a dip into her small capital, she was able to buy a Baby Austin for herself and so devote her time more specifically to her clients' convenience.

Driving in those days was a more adventurous pastime than it is now; tyres readily became punctured, especially by thorny hedge clippings in autumn; gears, clutches, brakes – all failed with unexpected certainty, demanding from the driver the exercise of skills unknown today if accidents were to be avoided on the steep hills of Torquay, let alone Dartmoor, where I often saw cars stuck on a steep road with a boulder behind one of the rear wheels and steam pouring from the radiator. My mother several times had to change a wheel herself when out with a passenger. On another occasion she got into a narrow track near Fingle Bridge and had to reverse down its bed of pebbles (it is still unsurfaced today, thank goodness). And yet again, one day she got the car jammed in gear and placed crosswise over a lane near Lifton, a position from which she finally extricated it without any assistance from outside. When other people drove at 30 miles per hour, she drove at 40. Her favourite sporting drive came in winter when high winds drove 60-foot waves over the front at Torquay. It has since been widened, so this game is doubtless less often possible. She would drive slowly along with us boys in the car and watch for the waves ahead to show signs of building up. When she saw a big one sweeping in from the bay she would accelerate along the front and just get by in time to hear it crashing on the road behind us. With her steady nerve and daring heart she was one of the best drivers I have ever known, safe, dependable, resourceful.

As I have said, my mother was an expert pistol shot. Somewhere in the house was an army revolver my half-brother had brought back from the war. One day it was missing. My mother stormed into the drawing room where my father was watering a plant and I was sitting reading. She accused him of having concealed it. He retorted angrily that he hadn't seen it. She brushed this aside, "You're not safe to have it." – "Nor are you." – "I believe you want to kill me." – "I wouldn't put it past you either." – And so on. Of course I was in tears over this altercation and left the room hurriedly, for it made me feel that my mother or father might actually shoot the other, that my world was on the brink of ending. Only in retrospect did I realise that what had come to an end after nine years of marriage was not my world but theirs, their love, their unison.

In 1926, when I was 9, the first of A A Milne's books on Winnie-the-Pooh, Piglet, Tigger, Christopher Robin, and the rest appeared and immediately captivated a large readership, among them my mother. In the school holidays (for I had now begun boarding school) she loved to read them to my brother and me, who, though we did not turn to them so much on our own, enjoyed her rendering of these innocent tales. She built up with us a whole fantasy world in which she herself had the role of Pooh, I was Christopher Robin, my brother was Piglet, and the part of Tigger was allotted to a recently acquired friend, Commander Stanley Cater, who had retired with a pension from the Royal Navy at the age of about 40 and lived in Torquay. He was a widower and had one son, slightly older than I was.

As the Pooh stories were read and reread and the adventures of the bouncy, energetic Tigger with the foolish yet sagacious Pooh were mulled over in the garden or on picnics, it gradually became apparent to me that Commander

Cater was a delightful companion, whether at the golf club or at Bobby's, was warm-hearted, amusing, adventurous, someone who liked doing the sort of things that we boys did, who had tales to tell of a wider world, who was popular and generous in the clubs. Nor was it long before I became aware he was not popular with my father. But to me he seemed to have so many of the qualities a boy admires – and which my father lacked – and indeed to have the warmth and cheerful friendliness a son desires and which my father seemed to conceal behind an unimpassioned mask, that I took to him as a kind of substitute father. Some sort of row broke out at the golf club to which we all belonged (I was of course only a very junior member at the age of 9), and the upshot was that my father resigned from that club and joined the other one. Thereafter my mother and Cater and we two boys often played a foursome while my father played with friends elsewhere. As I was not bad at the game and my brother was unusually skilled for his age, the two grown-ups quite enjoyed piloting us around. Whether to watch the rugger matches on Saturday afternoons in winter or to go on picnics in summer, my mother often invited Cater to come along too.

Quarrels over this friendship divided my father and mother ever more irrevocably. For all the rest of my boyhood the disputes and divisions caused me the most poignant anguish. With my father so apparently uninterested in me, yet in his way never unkind, so remote from the daily family affairs yet clearly enough its linchpin, I was in a perpetual quandary to know just what my feelings for him were. Since Cater was so pleasantly obtrusive and, as I came to appreciate much later, possessed great social charm in association with his thoroughly manly bearing, my affections were fastened often enough on the winning ways of our friend and at the same time came to be uncomfortably alienated from my uncommunicative father. What I did not understand at the time but grasped only many years later was that this was not simply an ordinary warm friendship between my mother and an entertaining companion who shared some of the tastes and inclinations that my father lacked. She was passionately in love with him and even (as I learnt some 60 years on) went so far as to rent a flat down in the town where she and Cater could meet. Emotionally, but uncomprehendingly, in all this I sided with my mother; but my mind was split between a mother who seemed to have all the care of bringing up her sons and a father who, as she no doubt only half-consciously presented the situation to me, should be contradicted on any matter of importance because of his lack of interest in the upbringing of the family.

Here again, but in a fresh permutation, the shadow of her own father fell across my mother's life. Like him Commander Cater was a travelled man who had seen many odd things; like her father's his personality was outgoing, energetic; both had a touch of the adventurer in them. In Cater, who was much closer to her in age than my father, she could enjoy the qualities that her own father had planted in her mind – but this time possessed by a man much better qualified by his age to be a lover and husband. The transition from her father to her husband had been along a road that at first seemed easy, because her husband being so much older and more experienced than she was seemed thereby akin to her father, but then as could only be expected the relationship disintegrated into a waste land. Now in Commander Cater the image of manhood that she had also derived from her father was reincarnated in desirable form.

One particular feature of Cater's life appealed to my mother. He was most unusual for that time in having entered the navy as a boy from a poor home and risen through the ranks to retire as a commander, not in some specialist branch such as signals or engineering, but in the executive class. While my mother, as was common in her generation, was inclined to assume that people were born to a "place" in the world, she delighted when a person's merit – provided it was not just trickery – enabled him (or her) to rise up the social scale. In fact, unlike snobs, she never judged a person by his social class but on what she conceived his character to be. She therefore took pride in Cater's rare achievement. My father, in contrast, regarded him as a bounder partly because he was an "upstart".

Despite my enjoyment of Cater's company, but because of my love for my mother and a still lingering regard for my father, I felt some unease about the relationship. To my anxious tread it seemed to present a slippery path. Of this I became sharply aware one winter. As Cater was an expert sailor and my mother enjoyed going out in the bay with him, they had jointly bought a small sailing boat called *Belinda*, and sometimes they took me out in her too. Often the deep blue of sky and sea and the houses glittering white round the bay present a picture such as appears on posters to attract visitors. But it is not always so. In winter, and sometimes at other seasons, violent storms may sweep across the bay, hurling great waves into the harbour and felling trees in the gardens. After a particularly violent gale in the winter following the acquisition of *Belinda*, my mother came into the drawing room one evening and told me sadly, "*Belinda* was smashed up in the storm last night". The boat had been moored in the outer harbour, but the protection there was insufficient. Only those in the inner harbour had been safe. My feeling, unexpressed, was that this particular cloud probably had a silver lining.

Several years later my mother, still devoted to Cater, remarked to me on her friendship with him and said something that perhaps was a surprising burden to put on a 14-year-old boy, as I then was: "Your father asked me if I would like a divorce to marry 'Tigger', but I refused for the sake of you boys".

At that age I began to lose weight, largely I believe from unhappiness, to which no doubt puberty added its stresses. From being well covered if never physically robust I became thin and "peaky" – a favourite epithet of my mother's – and I recall staring into a mirror with a worried expression to see whether any of my hair had turned grey from sorrow.

3 Self-division

As I have found in later years from reading other people's memoirs, I was far from being the only shy, sensitive boy who disliked school. I shall not weary the reader with memories that would seem as unbalanced for him to read about as they would be grievous for me to recall. But since they led on to my becoming a Taoist a few milestones, or perhaps flaming torches, on the dark road I traversed need to be delineated.

From the age of 6 till I was 9 I went to a local day school run by two spinster ladies, who taught me reading, writing and arithmetic on the foundations already laid by my mother. Travelling to and fro by tram, I would run upstairs to the top deck, open to the sky in those days, and enjoy the breeze on the wooden seats whose backs could be swung forward or backwards in accordance with the direction you wanted to face. Despite the storms at home, life was enjoyable at school. But at the age of 9 the time had come for me to go to a boarding school. My parents had chosen a preparatory school on Clifton Downs, Bristol, some 100 miles from Torquay. It was run by a bachelor, then aged about 60, while the domestic side was manged by his slightly older sister. My mother had bought all that I required for this new life – clothes, tuck box, sweets (especially Caley's Marching Chocolate, which was held not to be "sickly"), pens and pencils, and a smart pullover. My father had also specially marked the occasion by giving me a handsome pocket watch with a gun metal case, and my mother gave me a Bible.

Neither my father nor my mother ever made any spontaneous reference to religion in my hearing, though when I was much younger my mother had ocasionally taken me to church on a Sunday, mainly to show me what went on,

I think. It was a useful lesson against the time when I went to school. To my juvenile questions about God and Heaven and Hell she would reply in generalities that gave me the impression of something puzzling to the imagination, useful to society, comforting in sorrow, and trivial to her personally. Which of us indeed has done better?

Kicking a football around on my first evening at school after my mother had left me there at the beginning of the autumn term in 1926, I was struck by the bleakness of my new abode, with its bare wooden tables and benches, its unpapered, ink-stained walls, and its passages smelling of dust and disinfectant. The physical bareness of my boarding schools was a feature of them that I always found particularly dispiriting. At any rate when we assembled round the piano next day after breakfast to say the Lord's Prayer (which my mother had also taught me) and to sing a hymn, I felt nervous in these unfamiliar devotions but comforted by the sense of belonging to a community that was not entirely hostile. I came to recognise during that first term also that, just as life offers a pecking order in power, so it inflicts a pecking order in plight. One boy in particular was much worse off than I was because he was subject to nervous tics which made him the butt of our jokes and even of a cruel malice that sprang partly from fear of the strange and incomprehensible behaviour they generated, partly from our desire to remain one up. Now, as an adult and above all as a doctor, I am ashamed to admit we treated him badly, and at the end of the term he was removed to a more suitable school. It is a reflection on the primitive thought still prevalent in the 1920s that the staff did not seem to regard him as handicapped but rather to have some kind of "devil" in him.*

As the end of term approached and Christmas appeared on the horizon, one of the older boys, more experienced at relieving the boredom of school than I, inducted me into what must have been a favourite pastime of school children.

* At my second school (mention of which comes later) one of the boys had a congenital absence of one hand, only finger buds being present on a stump. I asked the headmaster (a clergyman) one day what could be the cause of this, and he said the boy's parents might have offended God in some way.

31

He had discovered that you could write to Gamage's shop in London and receive free of charge a wonderful catalogue filled with illustrations of toys, pets, household goods, anything the mind could conceive of or the heart desire. We both of us obtained the catalogue in this way, and I continued to do so for several years. (What a tragedy that that great store has now disappeared from Holborn and can no longer fill the hearts of exiles in boarding schools.) Naturally my little pocket money did not allow me to buy any of the goods displayed in the catalogue, but the dreams of what I might have bought were a good second best.

So I went home for my first holiday from boarding school. The excitement of Christmas and the comfort of being at home again gradually overbore the resolution with which I had learnt to survive in school life, so that when the time approached for my return I begged my mother not to send me. It was of course to no avail. I pleaded that I didn't seem to get on well with the other boys. She gave me some homely advice on adapting myself to their ways. So with reluctance I returned. Many years later she did tell me she regretted the choice of that school, but it had been recommended by someone. It is perhaps significant that when my brother's time came to go to a preparatory school she sent him as a day boy to an excellent one in Torquay.

An attempt to delay my return to school at the beginning of the following term took the form of a vomiting attack a day or so before the dreaded journey. It was not induced by any mechanical means but by sheer nerves – though again without avail. But later I was more successful. When I was 12 I managed to develop an illness which I realise in retrospect was entirely imaginary – though none the less real – and so delayed my return to school for an entire half term. It took the form of a persistent pain in my flanks, a sense of malaise, and headache. Our doctor diagnosed kidney disease, put me to bed, prescribed some medicine, and told my mother to get me Contrexeville water to drink. So crates of this delicious fizzy stuff came along, to be followed as I convalesced by a glass a day of Australian burgundy in round-bellied bottles. Cure, if such it was, supervened. I regained sufficient composure to prepare for a return to school for half a term.

Nowadays this illness might be called psychogenic perhaps. It was hardly plain malingering, though I think I was conscious at the time of playing up a bit, aware to some extent that mental distress was related in some way to a feeling of physical illness, even though such thoughts had only to enter my mind to be quickly rejected.

In the last year at that school another illumination came to me, when I was 13. A new mathematics master, Mr Clarke, joined the staff, and recognising that this was a subject I was keen on, he taught me a lot of trigonometry. Having won my attention and even devotion, he asked me to come along and have tea with him and his wife, both aged about 30 or a little under. Their home was a small house in another part of Bristol, warm from an open fire, lit with a pinkish orange glow in the autumn afternoon, cosily harmonious. Their exchanges were patient and natural, without strain or discord; their conversation with me was unaffected and kind, with each other unreserved and loving. The contrast with my own parents left me amazed. How could such a life be possible? It took me many years to find out.

Now that I was one of the senior boys at the school I was promoted to a small dormitory with three other boys, where on occasions we entered into a certain amount of rough and tumble, some of it of a vaguely sexual nature. But in fact this instinct, which in later life imbues us with almost every emotion from joy to despair, found little overt expression at school and was associated in my mind more with a sense of shame than of that natural innocence which anthropologists have observed in less sophisticated societies than ours. Consequently I was friendly but unresponsive when the headmaster took to inviting me to go down to his bedroom before I got up in the mornings to drink a cup of milk sitting on his knees in my pyjamas. For a week or so I thought the invitation sufficiently unusual to accept it. Thereafter a slight uneasiness about the relationship, and what other boys might say about it if it became a habit, led me to express at first reluctance to come along and then to default without explanation. The meetings were innocent of any but the most Platonic pleasure to the headmaster. To me they remain as the memory of a kindly old man, devoid of ill intent or ill effect, stretching out his hands to the embers before they finally cooled to ashes.

My parents had been in a quandary about which public school I should attend. My half-brother Alister had been to Charterhouse, but that was said to be "in the doldrums" when my turn came. So in the end they asked my prep school headmaster, and he recommended Kelly College, which lies a few miles to the west of Dartmoor and so was a relatively short distance from my home. I believe he regarded its small size – only 120 boarders and a few day boys – as being less likely to overwhelm my retiring nature than a large school might do. Whether he was right I find it impossible to say, for I would certainly have been a poor pupil at any school the kingdom could offer. My inner conflicts were often manifest above the surface in a diffidence that was apt to arouse, in anyone friendly enough to notice me, a combination of solicitude and impatience. This was not the stuff for a successful life at boarding school.

Founded by an Admiral Kelly in the middle of the nineteenth century, the school had not by then attained sufficient size to offer more than the minimum teaching facilities or attracted masters of broad enough culture to take the boys beyond the boundaries of the examination syllabus. Within those limits they were competent enough in my time, though with one exception: the teaching of mathematics was abysmally uninspired. The headmaster, the Reverend Norman Miller, was a bachelor in his early 40s whose favourite expression of displeasure was "pretty grim", so that he was often known simply as "Grim". Anything he deemed deserving of criticism, whether deportment, dress, conduct, or scholastic performance, he declared to be "pretty grim". In fact I think he found me pretty grim in the end. If so, the fault was entirely mine.*

Jesus has always seemed to me to have been a troublesome

* Some time after I left the school he resigned, became rector of a church in Bristol, married happily, and lived to be over 90.

and rebellious person, so that I was never able at school to reconcile this view of Him, which I had already formed, with the authoritative office that either the headmaster or another master who was also a parson exercised over us. The dual role of master in authority over us enforcing loyalty to the school ethos, and the Son of God upsetting authority was one that I used to puzzle over, as also I did over another duality, for, even if we repented of our sins, they could only bring us punishment from our masters – parsons though they were – yet from God we hoped that repentance would earn us forgiveness and reconciliation. Whether these clerical masters were saving our bodies from beastliness, our minds from indolence, or our souls from Hell, they presented a chivvying intention that, at least to me, seemed like a sheep dog tracking this way and that to drive the sheep, sometimes bewildered, sometimes recalcitrant, into the fold. Christianity was obscured from me for many years in these trampled fields.

Even so, the school chapel brought much colour into my life. This was partly because I went through a brief religious phase as puberty intensified my imagination, partly because I had a good enough voice before it broke to sing in the choir. Generally we sang the more boisterous, tuneful hymns that boys love to belt out, such as "Onward Christian soldiers", "O happy band of pilgrims", "All things bright and beautiful", and so on, as well as the melodious melancholy of "Lead kindly light", or "There is a green hill far away". So I missed a great deal when my voice finally gave way and refused to accommodate itself to a tenor or bass pitch.

To subdue our sexual instincts, a compulsory cold dip every morning – winter and summer – was merely the first each day of countermeasures that included PT exercises in the morning, games in the afternoon, and "prep" in the evening in association with what we boys generally regarded as a semi-starvation diet. Though the usual romantic friendships between boys were known, they were unobtrusive and rarely had any sexual expression. Stupefied by conformity, we were numbed emotionally, tired out physically, unawakened aesthetically, and steered firmly away from any kind of enthusiasm.

35

At the age of 16 I found myself discussing with my mother what sort of career I should aim at. In earlier days she had fancied me as an ambassador – "Dougal would do well in the diplomatic corps," she would say. Then she entertained the idea – and entertained is not too strong a word for the extent to which she let her fancy play on it – that I should be a barrister, though she realised that the private means I should need at the start of a career at the Bar would be so considerable as possibly to deny it to me. My complete unfitness for either of these professions may gradually have become clear to her, for my inability either to exercise the school's authority (I never became a prefect) or even to accept it (for I was unruly to the end) were part and parcel of a school record so undistinguished that any advice she received from the headmaster must have induced her to cast around for a profession less demanding of an authoritative and confident public presence.

The choice of medicine came naturally for several reasons. If one had to have an occupation, a "job" at all – and several members of my family were engaged in employment so tenuously defined that one could only ask just what they contributed to the advancement of society or themselves – a profession of some kind seemed suited to the sort of station in life my parents hoped I should occupy. Moreover, as a patient, my mother knew and on the whole liked doctors, for during my childhood she had, and continued to have, a series of illnesses. Yet so far from leaving her a hypochondriac the suffering and survival of her maladies gave her a sense of accomplishment, as though she had fought off the Furies and could laugh in their face. Likewise none of her friends was ever left in doubt about her sense of smell: she had none. Boasting of this defect, she would add that she did once get the smell of fresh air up her nose. It was when a cousin of hers drove her round Brooklands race track at 60 miles an hour before the first world war in the sidecar attached to his motorcycle.

When we consulted our Dr Stabb about the advisability of a medical career he warmly endorsed the idea, adding that of course I must train at St Thomas's (never "Tommy's" as

I have sometimes heard it miscalled). But so limited was the teaching at Kelly College in those days that not even in the sixth form, which I had now entered after matriculating, was any instruction given in biology, only further chemistry and physics.

My enthusiasm for biology had been aroused largely by reading *The Science of Life* by H G Wells, his son G P Wells, and Julian Huxley.[3] A year or so earlier I had asked for this fascinating work as a school prize, and I read it with deep attention.* So at the age of 16 I drifted through school for another year, bored with the inadequate teaching, disgruntled with the restricted life that was perforce mine, unhappy over the continuing dissension at home – an altogether unattractive and moody teenager, to use a term not yet born. My school reports were bad – "uncooperative", "a disruptive influence", "has not yet worked as he should", and so on. As the year wore on I agreed with the headmaster that it would be better for me (and I expect he added under his breath, for the school) if I were to leave at the end of the summer term when I should be just 17.

But, if my school days at Kelly lacked acclaim for me and lustre for the school, I did learn one lesson of deep and lifelong value. After I had been there a couple of terms I noticed that a boy in my form had a 1-inch-to-the-mile Ordnance Survey map of Dartmoor with the contours distinguished in shades of brown. He was a pious boy who had never had any other ambition than to follow his parson father into the Church. I coveted this map, and I was delighted to find in conversation with him that the Bible which my mother had given me for my school days had a special appeal for him owing to its coloured illustrations and clear type. (He could in fact recite large chunks of it already.) We therefore exchanged these treasures.

As the boys were encouraged to roam out for walks on Sunday afternoons and for the entire day on the whole holidays we were occasionally granted in the summer term, I

* When 40 years later I sat next to G P Wells at a dinner at University College London, I was able to thank him for having given me so much inspiration in youth, and he told me the book still continued to have a good sale.

took to finding my way over Dartmoor with the aid of this map, to which later I added a compass. In this way I acquired the art of travelling over desolate wastes, learnt to love the chatter and rustle of nature, and became self-reliant in the lonely moorland, unafraid of its dead sheep, quaking bogs, and rocky hillsides. Sometimes I would go out with one or two friends, sometimes alone (a practice discouraged by the school). On whole holidays I would walk and run 30 miles in the day, going into the heart of the moor perhaps on a visit to Cranmere Pool or some of the tors round there, enjoying the exertion, the open space, and the test of navigational skill. On shorter days out I might go up and sit by a stream on a hot summer's afternoon, drawing the fronds of the mountain fern through my fingers to release its fresh scent. The old stone rows, circles, and menhirs of the moor were marked on my map, and to find one and contemplate its magic was a special thrill as I wondered about the ancient people who had venerated them. The cushions of moss in damp hollows among the boulders, the ferns waving along the stream banks, and the gnarled oaks of Wistman's Wood or along the River Walkham lodged themselves in my imagination, and in the mist that sometimes descended suddenly on the moor they pointed like seers to my future destiny.

Always a keen photographer since the age of 10, when I began with a Box Brownie, I had by this time acquired a reflex camera which took either plates or films. One day I photographed a scene over Dartmoor in June by infrared light, developed and printed it, and sent the print off to the local paper, the *Torbay Herald and Express*. To my delight the editor accepted it. But I learnt something about life when I found that it did not appear till Christmas, when, given a page spread, it was displayed as a snow scene over Dartmoor, which the infrared effect made quite credible. Such was the first time I appeared in print.

My last night at school was characteristically unruly. In

time-honoured fashion I organised a midnight feast. With several other boys I laid up a stock of food in the photographic dark-room, which was in a separate building from where our dormitories lay. Careful planning had ensured that windows and doors were unlocked. Everything went smoothly to the scent of frying sausages till we were on the way back. As leader, I jumped out on to the terrace outside the dark-room first – almost on to the feet of a master on the prowl.

"What are you doing here, Swinscow?" he asked.

With what seemed to me at the time to be impudent aplomb in the moonlight I replied, "Just taking the air, sir."

It was an unfortunate end to my career. A stern rebuke and prognostications of a life of beggary if I did not mend my ways followed in the morning, but it was too late for authority to hold me now. Yet as my mother drove me away with my brother, who had by then also joined the school, I strangely enough, looking back at the receding buildings, felt a pang of sorrow pass through me at parting with an institution with which I had had such a controversial relationship.*

A year later, when I was just 18, my mother and I were in a Smith's bookshop at Epsom, Surrey, to which town our family had now moved to my regret, when I took from the shelf an anthology of English poetry. What, I asked my mother, did the word "anthology" mean; but she did not know any more than I did. Afterwards I wondered how I could have reached such an age and be so shamefully ignorant. And not only of anthologies but of poetry itself I knew nothing except a few patriotic verses and some set pieces for examinations. Of the incomparable, lifelong pleasure, of the complete transformation of my entire world that it was soon to begin giving me I still had no inkling. But as I stood in the shop turning over the pages, my eyes fell on

* The school had the last laugh. When it published after the war a list of the old boys who had received military decorations, my name was omitted (no doubt inadvertently).

a verse that seemed so discerning of my personal predicament
I bought the book on the spot. It was these well known lines
by Fulke Greville, Lord Brooke:

> Oh wearisome condition of Humanity!
> Born under one law, to another bound:
> Vainly begot, yet forbidden vanity;
> Created sick, commanded to be sound:
> What meaneth Nature by these diverse laws?
> Passion and Reason self-division cause...

4 Transformation

The afternoon sun shone down through the windows of the lecture room, adding its heat to the already oppressive air within. The backs of some 30 motionless students, pale in their shirtsleeves like rows of tombstones, partly shielded my gaze from the table on which the lecturer had placed some slices of human lung in formalin. Suddenly a question hung in the air like one of those coloured rattles mama holds in front of a baby to attract his attention.

"Who is that dreamy-looking boy on the back bench?" The words entered my wandering thoughts, drew them together, focused them on the speaker. My fellow students turned round to identify the culprit. Yes, good heavens, it is me he means!

"I'm Swinscow, sir."

"Well, tell me, young Swinscow, what do you think of the appearance of this lung?"

The lecturer was the beloved Joe Bamforth. Though as a pathologist his professional attention was directed mainly to dead tissues and organs, his skill as a diagnostician of disease in the living patient was legendary. A wonderful all-rounder, the kindness of his manner to student, colleague, or patient was more than ample compensation for his lack of Harley Street polish. And as a student engaged on a course of study leading to the London degree I was aware, as were others registered for the same degree, that we ourselves were regarded as a little lacking in polish. For, although the medical school was a teaching school of London University, many of its students came from Oxford and Cambridge after obtaining a BA or BSC there, so that at the beginning of our clinical training those of us who passed the second MB examination of London University were joined by an even larger number of students from the two older universities for us all to do the clinical course together. As our teachers were very largely Oxford or Cambridge men – they would not have been on the Thomas's staff otherwise – the students working for the London degree, despite its more exacting standards than those of Oxford and Cambridge (at least in those days) gradually came to realise that their status presented a small obstacle that must be added to the academic hurdles set by our examiners. As students we experienced little or no difference. But when we qualified, and staff appointments came to be considered, we would discover that preference passed imperceptibly into preferment. These old prejudices have long since died away, I believe.

When caught dreaming on the back bench I had been at St Thomas's for some two and a half years, having passed the second MB at the second attempt (I failed in physiology at the first because I did not do enough work for it), and before entering the medical school had spent a year at Borlands, well known in the 1930s as a crammer for the army. There I studied the biology (in addition to physics and chemistry) which Kelly College had been unable to teach me for the first MB examination.

At the end of my eighteenth year, when I passed in to St Thomas's, my family had moved to Epsom, in Surrey, a sad contrast to the broad landscapes of Devon as the change seemed to me, but the reasons for their going were, as I learnt little by little, as complex as they were compelling. Financially my father had been slightly overstretched for some years at Torquay. His investments had not done well, probably because he relied greatly on the advice of a stockbroker who, through no fault of his own, had been barred from practice on the Stock Exchange (he had been let down by colleagues). According to my father he was "the cleverest man in the City", but long experience has since taught me, a complete ignoramus on City business, that those stockbrokers, however clever, who will work for relatively small investors are much less reliable than my wife (at that time unknown to

42

my father or me) in forecasting future commercial and industrial trends. So the move to Epsom was partly an economy: my father could finance my student career more cheaply by enabling me to live at home while attending medical school. Moreover, during the previous year some old friends of ours had moved from Torquay to Epsom, mainly for business reasons, so that we should again enjoy their companionship on going there ourselves.

Here some complications enter the story. When I was aged about 8 and my brother 6, we met in the course of our wanderings around the roads near our home in Torquay some children of about our age who lived in a house 10 minutes' walk away. There were three of them – Mary, a year older than I, Eric, slightly younger, and Bobby, a bit younger still. We soon became fast friends; indeed we had no other friends among us, because children were sparse on those Torquay hills. Naturally our parents soon got to hear of this friendship, and the children then introduced their parents to one another.

The parents of our friends, Raymond and Anne Bussell, lived in a large house like our own with a pleasant garden and in addition a tennis court, on which were were allowed to play. Raymond had made a fortune trading in the Dutch East Indies, as they were then called, and his wife, whom he had met out there, was in fact Dutch. She had a sense of style that had a slightly Continental chic to it, black wavy hair parted in the middle, pretty, doll-like features, a charmingly hospitable manner, and a trace of foreign accent. Her husband was often in the Far East on business, and my father found her undemanding conversation as attractive as her always smartly dressed person. Both her company and her appearance flattered his self-esteem, and she was undoubtedly less abrasive than my mother often seemed to be. Nothing more than a warm friendship developed between my father and Anne; she merely gave him the opportunity for easygoing but stylish social intercourse, but at the same time the friendship gave my mother the opportunity to assert that my father was "dotty" on Anne, that he preferred Anne to herself, despite, or as she might have hinted, because Anne was "feather-brained", "a painted doll", "a silly chatter-box". In this way my mother could attach to my father some of the social reproach that she may have felt directed by their Torquay friends at her own tumultuous life, and could perhaps inject him with some of the sense of guilt that on occasion may have troubled her own heart. Meanwhile my father continued to enjoy what the world at large would have judged an innocent liaison and what anyone who knew the people concerned more intimately would have thought a very understandable diversion from a relationship with his wife that ranged from the numb to the quarrelsome. So when the Bussells moved to Epsom there was a sentimental as well as a financial reason for our family to follow them there.

Finally there was my mother. No change in our life and home of this magnitude could have been undertaken without her wish and indeed impulsion. In fact she was probably the prime mover. Her relationship with Commander Cater had followed a course so often taken by living organisms, whether in their individual lives, in their relations with each other, in their cities, their nations, their civilisations. Their friendship had a small beginning when they met at the golf club; it swiftly grew in intensity, demanded an ever greater frequency of meetings, multiplied the variety of their exchanges, reached a plateau of certitude and passion; from there it slowly began to subside, to float on a calmer sea under a less stormy sky, finally to break up on the rocks that the tumultuous incoming tide had formerly carried them over, and which now, as the tide ebbed and receded into the bay, left them stranded on some harsh realities in their lives. One of these was that neither my mother nor Cater had any money to speak of, and neither was qualified to earn any. So that when my mother told me, as I have related above, some four years before the time of which I now write, that she had declined for the sake of us boys my father's offer of a divorce, she doubtless had in mind the economic disaster that such a course would have been for us all. For where love fails to bind, money may succeed – as many families have found throughout the ages.

But actuated as she doubtless was by love of her sons and

anxiety about the financial foundations if she threw in her lot with Cater, my mother was also buoyed up by, if not exactly the hope (which would be almost indecent to pronounce), at least by the speculation that my father, now in his 60s, might yield to the erosion of time and in the foreseeable future come to the natural end of his life. This possibility was fermented in her mind by the prognostications of a variety of fortune-tellers she used to visit, often accompanied by an old family friend, Dorothy Clowes, occasionally by me. From crystal-gazing to reading the tea leaves, from dealing cards to palmistry, the techniques by which these seers forecast my mother's future were traditional but, as time proved, unreliable. My mother would consult one or other of them almost weekly at one time, and she usually made written notes of their forecasts. When I accompanied her I did likewise, and I have often thought of this note-taking with its prospect of verification in reality as my introduction to scientific method.

The fortune-tellers always had a, to me, surprisingly normal, everyday appearance despite their astonishing powers. They were all of them women, though the spiritualist mediums did include a few men also. We would be ushered into the parlour of a small terrace house, to find there a table on which the divination would be performed, together with two or three chairs set round it. On the table might be a crystal ball or a pack of cards. Often the curtains would be partly drawn across so that a calm, dusky seclusion would add its mystery to the proceedings. My mother had no objection to Dorothy's remaining with her during the session, or to my doing so if she had taken me along for a treat.

Naturally most of what these visionaries asserted with breathless fluency was of so general a character that verification could hardly be attempted. Some of it was clearly wrong or inapplicable. Yet just occasionally they said something that made the client pause. For instance a crystal-gazer told me one day that I should on no account leave the house on 18 December, which lay some two months ahead. When the day came I suddenly developed a heavy cold, and the weather turned so bad that to have ventured out in my condition would certainly have been foolish. So that was one up to them.

My mother also called in the aid of spiritualist mediums, either in a private seance or with other clients in a kind of church service. On one of these private visits she went with Dorothy to a male medium who professed to be in communication with the spirit of a medical man. The medium in his normal state seemed to be a man of limited education who spoke with a Devon accent, but when possessed by the spirit of the doctor he spoke with an accent that would not have disgraced St Thomas's Hospital and with a considerable knowledge of medicine, of which Dorothy could judge as she was by profession a nurse. On this occasion the medium went into a trance as usual and the doctor's spirit began to speak about my mother's life. Suddenly his utterance ceased and there was a strained silence. "Something is crossed in the room," he declared with foreboding. There was a pause. Dorothy uncrossed her legs. The seance proceeded normally, or perhaps para-normally is the word.

At last my mother came to realise that there could be no permanent relationship with Cater while her husband was alive, and he showed no signs of relinquishing a life that the fortune-tellers had hinted to her – or at least not dashed her hopes – would end in time to accommodate a fresh start with Cater. For his part Cater must have begun to take a similar view to my mother's. He was a widower on a pension who would like to marry again, but there seemed to be no immediate likelihood of that being possible. Between them they apparently decided that a parting would be best for both, not an irrevocable sundering of their relationship but at least some diminution of its immediacy, and with the prospect that, if my father died within a few years, as might be consonant with the age he had now attained, they would then come together again and marry. That my father must have had some notion of this plan is probable, for it would

46

indeed seem a natural contingency to provide for. In addition I recall that the substance of some of their quarrels at this time would take the form of his uttering the threat, "I shall cut you out of my will", or even "I've changed my will". Whether he did alter it then I shall never know; when he died nearly 20 years later he left everything to her.

And so, complaining that if she spent another winter in Torquay it would kill her, my mother organised the sale of the house there, the purchase of the new one, and the technicalities of the move. The death that she envisaged for herself was from rheumatism. The move itself was an unhappy event because the Torquay house proved to be surprisingly difficult to sell, and my father obtained a much smaller price for it than he had had reason to hope.

For several years after we were established at Epsom my mother went back to Torquay on short visits to stay with Cater and to visit other friends there. Her passion for him lived on, but his feeling for her cooled to a friendly warmth and finally yielded to a more prudent relationship elsewhere. He met, and in about 1939 married, the sister of one of the masters at Kelly College. They lived happily together for many years to come. Out of curiosity about my vanished youth I took the opportunity in 1960 of a meeting in Torquay that I was attending to ask an old family friend still living there to take me along to see them. "Yes, come along," she said, "let's go now, I often see them." So for half an hour I renewed my acquaintance with "Tigger" and met his wife. By then he was an old man in bed with bronchitis, and deaf, so that the only possible conversation was inadequate to give any expression to the curiosity, let alone the conflicting emotions, that I felt struggling within me, but his friendly benignity on seeing me – after the initial surprise – suggested that for him at least his marriage had brought a sweet oblivion to cover the old tumults. I never told my mother of this meeting.

The move from Devon, as I always think of it rather than the move to Surrey, took place in 1935. Four years before that, when I was 14, another stream had welled up in my life which, at first no more than a bubbling spring, later swelled to a river of such sweeping force as to transform not merely my developed attitudes but my whole personality.

One of my father's sisters had married a teak trader in Burma (or Burmah as it was then often spelt) called Hugh Nisbet, who published a chatty account of his life there under the title *Experiences of a Jungle-Wallah* by "Nibs".[4] He had three sons, who were thus my first cousins. The eldest of them, Ulric, just 20 years older than me, had gone straight out to the trenches on the Western Front from Marlborough School, been badly wounded at Vimy Ridge, and invalided from the army in 1916. When peace came in 1918, he had many advantages in the ensuing struggle to find employment in a postwar world. Tall, strikingly handsome, intelligent, educated at a good school where he had been captain of cricket, a brave soldier who had done his utmost for his country, he seemed to have a position in the world from which it was only necessary for him to project the lines straight into a successful future.

But despite these advantages he had, from the conventional view of what a man should achieve in his life, a fatal flaw that prevented him for ever from settling into a job commensurate with his ability and his family's expectations. He was an idealist, and an idealist of uncompromising rigour. Consequently a year at Cambridge after the war led to no qualification or recognisable attainment, employment in his father's firm in Burma seemed little better than sordid drudgery without the polo ponies he would have liked to own but could not afford, and a succession of jobs such as so many young men drifted into in the 1920s – going from door to door selling insurance policies or postal services or motorcar gaskets – left him disillusioned with the world's prospects and more firmly attached to his ideals, becoming condensed now on a still centre of eclectic mysticism. The effect of the war had been deeply disturbing – but idealism cannot be dismissed as merely a mental disturbance. To the emotional shock of warfare was added a cultural alienation from the rest of our family which at least to me, who shared it, was

48

sympathetically comprehensible. Though he remained on perfectly friendly terms with my parents, for example, they regarded him at this time as something of a failure, and "it's his own fault," they would add. He was "wasting his time on writing books nobody would read" – for he had begun to feel the quickening of an ambition to be a writer – and worst of all, he was "arty". The last defect in particular was held to have gnawed away the foundations on which his family and friends expected him to build a respectable and remunerative career.

It is hard for a reader at the present day to realise the intense hatred of the arts, especially the contemporary arts, that animated the professional and middle classes between the wars. While the remains of the landed aristocracy were largely indifferent to any art except that produced by artists who were safely dead, and the still large working class were understandably ignorant of something that played little part in the lives of most of them, the professional, industrial, and commercial middle classes – but of course there were exceptions – found a surprising amount of cheerful pleasure in sneering at anyone who expressed enthusiasm for contemporary art and were louder still in their contemptuous laughter at those people who tried to earn a living by producing paintings, sculpture, music, and poetry. Scorn of contemporary art was often the mainspring of jokes and cartoons, conversations over the Pimms Number 1, letters to the newspapers and press reviews, and led even to personal abuse when artists or their friends dared let themselves be caught at exhibitions.*

Despite a few pockets of resistance the scene has entirely changed today. Two influences have come to bear, I think, on public opinion and turned it round to giving, at least initially, a receptive response to all but deliberately offensive contemporary art. The first is the incorporation of different styles of twentieth century art in a degraded, easily assimilable form in advertisements. Cubism, surrealism, constructionism, abstract art – all have been put on parade to sell anything from cosmetics to railway journeys. The second influence on the

---

* As Osbert Sitwell amusingly recorded in *Left Hand Right Hand!*[5]

49

public mind is the enormous prices that rich people and so, of necessity, institutions are willing to pay for a picture with an authentic signature and an assured provenance. To hard-headed business men (as they like to think of themselves), who used in the past to sneer at the distortions in a painting by Picasso or the holes in a sculpture by Henry Moore, the prices the works of these artists now command in the market place are a guarantee of their pre-eminent worth. So that although the current prices for works of art seem alternately laughable and offensive, as does the trading in them by individuals and pension funds for investment, they have at least attracted to art in general the approbation of people who, in Wilde's words, know the cost of everything and the value of nothing. What goes up must go up higher has been a general rule in the art market, and it is one that any businessman can commend. From appreciating the cost of a thing to appreciating its aesthetic qualities is a transition that the auctioneer's gavel has knocked into the minds of many who once stopped to sneer and now pause to admire.

But that paragraph is by way of being in parenthesis. When my cousin Ulric was a young man stepping out into the 1920s, he had artistic yearnings but came from a background where art was no more than a patterned drain cover and literature was represented largely by a swelling tide of detective stories. My father, for instance, from the earliest time when I can remember this detail, namely, when he was about 55 and I was 7, read no books but detective novels, one being obtained every week from the local library – at Torquay the Carnegie Library, with an imposing portico beyond which were deft and helpful ladies. In his literary preferences my father was representative not merely of our family but of very many in Torquay. By contrast Ulric was discovering the world of the Elizabethan dramatists, for in addition to reading them in the ordinary way he spent some time cataloguing them in the Folger Library at Washington. Thus he laid the groundwork for a scholarly study he published some years later on the identity of Mr W H, the "onlie begetter" of Shakespeare's sonnets. At this time too, in the later 1920s, he visited Paris, and there he had the good fortune to meet an American woman artist who was studying painting, Christine Bacheler. She fulfilled his every dream, for as well as being a painter of mysterious power and a person of exquisite charm and tenderness she reciprocated his affections. They were married in 1929.

In 1932, now with a baby girl of 7 months, Ulric and Christine came over from America, where Ulric had been working for the bookseller Rosenbach,* to settle in England. Having no home they stayed with us in Torquay for a short while until Ulric took up a post, which he had obtained by correspondence while in New York, as caretaker of Compton Castle a few miles away. Owned by the Gilbert family (an ancestor was half-brother of Sir Walter Raleigh), the castle had some habitable rooms and some derelict. It gave them a roof over their heads, primitive cooking and living conditions, space for Christine to continue her painting, and an obligation to serve teas to members of the public who were allowed on certain days to visit the castle.†

Though Ulric was my father's, not my mother's, relation, it was she who really took to our visitors and made them feel at home, coming especially under the spell of Christine – as everyone did who met her. My father's attitude was that of a kindly, tolerant, courteous, and more or less indifferent host, not quite so warmly receptive, because in his view anyone who could not train for and find a "decent job" needed to mend his ways before he could be unreservedly accepted socially. My mother would not at all have dissented from this opinion, but her ever-generous heart encouraged her to help the lame ducks while her outspoken tongue would at the same time urge them to conduct themselves more competently. "Well, to be perfectly frank," she would say to

* Known as "Rosie" in the trade, he specialised in incunabula and Elizabethan books, committing the famous "Rape of York" between the wars when he persuaded York Minster to sell him a mass of treasures from its library. According to Ulric, Rosie would sometimes wander round his shop in New York, take down perhaps a Shakespeare Quarto from the shelves, gaze thoughtfully at the price on a note inside the cover, and with his gold propelling pencil add a nought to it.

† A visitor having tea there one afternoon looked askance at the meal Ulric had set before her and said, "Not very dainty, is it?"

Ulric, "I think you're too fussy"; or to me, "Quite candidly, when he was in Burma he just threw away his chances."

At any rate when my cousins were installed at the castle my mother would sometimes drive over to see them and in the school holidays take my brother and me with her. In the murky, stone-floored rooms of the more habitable parts of the castle I first saw Christine's paintings. They looked rather grotesque to me, deformed figures of men and women sitting, standing, or kneeling in angular disarray, sometimes twisted by the effort of their struggle with the elements or with some dissident spirit in their minds. My judgment of art had so far been moulded by my parents – at least by my mother, for my father did not express opinions on things like that – and she had brought me up to share her view that, as she used to say, "a beautiful picture is a picture of a beautiful scene." To this she might add, "Quite frankly, I think most modern art is just striving for ugliness"; and, "I can't see any point in distorting beautiful things."

Consequently, though my mother and I did take the trouble at least to look at Christine's paintings, and to acknowledge that they fell into the category of real though incomprehensible "art" rather than just amateur "daubing", as my mother put it, we neither of us leapt the fence of prejudice to explore, let alone to admire, what might lie beyond.

Owing to a tactless article written by a friend and published in the *Sunday Express* in December 1933, Ulric lost his post at the castle in a storm of accusation from its affronted owner. A variety of jobs followed, some of which Ulric relinquished at his own volition, some at his employer's. At the same time he was writing a novel.[6] They moved to a rented house in Reigate, Surrey, where he and Christine found that money was so desperately short that she travelled up to London to work on fashion catalogues. There she suffered the fate, pitiable and repellent for so imaginative an artist, of having to draw figures of women wearing the current fashions. She was at first amused to find that she was the only person in the workshop who could draw the whole figure acceptably: other workers were allotted faces, arms, hats, dresses, and so on according to their special talents. But her amusement changed to dismay when she found that the jealousies her talents stirred up among the staff were deemed to be so disruptive of harmony in the workshop that she was reluctantly dismissed. My mother gave them some financial help from her small means, and we sometimes went over to visit them.

Here for the first time I began to appreciate, as I was later to love and try keenly to understand, the mysterious world of Christine's paintings; but never perhaps wholly to penetrate their secret life, because although a feature of them is generally the setting of human figures in landscapes, almost every picture is elusively enigmatic. Sometimes calmly reflective, sometimes energetically striving, the men and women, often in the nude, seem to be working out a problem of their own, independently of anything the viewer may be thinking about them. Their gaze is preoccupied, whether with joy or with sorrow. Some of them look at us with tender concern, others with ironic understanding. Sometimes our world is of no interest to them: they show us theirs.

Falling under the spell of these paintings, and moved by the painter's dire need for financial and perhaps moral support, I bought first one and then a month or two later another, feeling that I was at last being able to obtain works of art that my newly awakened imagination responded to, and supposing with juvenile presumption that the trifling sums I could afford to spend would give some help to my struggling cousins.

Having taken lessons from a driving instructor and been brought up with my mother's excellent example on the roads, I passed the driving test and immediately acquired to my parents' dismay a very second-hand motorbike, a Triumph. On this (as it proved to be) dangerous machine I used often to ride over to Reigate in order to learn more about Christine's paintings. She has always been a lucid expositer of what she aims to achieve on any particular canvas, so that hearing her talk about them amounted to much more than an "explanation" of the picture: it was nothing less than an education in the appreciation of art.

Though dismally ignorant of literature at the age of 18, as the conversation with my mother in the Epsom bookshop betrayed, I was beginning to understand something about pictures, and I had for several years been under the spell of music, at first Bach and then Mozart and then, in striking contrast, Chopin, so that one of the strongest claims on my pocket money was gramophone records – the old "78s" of course – for which my parents generously gave me a cabinet gramophone at Christmas when I was 16. But now as I approached the age of 19 my imagination at last began to unfurl, and in 1936, by which time I was a student at St Thomas's, I went with a friend to the first Surrealist exhibition in London. I had of course gone with some idea of what to expect. Even so, that efflorescence of bizarre fantasy laced with satirical thrusts at our everyday lives filled me with a sense of joyful freedom that I had not till then imagined. With a stroke as decisive as grotesque it tore out of my mind the conventions with which I had previously looked at pictures and sculpture. Above all it showed me that there was a contemporary world where adults, in contrast to moody, puzzled teenagers like myself, were able to swim with élan into the depths of the sea and bring back the uncanny forms of life to be found there.

Belatedly now by many people's experience I began to explore with ardour the realm of literature, its peaks and valleys, its dark forests and glittering rivers – and French as well as English. By chance I picked up a second-hand copy of *Baudelaire and the Symbolists* by Peter Quennell,[7] and with excitement I was peering into another cave where jewels lay stacked or scattered all around. Improving my fragments of school French in which I had matriculated, I immersed myself eagerly in the poems of Baudelaire, Verlaine, Rimbaud, Laforgue, and many more. How inadequate my French seemed! So to discipline my learning of it afresh I made a written translation of Baudelaire's *Le Peintre de la Vie Moderne*, a long essay devoted mainly to the work, outlook, and character of Constantin Guys.[8] Baudelaire describes him as a man for whom "aucun aspect de la vie n'est *emoussé*" ("blunted" – his italics). To my agitated imagination, now pierced at every turn by the shafts of poetry and art, this phrase formed part of a sympathetic portrait that lay before my gaze among the Parisian publishers' books with deckle-edged leaves and paper covers, or with gilt-edged pages bound in buckram, that began to pile up on my table at home.

The lives of Baudelaire and Rimbaud had been the subject of excellent biographies by Enid Starkie, and it was after reading the second of these that I turned to reading, and indeed absorbed with amazement, that extraordinary poem written when Rimbaud was only 16, "Bateau Ivre", of which Dr Starkie wrote: "In this poem Rimbaud reached one of the highest peaks of his art, and produced also one of the great masterpieces of French poetry."[9] Just as the Surrealist Exhibition had swept away all the conventions, habits, and prejudices with which I had been looking at pictures, and furthermore gave me an entirely fresh vantage point from which to view life as well as art, so my immersion in the waters of this poem – and I read it over and over again for many days so as to extract every nuance from it – revealed to me a new concept not merely of the depths of my mind but of the wonder of poetry itself.

I was thus deeply preoccupied on that sunny afternoon when Joe Bamforth caught me dreaming in class.

In 1938 the Nisbets moved from Reigate to Salcombe in south Devon to take charge of a newly opened youth hostel there. The house where the hostel was established, then known as Sharpitor, later as Overbecks, had a beautiful but rather unkempt garden containing a variety of tender trees and shrubs and giving glimpses through them of the sea below and of the coast on the far side of the estuary. Here Ulric and Christine were to continue their avocations, he writing, she painting, while at the same time they provided for the needs of the youth hostellers. In the upshot the main burden fell on Christine, because for many months of the year hostellers would arrive, often without warning and in numbers that could not be guessed at, expect to have their healthy hunger satisfied with a large meal, and depart the next day after clearing up in somewhat desultory fashion. In consequence her health suffered, and at one time she actually sank into an attack of pneumonia, yet despite these afflictions she continued to paint and occasionally to sell a picture as people got to know of her work there.

The admiration that I felt increasingly for the visual arts, as I went to exhibitions in London and studied her paintings in Salcombe, was matched by the adoration I felt for her. After my mother, whose influence over me was inescapable even though I now resisted it and rejected it at every turn, Christine more than anyone moulded my responses to life and art, animated my emotions, and helped the chrysalis to split open so that I could cast off the husk, spread my wings, and fly away from home. In many ways these two women, my mother and Christine, who were to have a greater influence on me than anyone except subsequently my wife, were the converse of each other. Whereas my mother was plain-spoken, practical, impulsive, and opinionated, Christine was tactful and solicitous of other people's feelings, retiring in her bearing, allusive in her speech, unworldly yet discerning. Both had a keen intelligence, but while my mother tended to despise academic training Christine well knew its value. A criticism commonly on my mother's lips was, "He's clever in a rutty way" – that is, she admired people with a broad understanding of the world and scorned those who lived in an intellectual rut (as she conceived it) or had attained distinction as narrow specialists. In contrast Christine had appreciated the value of a thorough training in preparation for her life as a professional artist, not only serving apprenticeships in the Paris studios under recognised artists there, but attending a course in the history of art at Yale University, where she graduated in a single year, an achievement never since repeated and now I believe impossible.

Between Christine and me a deep understanding developed on the basis of, not exactly the intimacies of daily life, which were few, but rather of the aspirations that we had in common, so that from viewpoints set by circumstance far apart we were looking towards the same horizon. But she, being some 10 years older than I, and so at that age far more mature – an established artist, a married woman with a child – she led the way as guide and friend.

In this mood of devotion I went down from Epsom on my motorbike to stay at the Salcombe youth hostel in the spring of 1939. Travelling at 60 miles an hour over Salisbury Plain I suddenly felt the machine judder violently and had the presence of mind to declutch. The engine had seized up, not from lack of oil in the system but, as I was later told, owing to a fault in the engine's design. After letting it cool down I drove on at a slower pace (and soon got rid of that machine in part exchange for what was to my mind the king of all motorbikes in those days, not excluding the Brough Superior, namely, a Norton).

Arrived at Salcombe I indulged, though at a distance, my love for Christine, enjoyed lively conversation with Ulric on André Gide's novels, which we were then reading, and strolled in the garden to enjoy gazing down on the sea far below at the foot of the steep cliffs. Sometimes we would row down the estuary into the open sea for some fishing, sometimes walk round the neighbouring coastal paths.

One day in the course of this visit when I woke up in the morning I felt that a change was coming over me. It began some time in the previous day, and I had slept fitfully on its intimations. Now as a sunny morning encouraged me to go out into the garden a sense of harmony with nature permeated my whole being and filled me with unthinking, unseeing contentment. Though I was embarrassingly self-conscious as a young man, my "self" now seemed to dissolve away, vanish into nothing. For a whole day I remained remote, monosyllabic, unobtrusive, but infinitely happy, in a state of entire acceptance of everything around me. Walking among the magnolias and daffodils in the garden I felt all that bound me to everyday life fall away, the need for decisions, the urge towards achievement – all dropped into oblivion. An enor-

57

mous burden was taken from me, and I became dispersed into the trees, the sky, the far stretches of the sea. It seemed an ecstatic union.

Nor did it end as evening drew on, for I had felt the sweep of a universal wind through my mind, bearing away dead twigs and fallen leaves, clearing the ground of withered herbs, laying open to the sun new shoots already bursting through. It left me a changed person. From being contrary and over-critical I now welcomed unfamiliar ideas, became affirmative in my responses to the steps people took towards me, tolerant instead of censorious, receptive instead of opinionated, and perceived a harmony vibrating through the life of the universe where before I had been perplexed by its discord. These new-found virtues have not, unfortunately, consistently adorned my character, for I have often erred along the way as most of us do. Nor is one of the principal changes this illumination brought me altogether admirable, for learning to accept things as they are, to take with equanimity what life offers by chance, is not in itself a virtue. Though I may have gained the approbation of philosophers, I must surely have earned the scorn of statesmen. In my home I should be content, but in the wider world I should never govern.

During that 48 hours I had in some ways turned into my opposite, following thereby the way of Christine rather than the way of my mother. The impulses that must have been building up at the back of my mind over the previous two or three years I allowed, in this upheaval, to come to the fore and remould my personality. If I present this experience partly in psychological terms, that is the result of thinking about it over many years, pondering its antecedents and consequences, and comparing it in its details with religious revelations that I have since read about. That it had its origins in the way my mental development had taken I have tried to demonstrate, because an analysis of this kind must be rare in accounts published by people who are as relatively sane as my friends judge me to be; I have not seen one. But what I must emphasise is that to me its real significance cannot be explained in psychological terms, any more than the real significance, that is, the artistry, of *Kubla Khan* can be explained by scavenging among the many sources from which Coleridge obtained his imagery. The psychology gives the experience a certain kind of setting. But the meaning of it to me was the recognition of something sacred in the universe. In other words, just as the aesthetic quality of a picture, though it is an attribute of the pigments on the canvas, cannot be understood from a physicochemical analysis of them, so a spiritual quality in the universe is an attribute of it but not deducible from a rational study of its constituent parts. In contrast to many published accounts of mystical revelations or conversions – and my experience had both those aspects – the sense of harmony and liberation I attained had no religious context at all. It was the heart of nature with which mine semed to beat in harmony. Nor did it have any ethical imperatives: it did not make me more righteous in any way. Like everyone else I have had to puzzle over the great questions of right and wrong in a variety of engagements and to endure the knowledge of failure. But in the transformed state of that illumination I have always remained, even though nearly 50 years have passed since the star swelled into sudden brilliance over my path.

Tao never does,
Yet through it all things are done. – *Tao Te Ching*, Chapter 37

5 Cities of dreams

On Sunday 3 September 1939 I was at home listening to the wireless in the expectation of a declaration of war against Germany. It came with Chamberlain's announcement at 11 15 am. Like most of the people I knew I greeted it with a sense of relief.

It must seem astonishing that anyone could feel relief at the prospect of a catastrophe which we all knew heralded the devastation of our cities by bombing attacks and which followed closely on the first world war, with its multitude of personal tragedies still fresh in the memory of so many people. But what most of us felt was: the Nazis were determined on war whatever we did, Germany's invasion of Poland, whose integrity we had guaranteed, was an outrage against Europe intended as a challenge; at last we were sticking to our guns – such as they were – and were not again running away: after years of tremulous concession we had finally mustered the determination to see it through. Oddly enough, perhaps, it was the large body of middle opinion that felt like this, though it might be thought that the most patiently moderate views would have gathered there. But both the political left and right were opposed to our declaration of war. The left pronounced it to be a capitalist war, for the Soviet Union was now allied with Germany in a non-aggression pact. The right less vociferously but as insidiously regarded it as being a mistaken war, for the Germans in contrast to the effete French were held to be essentially like us. As later events were to show, both these views were startling errors. The German-Soviet pact simply paved the way for Germany to invade a too-confident Russia hardly believing in such a possibility despite warnings from the British government, while the similarity of the Germans to us became an increasingly unbelievable tenet as their brutality in occupied countries developed into genocide of the Jewish race.

From the occupation of the Rhineland in 1936 Germany had been presenting to Europe a challenge that had been daily growing in intensity, cohesion, certitude, and exhilaration, or so it seemed to many of my generation who thought about the matter at all. But our parents' generation, having suffered the horrors of the first world war so recently, were less inclined to admit the possibility of a second tragedy on that scale. Thus the resistance of this country to German expansion was consistently and for mainly laudable reasons ineffectual. And the legend had grown up, perhaps as a rationalisation of the emotional horror, that the first world war could have been avoided if only a little more wisdom had been summoned to the slippery slopes beforehand, a little more give and take been exercised, and more conciliatory diplomacy had governed relations between the European powers. This version of events was based on a confidence in the ultimate triumph of civilisation that the subsequent history of mankind shook severely, but in the 1930s it seemed plausible to many people. Historians have written their volumes on this turning point in European history, and politicians have drawn every possible conclusion from it. My object now is simply to present this scene as the background against which my friends and I grew up in those years.

When I was 16 (in 1933) the English master at Kelly set us the task of writing an essay on the view from our classroom window. The terrace and playing fields were visible and beyond them the wooded hills and the River Tavy. Below the terrace the school war memorial stood in the centre, a granite cross on its plinth. Here was my theme, it seemed to me, and so I wrote a jejune and sentimental piece on the war whose dead it commemorated, compounding sloppy ideas with pacifist benevolence. By this time I had become keenly aware that I was fairly closely related to, as indeed I was named after, Lord Haig, whom even his friends had come to regard as unimaginative to the point of being often mistaken in his generalship, while his more numerous critics declared him to have been heedlessly responsible for thousands of deaths that could have been avoided. This view was not of course current in my family (nor after all these years do I think it fair), but as a teenager I tended to differ from my family on most issues.

The vastness of the war's destruction had been brought home to me the previous year when I went on an exchange visit to France. My hosts at Doullens, near Amiens, drove me over to see the war cemeteries near Ypres and the trenches still preserved as a kind of museum at Vimy Ridge. The uncountable rows of tombstones and crosses, the names reduced to little more than a meaningless pattern at the Menin Gate, brought home to me in their myriad the loss of a whole civilisation. This fearful sight combined with my youthful contrariety to make me something of a pacifist, and many of my contemporaries at school as well as their elder brothers at university were turned in the same direction by the immediacy of the tragedy in their homes, the sorrowful acceptance of it by many of their elders, and the political failure to make any attempt that looked like being successful to prevent its repetition in our lifetime. Thus, at the worst, fear, ignorance, and youthful rebellion governed our opinions, at the best, idealism, faith in the future (under our control) of mankind, and the desire to create a new kind of world. Some young people, as in the notorious Oxford Union debate, declared they would not fight for King and Country.* Some, like the Cambridge spies, hating their parents or the society their parents represented, joined the cells of the Communist party, whose established tyranny in Russia offered a stability that the tyranny of National Socialism was threatening.† Others swelled the ranks of the Peace Pledge Union, and yet others, like me, too uneasy to do nothing yet

* Though it has often been said that in the upshot most of them did, in fact many prominent in the debate did not, for they found a better use of their talents during the war in the Ministry of Information.

† Winston Churchill made a vivid comment on their differences: "People say that the Nazi-Fascist and Communist systems are poles apart. So they are. But, if you went to the North or the South Pole, what would you find? A few more polar bears here, a few more penguins there. But in either place the same bleak, desolate landscape, swept by the bitter winds of death."[10]

too bewildered to do anything, worked out our ignorance in fruitless arguments.

In 1935, when I became 18, I looked through a window, admittedly a very small window, on to the European scene. I had become friendly with a fellow student at Borlands called Walter Merivale. He had come to Borlands from Westminster School because, like me, he had been unable to get any tuition in biology in the sixth form. Tall and of solid build, with thick fair hair, bushy eyebrows, and poor eyesight which necessitated his always wearing glasses, he had an extravagant manner that reflected a histrionic strain running through his family on his father's side, several members of it being professional actors. We became introduced soon after our arrival there when, during a practical chemistry session in the laboratory, the retort he was supposed to be heating over a Bunsen burner suddenly turned upside down.

"My dear sir," he said to me, "what the hell do I do with this sanious fluid?" – for the retort's contents were by now dripping on to the bench and from the bench to the floor.

"Keep it off your trousers," I suggested.

"Good god, did I come here to have my vital parts dissolved?" He glared round the room until salvation arrived on the scene in the person of the tutor, who got the experiment going again for him. Imagining that my few words of advice signified a greater knowledge of chemistry than he possessed, Walter asked me to take the whole experiment in hand when the tutor's back was turned and explain in simple language just what we were doing.

Westminster had taught him very little chemistry indeed, but to me it had always been the most fascinating of subjects, though I had failed to get the highest marks I expected in the school certificate examination because I was struck down by an attack of migraine in the practical. (It was an affliction I suffered throughout adolescence and till I was about 25, when it became rare and finally left me.) So it was with no great difficulty that I showed him when to mix this with that, when to boil, what to do with the distillate, and so on – all very strange to a man (though we were only 17) raised on the sport of Homer's gods and Horace's shepherds.

When the first MB was behind us at the end of the academic year Walter and I decided that some foreign travel would restore our depleted spirits, especially as with some discomfort it could be undertaken exceedingly cheaply. We therefore joined forces for a walking tour in the Black Forest through a scheme organised by Thomas Cook & Son, who provided a guide. The one allotted to us was a certain Herr Orssich, of Austrian origin.

As we strode along the paths among the pine trees or halted for a glass of moselle in mid-morning we needled him about the press reports of Nazi persecution of the Jews, then restricted to local murders and assaults, for the genocide to come was unimagined – inconceivable – in those days except no doubt in the plans of the people who had seized power. Orssich was a skilled apologist for the regime, which was presumably why he was permitted to guide young foreigners along its byways. Urbane, concerned, forthright, he could not have delivered his message more persuasively, even – and this did strike us both – chillingly. His message was simple, yet much needed – for "Europe is in a mess," he told us. Some nations were endowed (as history had shown) with superior qualities of leadership, among them Germany and Great Britain; others were decadent, notably France and Spain; yet others a danger to civilisation, pre-eminent among these being Russia. Others again could be brought into a civilised condition that they lacked at present, for instance Austria and Czechoslovakia – and that task would fall to the great civilising power of Germany.

Our first day's walk as it happened was rather a long one for a couple of unfit students, about 20 miles. After we had done 19 of them we came to a fork in the track. To the left, said Orssich, it was only 20 minutes to our destination, to the right an hour. Which would we like to take? Neither Walter nor I was willing to confess that all we wanted was to put our feet up, prick our blisters, and drain a glass of beer, so we said we would toss for it, heads to the left, tails to the right. It came down heads. Not till we reached the privacy of our room at the inn did we feel free to have a good laugh at the merciful relief to our weary legs that chance had allowed us.

To have let Britain down before Orssich by choosing the easy option would have been unthinkable.

At one small village where we stopped for the night a traditional brass band played in the square beneath lights hung in the trees while the villagers stood or sat around, the children yawned or played, and the lovers edged off into the shadows. At the end of the concert it played "God Save the King". Everyone stood bareheaded to pay respect to the King of the Englishmen in their midst. Walter and I were impressed, but not quite in the way Orssich would have relished. We realised of course that this was a routine welcome to British visitors, that Orssich had tipped off the players about our presence there that evening, and that their performance had been adapted to become an attractive shop window for a regime that wanted to show us a pleasing stretch of Bavarian life. What impressed us was the unassuming, natural manner in which we had been incorporated into this state-encouraged festivity. It was all so cleverly planned that there seemed to be no cleverness in it. But at that age Walter and I enjoyed a healthy streak of cynicism – a quality that is surely the seasoning of youth, the poison of age.

Despite his "Aryan" good looks and easy assurance Herr Orssich, pleasant companion that he was on our rambles from village to village, had too unconvincing a brief to advocate. Our newspapers had shown us pictures of Jews knocked into the gutter, of their windows smashed, and of blood congealing on the pavement – press photographs were slightly more restrained in those days than they later became – and we had begun to look along towards the horizons of German ambition just as the Germans themselves – though in a different manner – were being exhorted to do between the Sieg Heils.

The Germany that Walter and I saw on holiday impressed us as being altogether too stage-managed, a quality to which he with his dramatic temperament was sensitive. The contrast with what we had read about in the papers seemed slightly contrived, like a garden that has been cleaned up and trimmed for the day when visitors are expected. Yet, for all that, we had a delightful holiday in the fresh air filled with the scent of pine and spruce and warmed by the shafts of sunlight that glittered every day through the trees. As we could not speak German our impressions were superficial, though Walter did have a long conversation in Latin with a priest at a village church who made us feel his friends. Energetic walking during the day enabled us to drink wine in the morning and wine in the evening with impunity, more with hilarity, and by the time a few glasses of kirsch had been drunk as well the way back from some bar to our village inn was not always as clearly marked as it might have been.

As the boots stamped and the tanks rumbled in the succeeding years the pacifism of my schooldays made way for socialism; that is, I drifted into the middle-of-the-road majority of mainly unthinking, liberal-minded, ignorant citizens who believed (quite mistakenly) that it was only the left who were standing up to the dictators and, perhaps more truly, that it was only the left who promised a more equitable world in future. Few indeed had the prescience and will of Churchill and his adherents to see that the real political issue was not between left and right but between dictatorship and democracy, between, at a more personal level, bondage and freedom.

Yet, indecisive and fluctuant though my judgment of events certainly was, I retained sufficient sense to realise that the leftish-liberal opinions being hammered out all round me in the pubs of Soho and the columns of the *New Statesman*, though they might have some place in the building of a new world to which our youthful idealism committed us, were not going to stop Germany going to war or help us to win it when she did. Moreover there was an element of falsity, above all of expediency, in the well-meaning assertions of the left that was irreconcilable with the hopes of many young people then. It stemmed partly from Marxism. For just as in the 1980s we have become accustomed to hearing that truth is "relative" and goodness a "value judgment", so in the 1930s the liberal left came to regard liberty as a bourgeois illusion and loyalty as a matter of self-interest. Without being communists politically, many people accepted Marxism philosophically even, as has always been inexplicable to me, academic people in universities, who are supposed to have well trained minds. They wriggled this way and that round the central contradiction of Marxism – namely, that a philosophy which asserts the supremacy of our socio-economic status in determining our thought must itself be bound by the same restriction and therefore has no objective validity – wriggled, but never resolved it. They hoped it would pass unnoticed by the hoi polloi, and often enough it did in one of those compromises that convert philosophers into politicians.* But for me the truth lay in poetry, painting and music, in the freezing hands of a farmer delivering a cow of her calf before dawn, the backache of a mechanic stooping over his lathe as dusk falls, the breathlessness of an old man dipping his pot in the glaze at a Torquay pottery – not in political expediency.

> Then who would go
> Into dark Soho,
> And chatter with dank-hair'd critics,
> When he can stay
> For the new-mown hay
> And startle the dappled crickets?
> – KEATS. (In a letter to Haydon)

I thus earned the contempt of the serious left-wingers committed to a radical or revolutionary change of the social order. Their commitment seemed too closely akin to that uniquely human impulse to enjoy destruction for its own sake, ranging in its expression from defacing walls to defacing people; and their satisfaction seemed to derive more from a sense of betrayal than of creation.

From 1936 a frequent topic of conversation and dissent in families was the Spanish civil war, in which Germany, Italy, and Russia were all dabbling to the detriment of the Spanish people. Again among my contemporaries (I was then 19) opinion was polarised more by emotional adjuration than rational debate. Feelings were excited, and under the official British policy of non-intervention many people asked, Can't we do something? For the dictators were clearly flexing their

* For a neat pricking of the Marxist bubble see Bloom A.[11]

muscles in Spain in preparation for tougher battles. Mild-and-bitter spilt on to the stained mahogany of the Swiss Bar in Old Compton Street, an accordionist played in the Golden Lion, and wine flowed at the York Minster under Monsieur Berlemont, but the arguments often seemed as unconvincing as they were emphatic.

One day an old schoolfriend of mine, Gordon Hughes, who was not medical, suggested we should join an ambulance unit in Spain. The proposal seemed for a moment tempting, an adventure in what we conceived of as a good cause. But we both had the sense to turn it down. In my case acceptance would have led to unpredictable delay in my qualifying as a doctor, as my parents forcefully pointed out, and the growing unrest caused by German expansion made that a first priority. My friend Gordon was likewise spared for a more decisive destiny in the war against Germany, when he piloted reconnaissance Spitfires, was twice shot down but survived, and won the DSO and DFC and bar.

So I gradually slid into the belief that war was inevitable, not so much because Germany would ultimately make a demand that we should be bound by honour or for our own safety to resist – though that is in fact how war did come in the end – but rather because the Nazis wanted war at any price. They intended to provoke it in the knowledge that they would have the support of almost the whole German nation in the challenge it presented to what they considered to be their manhood and for the opportunity it offered for avenging the defeat of 1918.

In 1938 the Munich crisis brought us, in addition to a sense of shame at the betrayal of Czechoslovakia, an anti-aircraft gun placed in the middle of Westminster Bridge, where some of us walked out from St Thomas's to inspect it. Pointing to the sky in the direction of the Continent, in its solitary state and unimpressive size it might almost have been taken for the gnomon of a sundial. Still, it was a reminder. Thomas's polished up its plans in case of war, and a new sense of urgency drove us to our studies.

While statesmen alternately travelled and trembled in 1939

I was completing in June my midwifery course by attending labours under expert tuition at St James's Hospital, Balham. Owing to the disturbed state of Europe I particularly wanted to visit Paris before, as then seemed sadly possible, the frontiers closed for ever. The home country of the poets I so much admired, especially Baudelaire and Rimbaud, beckoned me across the Channel to the last dream of my youth. However, this one began with a bedroom farce.

Required to attend 20 deliveries in, if I remember rightly, two weeks, I took every fourth one in turn with my fellow students as it came, day or night. The deadline for my release was the evening two weeks hence. As labour succeeded labour at irregular intervals I was pleased to note that I was ahead of schedule, so that number 20 was completed a few hours before I was due to leave the hospital, and I was glad to think that I should have a short rest after changing and packing for the holiday. But now by an unforeseen chance a spate of women went into labour with the result that just before I was due to leave a 21st, a supererogatory, case called out my consultant tutor, and so I had to drop everything to attend that. For much of the night I was assisting the consultant until all was safely accomplished with the delivery of a healthy girl in the morning. Then followed a wild dash to Victoria Station, where I literally threw myself into the boat train just as it was blowing its whistle and was about to move off.

Arrived in Paris, I went first down to Lyons and took a small train up to Geneva for a day to see the paintings from the Prado, removed for safety from Madrid during the Spanish civil war. The vast wealth of Spanish painting is only fragmentarily represented outside that collection, so that to stand in front of wall after wall in the house where they were on display, to enter room after room, and see for the first time such glorious paintings by El Greco, Goya, Murillo, and so on was to gaze on a new, astounding range of European art. El Greco has always seemed to me to have a special love of yellow, and I was amazed above all by a large painting of St Peter with a small grey head at the top, small grey feet at the bottom, and the whole canvas in between covered with a billowing yellow robe, an intricate mass of greenish, bluish, greyish, yellowish yellows.

So back to Paris for a week, not in my imagination the real Paris, but Baudelaire's:

> Fourmillante cité, cité pleine de rêves,
> Où le spectre, en plein jour, raccroche le passant!

Exploring picture galleries, bookshops, and cafés, wandering through narrow streets or leaning over a parapet to watch the Seine flow by, I constructed in my imagination the city of my favourite poets. For lunch I used to buy a bag of cherries and eat them on a quiet seat in a park or simply by the Place de la Concorde. This was to economise so that I should have more to spend on books. Finally I had no money left, only my return tickets, and I had to walk across Paris to the Gard du Nord from my hotel in Montparnasse to catch the train for Boulogne.

Within a year all had gone – not the city blocks, the parapets, the old streets of Montmartre and Montparnasse, not the dark bookshops and the pert tables under the awnings, but the dream; not the French cities conquered by the German war machine but the French spirit eaten away at its core.

In June that year my first publication saw the light of day – a poem entitled "Renaissance Scene". It had been accepted by T S Eliot for the *New English Weekly*.*

* As Gibbon wrote[12] of his first published essay: "I have expatiated on the loss of my litterary maidenhead; a memorable area in the life of a student, when he ventures to reveal the measure of his mind. His hopes and fears are multiplied by the idea of self-importance, and he believes for a while, that the eyes of mankind are fixed on his person and performance". Now all I can ask half a century later is that anyone writing my obituary will record that my first publication was a poem.

6 A new figure

After qualifying in 1940 when I was 22 I needed to serve for six months in a hospital appointment before being eligible for military service. Now I learnt one of the hard lessons of life: not everyone wants us.

The St Helier Hospital, Carshalton, needed a house surgeon, so I applied for the job and was duly summoned for interview, my first experience of anything like this. A small committee put to me several questions of a routine nature about my student career, and then one member asked, "Have you any special interests in medicine?" For some reason this seemed to me to be a more difficult question to answer than my interlocutor probably intended. Having just qualified, I had a rather unformed view of the various branches of medicine, surgery, pathology, and so on that had come into my education, and being faced by a future that total war made uncertain, I visibly racked my brains. Finally I said that I was interested in the idea of medical diatheses, that is, constitutional susceptibility to particular diseases that seemed to be characteristic of some patients. It was a woolly and unconvincing reply. The committee could hardly conceal their private thoughts that I must be deficient in the harder virtues they were looking for, and I left the room aware that I had not given an entirely satisfactory impression of what I hoped was nevertheless a marketable skill. A letter two days later confirmed my fears and dashed my hopes. To be rejected for a post is a common disappointment, but the first time is the worst. For me it was the only time; perhaps others are not so lucky.

A week or so later I received a letter from a government department directing me to a post in a Yorkshire hospital which I had never heard of. It seemed remote from the heart of history at that time (though years later I came to love those rose-filled hedges and limestone hills of the West Riding). So I went up to St Thomas's to see what the secretary could offer me. He suggested I apply for the post of house surgeon just become vacant at the Woking Victoria Hospital, which was in the St Thomas's sector. Consequently I travelled over to Woking on the day appointed for interview and was sat on a bench in the corridor to await a summons from the committee. As I looked around, a man who was evidently a member of the committee – and in fact proved to be the secretary of the hospital – walked by in conversation with the matron.

"We're just going to interview an applicant for the post," I heard him saying; "he's got a funny sort of name – hope he'll be all right."

This time I was more sensible at the interview, gave an acceptable account of my medical interests, lived down the disadvantage of my name, and was offered the post. I took it with gratitude.

The consultant physicians and surgeons at the hospital, most of whom had higher qualifications, were also in general practice locally. I was the only resident house officer, attending to everything day and night in the busy casualty department and the wards, which then accommodated about 30 adults and a dozen children, though sometimes more had to be crammed in. One ward was left empty in reserve for air raid casualties, a wise precaution as time was to show.

Here my medical education began afresh, for almost any kind of case could come along or be sent to the hospital, and the nurses often knew what to do better than I did. Their instruction, together with what I learnt from the visiting consultants, was a crash course in clinical medicine round the clock, and I was often so tired that I dozed off in the armchair thoughtfully provided in my flat above the casualty department.

Nor was it only diagnosis and treatment that I learnt about. One day a woman of about 30 came into the casualty department with a wound across the bridge of her nose, the result of an air raid in London a few weeks previously. She required a renewal of the dressings on it. While I was attending to another patient she began to make a fuss to the nurse about being kept waiting, complaining that the disfigurement was more than enough to suffer without the neglect of the doctor being added to it. So I went over to her and said, "For goodness sake keep quiet – there are people being killed and wounded far worse than you everywhere." A harsh and impatient rebuke. She burst into floods of tears, sobbing about the loss of her good looks and that I didn't understand her plight. Remorse overcame me for speaking so hurtfully, and I tried to comfort her. But it was a lesson that sank deeply into me and a memory that has saddened me all my life.

A few weeks later a flight of German bombers flew in at 2 o'clock in the afternoon and hit the Vickers aircraft factory at Brooklands near by, causing many casualties. The bombers had got through without being detected in time for adequate warning to be given and pinpointed the factory by the old motor racing track despite its having been skilfully camouflaged. Within half an hour about 20 of these casualties reached the Woking hospital, and the surgeon on duty that week, William Smellie, having heard of the raid arrived at about the same time as the patients. Between us we sorted them into those requiring urgent treatment and those for whom treatment should be deferred. One man lying unconscious on a stretcher appeared to be a Negro. Only when we cut off his shirt and found his body to be white did we realise that his dark, frizzled hair, black face, thick lips, and broad nose were the result of the terrible burns he had suffered. His life seemed to be ebbing away, so we gave him morphine and set him on one side while we attended to other urgent cases.

Most of the injuries were burns, with some deep wounds in a few patients, some of them requiring abdominal operations. The patients were brought into the operating theatre one by one, treated, taken out to the ward, and put to bed. At about midnight I swayed unsteadily and sat on the floor just after Smellie had finished stitching up a patient's abdomen. A nurse brought a cup of tea, for I had had nothing to eat for 10 hours; I recovered, and we carried on till about 3 am.

At last we came to the patient we thought was dying. Life still flickered, so we treated him for the burns that covered about half of his body. He was fortunately completely unconscious of his condition. Visibly fighting every inch of the way over the next three months, he made a complete recovery, though he did later need skin grafts to his hands. A week after he was treated he was found wandering in the road outside the hospital one night in a toxic confusional state and was returned to bed without harm. When the time came to remove his bandages for the first time – and they covered much of his body – I gave him a general anaesthetic and then gently peeled them off the burns. As they came away thousands of bluebottle maggots fell out and wriggled about all over the operating table, among the discarded dressings, and on the floor. One of the nurses was so overcome by the sight, experienced though she was, that she fainted. Though these creatures were uninvited, we took consolation in the idea that they were supposed to be beneficial to the extent of cleaning up the pus that accumulated in the dressings. There were of course no antibiotics in those days, but thanks to the treatment these casualties received from Smellie, and the unremitting care of the nurses, they all survived.

Neither the nurses nor any other member of staff thought too much about the hours they worked. They did of course have duty schedules, but they often regarded them as elastic, and the sisters and senior nurses would sacrifice some of their leisure time if the patients needed attention. I was allowed Saturday afternoon till midnight off duty, and on two or three weekends in my six months there I was given leave from Saturday lunchtime till Sunday evening. The general practitioner consultant doing emergency duties for the week was always available round the clock, though naturally enough he would sometimes guide me on the telephone into solving a problem without his personal attendance, especially in the middle of the night.

As the only male on the premises for most of the time – or

at least the only male out of bed – I enjoyed the ever-ready cups of tea, the bantering of the nurses, the jokes about the patients, and the gossip about the doctors. Despite the hectic pace, there were intervals of ease. Hospital life was fun then. Nor was it only the nurses with whom I talked or the sisters who came to my flat for some sherry in the evening. My duties sometimes took me along the corridor to discuss a patient with the lady almoner (now called medical social worker), Josephine Earle. Her efficient dealing with the patients' problems stemmed partly from the thorough training she had received from Bedford College and King's College Hospital, and partly from the detailed knowledge she had built up of the various services that were available to help the patients receive further treatment or care after they left hospital. A less popular duty in the era of the voluntary hospitals that sometimes required firmness as well as tact was to get those patients who could afford it to make a contribution to the cost of their treatment, for the hospital received no state subsidy and the consultant staff gave their services free.

In her white coat worn over a mauve or green jumper and dark skirt, with her blond hair and slender figure, her peach-like complexion, her serious glasses, she was brisk and demure at her desk. She too came and had sherry with me sometimes after the day's work had ended, and when she took her glasses off the harmonious contrast between her lion-brown eyes and pale yellow hair was striking.

One evening in mid-winter we were invited out together by a widow who was a voluntary worker at the hospital. After the meal, as we walked the mile or so from her house to the point where our ways parted, she to go to her lodgings, I to return to the hospital, the snow was falling lightly through the still air into the shadows all around us, for no lights were allowed to show anywhere in the "blackout" as a precaution against air raids. Lying on roofs and gardens, the snow gave a faint luminosity to the scene, while the falling flakes alighted on our faces and melted down our necks. As we walked along the deserted roads, where the only sound was the rustle of the flakes on the leafless hedges, barely audible until we paused as though to listen to the ticking of a watch, we hugged and kissed each other without a word in defiance of the frosty darkness that united us in our human warmth.

As though rowing in from the bay with the wind and tide behind me, I felt the weight of the oars lifted, the resistance of the water swept away before me, the scudding of the bows towards a fast approaching shore. The images of the women who had formed my expectation of femininity, and the image of myself too, became agitated and broken up; they were obscured as though I were seeing them reflected from the surface of the water which became ruffled as I sped across it. The past and the future were forgotten. I was beckoned to a country I had not visited before.

Thereafter the sherry was poured out more often, and by way of more recherché entertainment Josephine and I would go up to London during my Saturday off-duty time which, lasting till midnight, enabled us to enjoy a French or Russian film followed by a meal in Soho. There we would sometimes meet my cousin Ulric, whose wife Christine was now back in her native America, or a medical student friend of mine, Peter Johnson, still struggling with his exams and writing poetry. Putting the world to rights and making plans for a new society after the war, we talked over cheap meals in small restaurants that might go up in smoke at any moment as the bombs crashed down on the city around us. On one memorable evening near-hits rattled the crockery on our table more than usual. On 8 March 1941 Josephine and I were having a meal upstairs at the York Minster, with all its notices round the walls telling the Free French to keep their mouths shut (that pub was a favourite resort of theirs), when an aerial mine fell on the Café de Paris near by, killing 150 people and, as she subsequently learnt, blowing her half-brother Robert (of whom a sketch appears later in these pages) out of the door backwards and unharmed as he was entering the building.

For six months or so I had been renting very cheaply a room in a house in Brechin Place, South Kensington, where Peter Johnson also had one, and on several occasions I took

Josephine there to meet its pleasantly bohemian household. It was run by an artist called Garth. A friend of his, a girl called Dolly, occupied a cubby-hole under the staircase. A sculptor who had recently won a prize in Rome and entertained us on the Spanish guitar lived in a large room on the first floor, much of which was filled with a large pile of coke on the floor boards, as he needed a permanently lit stove to keep his models warm and his plaster sculptures dry. The distinguished pianist Eileen Joyce occupied another room and would allow us to listen to her practising sometimes. And yet another inhabitant, a girl called Betty, was separated from her husband and had her young daughter with her. Many years later she married Peter Johnson as his second (but not his last) wife. Garth, as well as being a skilful maker of toys and decorative constructions, enjoyed cooking and so often prepared a meal for the household. There was just enough crockery to last two and a half days; we then joined forces to wash it up.

When my six-month hospital appointment neared its end, in March 1941, I was worried by the prospect of trying to fit together the stability that love needs with a future where chance would overrule choice at every turn, perhaps disastrously. I therefore suggested to Josephine that, though it would be possible for our friendship to continue without any further, deeper commitment, it might be best to end it now, on my departure from the hospital, rather than let it drag on into confusion. In my present position, poised to venture heaven knew where, the prospect of marriage seemed daunting. Nor, though I realised that the old patterns in my mind had been torn up, was I entirely reconciled to seeing their fragments lying on the ground, despite the attractions of the new figure among them. For her part Josephine did convey to me the impression that I represented more closely the kind of person she was seeking, that there was already a place in her heart for me. In a more emotional manner than these sentences might suggest we talked it over. I could not resist the appeal of either her feelings or my own impulses, and I proposed marriage in the near rather than the distant future. She accepted, though perhaps with a lingering doubt whether happiness could possibly be distilled from the calamities that now beset us all. Yet in the end our anxieties and frustrations melted away. It was the best decision – she has made the same declaration as I do – the best decision either of us ever made in our lives.

Returning home to Epsom next day I wondered, as the Southern Electric rattled me along, how I would break the news to my parents, in what words exactly I could throw a message over the walls between us.

My father, ever cool and remote, puzzled and slightly irritated by a son with whom he may have felt he had nothing in common, now seemed to me much more likeable than when I was a boy, more lovable partly because more pitiable. I had come to understand some of the forces that had shut him off from me earlier in life, his desertion in spirit by my mother and the removal of her sons from the orbit of his affection. But just as in my boyhood my emotional bridge with him had been destroyed by my mother's passion and his withdrawal from a second failed marriage, so now in manhood my intellectual and aesthetic interests had become so different from his own that no conversation on anything except trivia was possible. Though I had grown to like him much more, it was therefore as difficult to communicate with him as ever.

With my mother the case was different. Her relationship with Cater, as described above, had begun to cool on his side some years previously and was finally severed by his marriage just before the war. Having to bear this heartache alone, she had turned for some consolation to the love of her sons. But both of us were by then young men struggling for emotional independence. To her love now inappropriately, as I felt, intensified, I responded by becoming aloof.

At the same time, relations between my father and mother had improved. She had come to realise that the end of her affair with Cater implied an acceptance of her home and husband with philosophic resignation. Still, if he made some remark, she would usually preface her reply with "Don't be so silly, William," but a new spirit of tolerance had come to modify the tone if not the language of her irritable responses.

And the war too had helped to draw them together again, gave them a context in which their own strife was easily buried beneath the conflict that embroiled us all outside. My younger brother had joined the army; I was shortly to do so. An air raid warning in the middle of the night sometimes sent us down to a room under the house where we had placed some mattresses, and then my mother's main complaint would be not of the enemy bombers droning overhead towards London but of my father's peaceful snoring. Home was really a haven after all.

So to this family of mine, these familiar yet strange people who had made me, I returned to announce my engagement. My half-sister Daphne was staying in the house at the time. My mother was also there when I arrived, but my father had gone down to the Boots library to change his weekly detective novel. The account of this occasion which my mother was accustomed to retell with some enjoyment in later years ran as follows:

"Dougal flumped himself down on the sofa and said, 'Well, I may as well tell you I'm engaged to be married'. And Daphne said, 'What on earth will Pa say?' And I replied 'Why should Pa say anything?'"

This picture of me so unsure of myself, my half-sister conventional and querulous, and my mother concerned to defend her son and put her husband in his place, rings true in every word, I am sorry to say.

PART 2

7 To and fro

The Southern Electric rattled me on the way to Crookham, the Royal Army Medical Corps Depot. In the rack above my head was a cardboard box containing my new uniform bearing the insignia of lieutenant, for I was now a commissioned officer in the RAMC. In the bag beside me was a heap of books, among them the *Tao Te Ching* embodying the philosophy of Taoism.

It is a philosophy that gives guidance on a great variety of human predicaments, and perhaps surprisingly for a system whose pervading tenet is the oneness of all living creatures it speaks dispassionately of war:

> The best charioteers do not rush ahead;
> The best fighters do not make displays of wrath.
>   – *Tao Te Ching*, Chapter 68

Examples of obedience to this pair of maxims as well as infractions of them came my way in the next five years, but experience proved, as it is apt to do of many maxims, that the circumstances in which their application seemed appropriate often made their validity questionable.

From the first I enjoyed the open-air life of the army. A cup of cocoa and physical exercises at 0630 on the brisk sunny mornings to which we awoke for much of that spring were invigorating. Marching to and fro on the square gave us some of the harmonious exertion of dancing or the spiritual solace that may be obtained from the ritual repetition of a sacred text in the courtyard of a monastery. Enough to be bracing, it was not so frequent as to be boring. But in conversation I was surprised to find that in many of my fellow recruits a petty individualism absorbed during their medical training had destroyed their capacity to feel any zest for these harmless evolutions.

The lectures were clear and systematic, so that even to an auditor like me, all too prone to inattention, they seemed to be exemplary in driving their message home. One lecturer in particular set me on an unpremeditated course some years later. We were sitting at our desks in the lecture room for a talk on army psychiatry when a small, neat, middle-aged, rather gnome-like man came in and stood before us on the dais in the uniform of a colonel and wearing medal ribbons from the first world war, including the military cross. His stance was calm; the audience fell quiet. This was E A Bennet. A padre on the Western Front in the previous war, he had left the church in the 1920s and taken a medical training as a basis on which to practise psychiatry. Soon afterwards he became friendly with Jung, visited him frequently, wrote a book about him,[13] and practised at the Maudsley Hospital and in Harley Street, not specifically as an analytical psychologist (the name by which close followers of Jung's teaching identified themselves), but as a psychiatrist influenced by Jung's ideas. The unobtrusive strength of his personality impressed me in that hour's lecture, and I resolved to meet him again if it should be possible after the war, an unimaginable future in 1941.

While I was at the depot my sister-in-law Jean, a half-sister of my wife, had an unusual experience that would certainly have fascinated Jung if he could have known of it. She was staying in Kent with some friends, a doctor and his wife. They had a son who was a lieutenant in the Royal Navy. Jean had never met him but knew what he looked like from photographs of him in the house. One day during that visit Jean was weeding a herbaceous border on a warm, still evening after tea when she felt impelled to turn round. On doing so she saw her hosts' son in naval uniform walking up the drive, and as she watched him he gradually sank away into the ground. She knew he had been reported missing when his ship was torpedoed some nine months previously. Later she returned to the house to wash before dinner, and on coming downstairs she saw his head in "a kind of cloud" by the staircase, as she later told me. On entering the drawing-room she said, "I've seen a most extraordinary thing this evening..." when her hostess interrupted with, "You don't need to tell me – I've seen him too."

Four features of this apparition are of special interest. The first and perhaps most important is that the veracity of the witnesses is beyond question. Secondly, there was no emotional bond of any kind between my sister-in-law and the young man: they had never met. The third exceptionally striking feature is that two people saw him independently, as became apparent in their conversation at the drawing-room door. And fourthly, my sister-in-law had no other super-natural visitations in her life, if that is what it was. As was subsequently ascertained, the lieutenant had in fact met his death nine months previously in the battle during which his ship was sunk.

From the depot I went to a field ambulance near the south coast, first to its headquarters and then to a detachment commanded by a major who had been a Territorial officer. He was an energetic young man with a keen eye, a ruddy complexion, thick dark hair, and an emphatic manner of speech, and might have been an excellent instructor but for one defect: he disliked delegating authority for administrative matters connected with the field ambulance (though medical judgments he did not interfere with). Consequently I learnt very little about the forms and procedures that make the army tick over. His reluctance in this respect stemmed from his love of the unit, his desire to perfect it in every possible way, to make it glitter with competence in an army that at that stage, a year after the evacuation from Dunkirk, was still bewildered about what its role might be in the immediate future and whether it would have the capacity to fulfil it. No wonder he disliked the thought of putting any part of it in the charge of a novice like me, especially as he must have thought me something of a misfit, for considerable piles of books used to trail around with me, many from that great institution the London Library (and every book was returned to them too).

For I spent the odd hours reading up a subject of special interest to me at the time, namely the legends of the Holy Grail – at first sight hardly relevant to winning the war: but first appearances were deceptive, and these legends were not so remote from the realities of the day as they may have seemed to be.

The story had begun six years previously, when I was 18, and I read with the enthusiasm of a boy on the threshold of manhood (and a keen motorcyclist) T E Lawrence's *Seven Pillars of Wisdom*.* He too had enjoyed the old tales of adventure and romance told of King Arthur, Lancelot, Perceval, Guinevere, and the rest of those courtly if shadowy heroes and princesses. His predilection had led me in turn to study them intermittently while I was exploring the French symbolist poets mentioned above. Then the outbreak of war brought into prominence two of the themes of these legends. One was the need for adventure in order to attain manhood. The other was the quest for the vessel of feminine love symbolised by the Grail and becoming increasingly obscured by the masculine reordering of society in response to the needs of the war. Far from being recondite, these studies had practical, immediate significance for me. They constituted a framework, though only one of several, by which I, like millions of others in their different ways, became adapted to an existence so alien as the military life afforded and to a stance so unwontedly hostile as warfare demanded.

It may be too simple to say that what the Nazi myths were to the Germans the Arthurian legends were to me, though the war was often described as a war of ideologies; and as well as several other kinds of war I think it was that. But in the totality of the war's subjugation of our lives I tried to meet its challenges on terms that my inner being could accept.†

* Despite the oddities of his character that have been successively exposed over the years he remains for me a remarkable man. Which of us would not be found to have shameful or antisocial corners in the labyrinths of our lives if we had been subjected to the same intense scrutiny as he has been?

† Another example will be given from the reading of the editor when I was on the staff of the *British Medical Journal* many years later.

What seems fortuitous always has a traceable history.* There were certainly reasons stretching much further back in my life why at the age of 18 I should have been enthralled by Lawrence's strange masterpiece. But if for the sake of brevity we take that as a starting point, it is possible to trace the line forward from my interest in the Arthurian legends because he had enjoyed them, through the play of my imagination on the valour of the knights and their quest for love, and thence to the concentration in my mind of a desire to prove myself in the art of growing up. This well of imagery was thus one of several that I could draw from to gain strength, guidance, purpose for the role that the war had allotted to me as to so many other people. Fantasy can provide a template that moulds our destiny and directs us to achievement, or it may come into flower as a dream at once deceptive, immobile, enchanting, a substitute for living. Surely everyone experiences both types in varying degrees but are wary of confessing to the second?

In contrast to these speculations the field ambulance provided me with some hard work taking medical parades at neighbouring units lacking a medical officer of their own, while the commanding officer of our detachment led us out on route marches to toughen us up. Despite a weedy appearance I have always been able to stand up to this kind of thing, so that when one of my fellow officers complained privately to me of what he called the CO's sadism in exhausting us on marches with heavy equipment and sometimes wearing gasmasks, I could not agree with his strictures. In fact later when it was my responsibility to give advice in the combatant units I served in I always advocated rigorous training – and took part in it myself.

But one thing I did find difficult to stomach was the heavy drinking in the evenings. We often went along to the pub and knocked back 10 or 12 whiskies, usually neat. Though I have a good head for alcohol, enjoy it, and in subsequent units

* Boswell[14] had this to say in his diary: "If a person would keep an exact list of all the books or parts of books he has read, it might be seen how a wit or a philosopher is gradually formed according to the materials furnished to him."

often drank a great deal, I look back on my first unit as one where the drinking was frenetic, as though a schoolboy were testing the capacity of both himself and his companions to hold their liquor. To drop out would have been unthinkable disloyalty to the ethos of the officers' mess.

A series of orders from above together with some pleas from myself got me transferred early in 1942 to a unit that seemed to be preparing for a more active role than had so far come my way. But meanwhile on 17 July 1941 Josephine and I were married in London. Only a couple of days' leave was obtainable because I had so recently joined the army, but we were not entirely deprived of a honeymoon in that a few weeks later I was posted to Liverpool for a fortnight's course in tropical medicine, and Josephine was allowed to accompany me. Unexpected joy in those troubled times though the honeymoon was, I must dwell here in tribute to the teaching I received from the Liverpool School of Tropical Medicine. There I found a vast subject, but brilliant lecturers, and they laid the whole scene out in my mind like a new lawn in spring, with order and clarity and purpose. At the same time their practical guidance was admirably reinforced by the army handbook on tropical diseases, a masterly work that would fit into a battle dress trouser pocket.[15] The army is often depicted as having been led at that time by dunderheads who were contemptuous of science and blind to the role of technology in twentieth century warfare, but in the medical services this was not true.

After attending this course I spent a few weeks in medical charge of some units in Essex, where one day I was detailed to visit Clacton to examine a group of 100 men, all aged 35, to determine their fitness for army service. The men were assembled in a disused hall of dingy aspect, which had a small office leading off it where I questioned and examined them. As each of them came in to see me I noticed how short they were and that many of them had grey hair. On examining them my eye fell on bent fingers, swollen knees, stiff backs, chests with little or no expansion, ear drums that were perforated. At 35 many looked a decrepit 50; few still had the spring of youth in their step. They were men without zest. To be examined by a strange doctor in uniform for fitness to join the army is not everyone's idea of an afternoon by the sea at Clacton, and I could only sympathise with the apprehension or bravado that some of these men showed. Yet one of them with more life in his eyes and a sturdier deportment probably summed up what many of them felt. When I said to him, "I can't really find anything to worry about here, you seem all right to me," he replied, "But doctor, I'm an old man."

And that was the main trouble. Diagnoses could be attached to a swollen joint here, a bent back there, or an ear that had been discharging ever since infancy, but the sum added up at the age of 35 to a total of "old age". Eliminating the causes of this premature aging formed part of the vision that many of us believed might be turned to reality in a postwar world if we should live to see one; at the time it seemed as obscure as the surface of Venus under her cloud cover. But the observation of time's mark on these men brought the ambition vividly to life.*

Early in 1942 I at last reached a unit that was preparing to get to grips with the enemy. Stationed at Largs in west Scotland, it consisted largely of officers in military intelligence and planning when I got there. The officer in command was a Major F Turner of the Grenadier Guards, then in his 40s. He had served as a professional soldier in the Grenadiers all his life, including the previous war, and had been commissioned from the ranks. Known as Fred throughout the brigade and to everyone who enjoyed his friendship, he combined a calm confidence based on a lifetime's experience of army regulations and practice with an astute but sympathetic understanding of service life that made even those officers and men he disappointed feel he had taken the right decision.

In the evening of the day I arrived he called me across in the mess, stood me a glass of beer, and said, "Doc, I don't know how you go about things, but I'd like your cooperation. How do you see your job?"

* And after the war my first published medical paper was on the relation between suicide and unemployment during the 1930s.[16]

I told him that in addition to the medical care of the unit I would give him any help I possibly could.

"My aim is to help you as commanding officer to keep everyone healthy." Not very well thought out words perhaps, but he seemed grateful to hear them.

"Thanks, Doc," he said, and then made a bit more explicit the cause of what had seemed to be a slight anxiety in the tone of his voice, a questioning reserve in his gaze. "One of the chaps I had as MO last year didn't quite..." He paused to drink some beer and then looked me firmly in the eyes, "some MOs don't quite get the hang of working in a military unit." At the back of my mind I wondered whether my new CO expected some kind of compliance from his medical officers that would interfere with their care of the sick or even run counter to medical ethics. But as my service in the unit quickly proved, nobody could have been more exact in observing my medical prerogative or more scrupulous in accepting medical decisions offered in relation to individuals or the unit.

After a time I discovered what had been bothering him. The trouble had been a medical officer who regarded himself simply as a doctor and had no intention of accommodating himself to the discipline of the army. Most of his spare energies were devoted to trying to wangle a posting to a military hospital, where, as he put it, he would be able to keep up his profession. He would have been from the same mould as those I encountered at the depot who saw only childish play-acting in the drilling on the square and were discomfited by the thought that it was beneath their professional dignity. While businessmen, lawyers, architects, school-teachers, accountants, and dons generally had to turn themselves into amateur warriors and lose all contact with their profession, a (to me) surprising number of doctors, already fortunate enough to be practising their profession in the armed forces, used to bemoan their fate in being deprived of the opportunity to practise "real medicine".

Soon afterwards the unit's role became more clearly defined though its destination remained mysterious. We were to be the headquarters of a new invading force – but invading where? – and were issued with shoulder badges showing a dagger on a shield. But secrecy had to be absolute. We received instructions to say nothing about this badge or our unit. For me the order of silence was soon put to the test. One Saturday afternoon I took the train into Glasgow to see the sights of a city that I had not visited before and went into a pub for some sandwiches and beer. There was quite a crowd. While I was standing alone drinking the beer a young man, short and dark-haired, who had been standing near me for a minute or two, asked me in a slight Scots accent whether I knew Glasgow well. I told him I hadn't been there before.

"That's a new badge you've got on your shoulder," he said, "what unit would that be?"

The question came so abruptly, after so minimal an acquaintance, that I was silenced by its sheer effrontery and moved off down the bar without replying. At the time I thought he was probably someone without much experience who mixed with Nazi or communist sympathisers and was trying to get scraps of information for them, giving the wheel of history a little turn as it were. But later I had doubts about that. Could he have been a not very well trained agent of our own intelligence service? Perhaps he had been told to go round the pubs after our badge had been issued simply to test our reliability.

As I was to discover in all three countries where I took part in invasions (uncontested in the third), the allegiance of our associates proved to be one of the most complex – and even hazardous – puzzles we had to solve. Every nation, including our own, had both friends and enemies of our cause. And every officer was known to have information of value to an enemy. As a medical officer I was a fair target in that Glasgow pub to both sides in the war.

Over the next few months our unit expanded and became the headquarters of the First Army. Even the desk planners were expected to take plenty of exercise to get fit, but I must say they usually found their duties in the office to be rather more pressing than mine when it was a question of a cross-country run, and often I would go out by myself scrambling over the hills at the back of the town.

One man, a Guardsman, went missing one day after a run and finally came to view again a couple of days later. He was brought to me to be examined because he seemed to be rather confused. I felt convinced that for at least a large part of the time of his absence he was not really aware of what he was doing. Some domestic difficulties had apparently been swirling round him and finally rolled him like a pebble up against the breakwater of army regulations.

Three weeks later I was on 48 hours' leave with Josephine at the Strand Palace Hotel in London when the room telephone rang at 0830 in the morning. The call was from Chelsea Barracks. Did I know Guardsman So-and-so? Yes. He was due to go before a court martial that morning, so could I come along and give evidence on his mental state? The officer who telephoned added rather strangely, as it seemed to me then, though there may have been some legal reason for it, "You don't have to come, but we'd be glad if you would". Of course I did and gave evidence on the Guardsman's behalf that he was suffering from hysterical fugue, that is, his normal personality had become submerged in a more or less automatic state in which he had run about for a day or so hardly knowing what he was doing. Whether a psychiatrist then (let alone now) would have agreed with the diagnosis I doubt, for hysteria is an ill defined and much questioned concept, but my evidence got the Guardsman off, and I think justifiably. His mental state was certainly abnormal, and he was not malingering. But sometimes there was no clear division between the patient's deliberately deceiving the doctor and unconsciously deceiving himself.

Another case made this point that same summer. Though perfectly simple on the surface, it yet had roots that ran deep into the patient's personality. A unit of the Pioneer Corps stationed nearby had no medical officer of its own, so I had it in my care. One day a soldier from it in his middle 30s complained of a sore hand. The middle finger was contracted firmly down on to the palm, and the man said it had been like that for a year after an accident with a hammer. There was no physical cause of the condition, and from the way he spoke about it I suspected he realised the advantage it gave

92

him of being graded unfit for a combatant unit owing to his inability to handle a weapon. Yet he asked me if I could do something for it. So for a fortnight I saw him every day except Sundays and by suggestion combined with gently pressing on his finger restored it to its normal position. He was delighted. His unit was posted away for a couple of weeks, and when he came back his finger was contracted on the palm again. I failed to persuade him to try a second cure.

This man was more or less illiterate, married with no children, had had a succession of poor jobs, and felt quite comfortable in army life provided he did not have to fight. Just as a dog will sometimes gain attention and sympathy and a bit more devotion by dramatising a slight injury to its paw, so this man no doubt at first aroused the sympathy of his comrades and the indulgence of his officers by exaggerating the effects of a minor injury. Later on he forgot it was a play: the drama became real life. And yet at his own request, despite all the sorrows, the failures, the defeats of his life that had been slyly channelled into his useless hand, it could be restored to normal by the power transmitted in words, just as a wounded king in mediaeval legend could be healed by the words of a magic formula and the fertility of his land released.

That summer I completed an article on the Holy Grail and sent it off to *Folklore*. Its themes were the loss and recovery of femininity in Christianity, and the quest for permanent values in individuals' lives. Now it embarrasses me as too briefly worked out, the product of too hurried a life. But, if the writing of it was a rushed affair, its publication ran true to form, for it did not appear in print till two years and an African campaign had passed by.[17]

8 Into Africa

At last the day came in October 1942 when we embarked on a troopship at Gourock and sailed in darkness down the Clyde. Only a handful of people on board knew our destination. I was not one of them. Further and further south we steamed in calm seas to warmer climates, far down into the Atlantic. Then we turned northwards again. Physical training, weapons training, and games on crowded decks kept us busy, and in the evening concerts and "brains trusts" (made popular by the BBC feature) made an innocent diversion. One evening ended with a brigadier announcing we should all stand up and sing "Abide with me", that haunting hymn that is now said to be droned out at football matches between mouthfuls of potato crisps. Unfortunately, few people knew the words after the opening line, and it degenerated into a more or less tuneful moaning at the bar. Later that night we passed through the Straits of Gibraltar, the rock standing black against a dark sky, with our ship casting up phosphorescent furrows at its bows, leaving the luminous wavelets to sprinkle away at either side.

By now we had learnt of our destination: Algiers. The first landings had taken place, and as we approached the city a few hours later we watched the early morning sun glittering across its white buildings set on low hills along the shore beside the blue satin of the sea. All was now quiet after some of the initial assault troops had had some minor skirmishes with the French.

In the streets of the city or in the bar of the Aletti Hotel it was quite usual to be approached during the first few days by friendly Frenchmen or Arabs asking for cigarettes, corned beef, aspirins – and information. In return they offered hospitality of various kinds. The French colonists in Algeria, in contrast to those in Tunisia, were mostly hostile to the Allied cause. Although nationals of a country that was still our ally, they hoped in their hearts for a German victory. The Arabs hoped for a French defeat.

Through the quiet streets and alleyways people moved warily, sometimes a little too quickly, sometimes loitering questioningly. A stranger's eyes would catch one's own from a doorway or window, or he would turn abruptly away as one looked at him. Doubt, suspicion, fear, all lurked in faces that were composed to seem unconcerned. Hatred occasionally glinted, but usually lay hidden behind a guard of reserve.

The surreptitious dealing in the streets was reflected in offices and hotel rooms by the bargaining between contending parties representing the many factions of French political opinion. Here a hand would be raised to conceal a smile, there to cup an ear straining to catch a whispered proposition. Everywhere voices were low, eyes alert.

One evening I accompanied some of my fellow officers to a brothel called The Sphinx in the Arab quarter. It was open to other ranks in the afternoon and officers in the evening. A lesbian performance was enacted for about half an hour on a broad couch in its main hall, while we sat round drinking beer, and one officer from another unit was rash enough to entrust himself to the attentions of these ladies (but ineffectively as it happened). They did not succeed in tempting any more of us to sample their wares, and I sympathised with the feelings of a Scottish friend with me who said, "I'd as soon go with a dummy in a shop window."

We had on our staff a French lieutenant acting as a liaison officer. He had escaped from France at its downfall, joined the Free French in London, and from there been seconded to the First Army. As a patriotic Frenchman he felt he was fighting the war effectually by serving in the British army, but he nevertheless held us in great contempt. His antipathy had two causes: the first was that we had betrayed France by withdrawing at Dunkirk and then sinking the French fleet at Toulon. The second was that we had absurd pretensions to culture while at the same time pouring scorn on French achievements. All the same, he was an exhilarating companion in the mess and, as a patriotic Frenchman who could talk about Racine, evoked my respect. One day he also surprised me. We were talking about that world after the war that sometimes filled our thoughts, and I asked him whether he intended to stay in the French army.

"Oh no," he replied, "I shall emigrate to America. France is finished."

When Admiral Darlan was assassinated in Algiers on Christmas Eve 1942 I was further east in Constantine, where the political tremors could also be felt. The assassin, a Frenchman of 20 called Bonnier de la Chapelle, was promptly tried by court martial and executed two days later. Calm was restored in the rear, and the army could press on without fear of trouble there. Darlan had been a help to us in the landings, but to continue working with such an untrustworthy ally had been a source of much political anxiety to the British.

In addition to the French quarrels among themselves there was a strong Arab movement hostile to the French colonists and also strife between the Arabs and the Jews in Constantine itself. The result was a succession of riots in the streets, many of them essentially antisemitic in form, though the real cause of any particular outbreak in this network of alliances and enmities often lay in decisions taken by political schemers far from the local fighting. Turbans, fezzes, forage caps, and kepis all hurried officiously to and fro through the crowds of merchants, sprawling beggars, dodging boys, and women enveloped in black with two slits for a pair of sparkling eyes.

The site on which Constantine is built must surely be the most spectacular in the world. It is a gigantic boss of rock jutting out of the surrounding dry scrub and cleft through its middle by a gorge 1000 feet (300 m) deep with vertical sides. Bridging the gorge at the top were, in those days, 22 tiny bridges, and at the bottom of this dark fissure were hot springs where the Romans had constructed baths nearly 2000 years ago. The pools down there in the Roman stonework, from which one could gaze up at a crack of sky laced across by the bridges, were derelict, stagnant, a breeding ground for malarial mosquitoes, slime-covered remnants of a lost luxury.

By now the First Army headquarters had been split into two sections – a forward, of which I was the medical officer at Constantine, and a rear section, where another MO, Captain James Smith, was in charge. Moving eastwards again as our army fought towards Tunis I spent a short time camped at a delightful spot in an outlier of the Atlas Mountains called Laverdure from its perennially green vegetation in an otherwise arid land. Here I made one of the few important decisions of my life, whose every consequence was unregretted. An officer temporarily on liaison from the 1st Airborne Division called Sir Richard (Dickie) des Voeux had joined our mess for a few weeks, when I got to know him well and in conversation learnt about life in his division.* Resolved to join it, I applied to my commanding officer, Fred Turner.

"Certainly not," he said, "we can't spare you at the moment."

Flattered—and so being left to think he must have taken the right decision—but disappointed, I continued towards Tunis with the advanced headquarters, next camping by contrast to Laverdure on a sun-scorched hillside of cracked earth and rustling grasses. In and out of the cracks ran giant orange centipedes 2 cm wide and about 15 cm long.

The medley of units in my medical care were mainly concerned with gathering intelligence. One of them used to set up its radio equipment at a suitable point and intercept messages that the units in the German army facing us were sending to each other, and with great speed and skill decipher them on the spot, identify the units sending them, and transmit the information back to Headquarters, which could then order an air attack on worthwhile targets. The Germans were of course playing the same game, and each side was trying to confuse the other with false messages.

This unit to which I was attached regarded itself as being in friendly competition with a motorised reconnaissance unit

---

* Sadly, he was killed at Arnhem, the last baronet of his line.

called the Phantoms, which was also in my care intermittently. It too was engaged in identifying the whereabouts
of enemy units and sending the information directly to Army
Headquarters and even further back. The Phantoms had
attracted exceptionally good officers, the two I dealt with
being Major Hugh Fraser and the adjutant Captain John
Profumo. But this type of unit was not popular everywhere in
the army (though I myself belonged to one for the second half
of my war service). For just as boys' public schools are
nowadays accused of creaming off into their sixth forms the
best from the girls' schools, so the irregular units were held
to have attracted the best officers away from their own
regimental units. There was something in this argument, but
it had a counterpoise. Units of this kind (I am not now
speaking of the Phantoms or any particular unit) also tended
to attract misfits, people who had made a nuisance of
themselves, troublesome men whom the commanding officer
of a conventional unit was glad to be rid of. Such men might
be better soldiers than the average – or worse. Their new
unit would find this out fairly quickly and had the power to
get rid of men who were a liability. Reliability in battle rarely
went with a psychopathic personality.

One of the officers in the radio interception unit to which
I was attached, Captain Rollo Biddulph, caught my
attention at Constantine, where I first met him. During a
walk along the city's outskirts we passed a plant with large
leaves and a purple flower smelling of carrion, probably in
the arum family, and he remarked to me, "Une fleur
maladive". This phrase was from the dedication of Baudelaire's *Les Fleurs du Mal* to Théophile Gautier, a book I was
carrying in my rucksack together with the *Oxford Book of
English Verse* (India paper edition, now regrettably dis-
continued). At once I realised that here was someone on the
same wavelength.*

Now we were camped above the Medjerda River, where
turtles swam up and down the stream and snakes in their
thousands lurked along the banks in the wet vegetation. Here

* Surprisingly so, as it happened: 45 years later his youngest son
married my youngest daughter – second time round for both of them.

another strange case came my way. A young captain was brought into my aid post deeply unconscious, having suddenly collapsed at work. He was a highly qualified scientist working on some intelligence project. On examining him I found his whole body, including his face, was anaesthetic to pinprick; in fact he was completely limp and unresponsive – or was he? There was something odd about him. And it was his eyes. The lids were almost but not quite closed over them and every so often showed a slight tremor, rather as a child pretending to be asleep will watch its mother through half-closed lids. So I told the orderlies to leave the tent and spoke to him quietly alone. Quite quickly he recovered his normal state of mind, sat up, rubbed his eyes, and asked the traditional question, "Where am I?" Apparently he was due to go on a hazardous mission, and this was his reaction to the prospect. During my conversation with him he gradually returned to a normal state of consciousness, as a sleeper awakes. But what has always surprised me was the total anaesthesia and apparent unconsciousness allied to high intelligence – an unexpected and indeed improbable combination.

The hazards of war were not the only troubles that brought patients along to my aid post. Even in remote places both women and wine could also exact their tribute from the careless soldier. Reporting sick one day with a discharge of what was obviously gonorrhoeal pus, a soldier told me it was the result of an injury he had received when climbing through one of the hedges of prickly pear that marked out territories there, though as he uttered the words he did look at me questioningly, wondering how far I would go along with him, I suppose. Having become incapacitated through a love which was certainly not vegetable, he may have hoped to escape some kind of disciplinary action by throwing up this explanation and seeing what came down, yet so incredible must even he have seen it to be that I suspect he told it more to dull his own regret or remorse than to deceive me. For to acquire a venereal disease sometimes wounded a sensitive man's longing for feminine love. He could not accept with equanimity the contrast between the beauty of the woman's body and its diseased state, between the pleasure she gave him and the pain that followed. Many soldiers suffered the anguish of a shattered myth, an anguish that they tried to bury in oblivion, when they reported to the medical officer in conventional, emotionless words, "I think I've got a dose of the clap, doctor." They knew there was no easy cure for it (this was before the days of penicillin). One man at Headquarters who became infected loaded his rifle and shot himself in the head without even reporting sick.

Again, every army finds a place for men who are there mainly for the beer. One of these, who had been a professional soldier for a good many years, dodging up and down over the ranks of private, lance corporal, corporal, and back to private in a cycle of trust and retribution as the trust was found to be misplaced, was brought to me under arrest. In fact he had demanded to see the medical officer as soon as he was arrested for being drunk on duty. I examined him rather cursorily because I had no idea of the plot that lay in his mind. He had no special complaints except that he felt dizzy and readily agreed with me that there was really nothing wrong with him. Some weeks later I was surprised to be summoned to give evidence on the question of his drunkenness, for he had elected to be tried by court martial instead of summarily. An experienced defending officer cross-examined me as follows:

Defending officer   Captain Swinscow, you diagnosed Private X as being under the influence of alcohol?
Swinscow   Yes.
Defending officer   How did you reach that diagnosis?
Swinscow   I examined him and noted he smelt of drink, was unsteady on his feet, his face was flushed, and his speech was rather thick.
Defending officer   Did you test his sense of balance – make him walk along a straight line?
Swinscow   No, I didn't think that necessary.
Defending officer   Did you give him test sentences to speak?
Swinscow   No.

That was enough. After that it was downhill all the way for me into perdition. My examination had been too superficial because I had never expected it would end up being scrutinised in a court of law – something that my patient of course knew all along would happen. He was promptly acquitted. Years of experience had taught him how to tie up the legal process and a young medical officer in a neat parcel and throw it out through the tent flap.

The malaria season was about to begin, so with some orderlies I spent a couple of days cutting back the banks of the river – and many snakes I'm sorry to say too – in order to eliminate pools in which mosquitoes could breed near our camp. Then the great day came in February when we received tablets of the new antimalarial drug, mepacrine, for distribution to everyone. It had been manufactured by ICI as an alternative to quinine and an answer to the German atabrin. The day after it was issued the entire army was hors de combat with gastroenteritis. This was not a side effect that clinical trials had led the medical authorities to expect, so three days later, when the next dose was due, they instructed the regimental medical officers like me to issue the tablets again. And again the army was knocked out by gastroenteritis – mild, but it would have been alarming if the Germans had attacked, for they would have found most of their opponents squatting over old biscuit tins. Many years later I discussed this episode with an intelligence officer who had been there at the time, and he told me that by chance the Germans had issued atabrin on the same days we had chosen – and with exactly the same results. They could not possibly have attacked us. Thereafter it was taken with very little ill effect except for the bright yellow colour it dyed our skins.

The Luftwaffe bombed our positions from time to time but not very accurately. After one of their raids a casualty brought to my aid post was a badly burnt soldier groaning in agony. Now I remembered some advice given to me when I was a student at St Thomas's: in emergency don't hesitate to give morphine intravenously. The soldier was a tall man of powerful physique, so I slowly injected a large dose, $\frac{1}{2}$ grain (32 mg) into an arm vein. The effect was instantaneous and wonderful to see. He ceased to groan, his features relaxed into a blissful smile, and his body became rested and composed as the opiate flowed into him. The thanks he gave me were moving. Sent back to base hospital, he made a good recovery.

I mention this rather ordinary case in particular because the relief of pain and suffering always seemed to me to be the first essential of treatment. In battle one can sometimes do little else. Yet in later years and civilian life I have known of bitter complaints from patients whose pain was not adequately relieved when it could have been, and heard criticisms by doctors who have encountered such cases. To help patients through grief or "depressions" or to mitigate the frustrations of a misconceived lifestyle, doctors will pour out tranquillisers and hypnotics like coins rattling from a fruit machine when you are in luck. But for a patient in severe pain some of them do too little. I believe this is largely because students' attention during their training is focused on identifying the cause of the disease and treating that cause – in itself an unexceptionable procedure. But so sharp is the focus that removal of the symptom is a peripheral aim while removal of the cause as soon as maybe is the central. Like other symptoms pain is apt to take its place in a chain of diagnostic thought, to be regarded as a clue to a cause, rather than the essential suffering from which the patient seeks relief.

A casualty from another air raid probably did not fare so well. He was an Arab boy of about 14 brought to me with a severe wound of one arm, and not surprisingly he was howling pitifully. I tried to give him morphine, but he struggled so violently against the unaccustomed assault of a syringe that it was impossible to hold an arm still enough for an injection. Managing to inject the drug into a thigh, I was amazed at how hard the muscles were, just like the wood of a tree trunk. He calmed down in time, but his father would not allow him to receive any treatment in hospital and took him away.

A peculiar epidemic then struck down some members of the unit. A soldier reported sick complaining of feeling hot and tremulous. His face was flushed, pulse rapid, and pupils dilated. His temperature was normal. When a second and a third and more came along I suspected some kind of poison, and the symptoms suggested atropine. But how? They were all being treated for mild dysentery, and the standard mixture contained belladonna. A radio message back to the base hospital which had sent the mixture up to my unit quickly elicited the answer: it had been made up incorrectly and contained belladonna at 10 times the required strength.

On 12 May 1943 Tunis was captured and the German forces in North Africa capitulated. Their commander, General von Arnim, was brought to our unit for an initial interrogation before being sent back as a prisoner. The end had come for him, and a kind of end had come for me too. I called on Fred Turner

"Sir, you can't really need me any more?"

"All right, Doc, but don't do anything rash."

So I applied to join the 1st Airborne Division and was accepted after a medical examination that showed nothing worse than a kink in my spine due, as was later discovered, to two fused vertebrae, probably as a result of an undetected fracture when I fell down some stone steps at school; and of course my slightly peculiar left foot, which gave no trouble.

But meanwhile I went with my unit to Carthage, where we camped among the fly-infested ruins, to await a formal posting. Its great bowl-like amphitheatre, open to the sky, was the scene of an address by Winston Churchill on 1 June. Over 5000 of us sat on its stone benches or stood around and heard every word as though in a small room. On the stage below us Churchill held our attention and made us feel we were at the heart of contemporary history. He himself recorded: "I have no idea what I said, but the whole audience clapped and cheered as doubtless their predecessors of two thousand years ago had done as they watched gladiatorial combats."[18] That evening he attended a dinner and gave the guests a picturesque account of his address: "Yes, I was speaking from where the cries of Christian virgins rent the air whilst roaring lions devoured them – and yet – I am no lion and certainly not a virgin!"[19]

When our unit was dispersed I was posted to Algiers to await transfer to the 1st Airborne Division. On the way I had an enjoyable five days' leave with my colleague, Captain Smith, from the rear Headquarters, when we travelled in a 15-cwt truck through the Atlas Mountains. The cedar forests interspersed with great stands of the cork oak were a beautifully cool contrast to the hot plains below. In Algeria we went up into a region where the Kabyle dwell, a pale-skinned race with blue eyes and reddish-brown hair. Pausing at the top of a pass to admire the view, we had got out of our truck and were gazing across to distant ridges when a party of Arabs came along on their camels. One of them dismounted and walked up to me, stood a moment facing me, and then in a flash whipped out a knife and pointed it straight at my stomach. But equally quickly I caught a glint in his eye that told me: this man is trying to frighten me – he means no harm. So, looking at him as though I were a customer in an ironmonger's shop, I said, "Combien pour ça?" He sold it to me for the equivalent of about a pound, a beautiful hand-made knife with a wooden scabbard and a blade so sharp that I have never seen its like – still razor-sharp today after many year's use as a paperknife. We shook hands on the deal and went off in our different directions down the pass.

Arrived in Algiers, I found that before joining the Airborne Division I was required for a few weeks to take medical charge of an American unit at Tizi-ouzou. This delightfully named little town occupied a dust bowl in the mountains and was in fact the capital of Algeria, surprisingly in view of the far greater size, importance, and facilities of Algiers. I arrived to find myself looking after a group of young American officers being trained for duties in an organisation called by its acronym Amgot, that is, Allied Military Government in Occupied Territories.

These men were being prepared to take up posts in Italy after the Germans had been cleared out and were attending lectures on the Italian language and customs. So I went along too, and at the first assembly was surprised to find that every single person except me had an Italian name. In fact the whole unit consisted of Americans of Italian origin. More remarkable was a discovery I made many years later from a history of the Mafia, for many officers in Amgot were said to have been connected with that organisation. The authorities back in the USA, in their search for people with some basic knowledge of the Italian language, had deliberately recruited Mafia adherents because they were known to be reliably hostile to Mussolini and the fascist regime. Their loyalty to the Allied cause was unassailable.

But my lot on the contrary seemed to me to be typical young Americans – innocent, enthusiastic, eager, and hard working. In the bed next to mine in the dormitory one of the officers spent his afternoons, when the heat was very great and we had a siesta, reading a one-volume encyclopedia from cover to cover, straight through from A to Z. I asked him if he managed to remember what he read, and he replied, "Well, I guess I get a general picture of it all." I felt slightly shamed by his industry as I pulled my *Oxford Book of English Verse* out of the jacket pocket it fitted so well. (Its India paper stood up to being flooded in the Tunisian desert when a freak rainstorm one night covered it and me on my Safari bed before I awoke to what was happening. It travelled throughout the rest of the war with me and is on my shelves still.)

The camp was serviced in part by staff from the French army, and one night they organised a concert in the town hall. In the darkened auditorium we sat with the sweat running down our faces and bodies, billows of tobacco smoke hanging under the low ceiling, alternately attentive and chattering, when the last turn was announced. A French corporal would play the trumpet. And what a performance! I never heard such trumpet-playing before or since. He brought the house down again and again. A large man with a great barrel chest, liquid with sweat like all of us, he stood on the lighted stage and played old French airs and gallops and hunting tunes on the trumpet, and also on a long hunting horn, with unforgettable brilliance, transforming the breath from those great lungs into melodies billowing away to the horizon. Such virtuosity! Such panache! We could not let him go.

After six weeks of waffles and canned chicken, sometimes together and sometimes separately, often with maple syrup on top of both, and no medical complaints, I relinquished my charge of the unit to an American medical officer and was posted to a field ambulance in the 1st Airborne Division rear party stationed in Tunisia near Sousse. The main body was in Sicily. Then at the end of 1943 we were ordered back to England to prepare for what was now beginning to gain some definition in our sights, the invasion of Europe in 1944.

Arriving in the middle of January, I was granted a fortnight's leave. Josephine was waiting for me at Waterloo Station, and was rather shocked to see a thin figure with sun-bleached hair and skin stained bright yellow from mepacrine come towards her. We had an enjoyable and expensive leave at the Savoy and other hotels, the longest time we had been together since the tropical medicine course at Liverpool in 1941. During the first five years of our married life we saw each other for an aggregate of less than three months.

While I was away she had been serving in the WAAF as a leading aircraftwoman in Balloon Command, first at Kidbrooke, east of London, and then at Biggin Hill to the south. At Kidbrooke an air raid in the night had precipitated the staff into taking up action stations, when, stumbling on an unforeseen obstacle, she tripped and broke her nose, sustaining an extremely painful injury. Biggin Hill, famous for its fighter squadron in the Battle of Britain, promised to be more interesting, though not quite in the way she expected. She had been transferred there to take part in the efforts being urgently made to stop the pilotless planes (buzz bombs) from reaching London, and in fact the balloons had brought some down. But soon after arriving there she was startled to be informed by another aircraftwoman, "I tell you, Jo, this place is chock-a-block with lesbians."

9 Into Holland

Few people, I suppose, can have had the experience I did in those days of being deliberately shot at six times in succession – and missed!

Eight months previously, on returning from my disembarkation leave I had been posted to the 1st Airborne Reconnaissance Squadron as its medical officer. The commanding officer, Major C F H (Freddie) Gough, had had a bold career in the first world war in the Royal Navy as a midshipman. By now in his early 40s, he was much the oldest officer in the squadron, and he looked more venerable because his hair had already turned white. When I reported to him, I entered the room and saluted. He turned to the adjutant sitting beside him: "There you are – why doesn't everyone salute like this ropey quack?" In fact the squadron was both smart and efficient in the performance of the niceties to which the army attached importance, but Freddie sometimes liked to think, as a doting father will proudly declare of his young son "he's a bit wild at times", that it was apt to fall short of purely conventional and so rather trivial standards. It was essentially a fighting force; things like proper saluting were taken for granted. And if saluting were asserted to be a bit slack (even though it was in reality strictly performed), then it must have fallen off a bit because the fighting qualities of the squadron had for a time taken precedence and were that much more keenly tempered.

Now on 17 September 1944, with parachute training and many exercises by day and night behind us, the 1st Airborne Division commanded by General R E Urquhart, had landed on the dropping zone outside Arnhem with the task of getting to the bridge across the Rhine and holding it till the Second Army came up to relieve us.

Military parachuting is very different from the peacetime sport. Speed in leaving the aircraft is of the essence so that the entire group (or "stick") shall be close together when they reach the ground. For the same reason the drop is from a low altitude – about 700 to 1000 feet (200 to 300 metres), and we carried heavy equipment strapped to the body. As we approached the ground we let this down on a rope; when it touched down we felt a slight lift, a momentary slowing of the descent. In the course of his descent a parachutist experiences a distinct crossover point in his perception of the ground: until that point the ground seems to be coming up to meet him; then suddenly he feels himself to be falling to meet the ground.

On leaving the Dakota I had heard the reassuring musical notes, like the tinkling of a Chinese glass lantern, as the parachute opened. It was a sunny afternoon with a mainly blue sky and hardly any breeze, perfect for parachuting. Heathland stretched out below us, and blocks of conifers in commercial plantations formed a pattern clearly recognisable from the stereoscopic photographs with which we had been briefed. We had no difficulty in reaching our prearranged rendezvous at the corner of a wood. A few shots were fired at us as we came down, but fortunately nobody in the squadron was hit. Gliders had transported the squadron's jeeps fitted with machine guns and radio sets, and with them came my medical jeep and trailer bearing first aid equipment. Most of the vehicles were successfully extricated on landing, among them mine, but a few could not be dislodged from badly damaged gliders. Losses of vehicles on operations of this kind are to be expected, and the squadron's were no worse than those suffered by the division as a whole. In less than an hour we had formed up and set off over the heath towards Arnhem and its bridge across the Rhine.

To reach the city we had to traverse the nearby suburb of Oosterbeek with its attractive houses among tree-lined streets interspersed with woodland. Heathland runs along its boundary, and advancing through it we soon came under fire, for with their usual skill at responding quickly even when surprised the Germans had taken up strong defensive positions, while the Dutch ran for cover or came out to see what was going on. One of our troops of a dozen men sustained casualties from machine gun fire, so I went out with two orderlies wearing Red Cross brassards and bearing a Red Cross flag to attend to them. The Germans immediately fired on us so heavily that we had to lie flat on the ground to take cover.

Some confused fighting followed, and then in a second lull I ran down a hillside to a wounded man to give him aid. Quite near him I was pinned down again by machine gun fire and tried to merge myself inconspicuously in the heathland. Unfortunately, the slope on which I was lying was faced beyond a stream by a corresponding slope up the other side, at the top of which was a small wood concealing an enemy mortar bomb detachment who could see me perfectly clearly though I could not see them. As I lay in the heather pressing myself out of sight of the machine gunner, the mortar detachment dropped a bomb a couple of yards in front of me. I then heard the plop of a second bomb as it left the barrel, and after what seemed a long time it exploded the same distance behind me. How long is this going on? I wondered. The answer came immediately with another plop from the mortar barrel and an explosion just to my right. The thought flitted through my mind that the Germans were much more skilful than anyone else in their use of this particular weapon because, as I contended, they have a cultural affinity with the mortar bomb's parabolic flight, its trajectory having some resemblance to the gothic architecture that they favour and their elongate female nudes. To use a different figure: the ellipse was to Gothic art what the circle was to the art of the Italian Renaissance. Yet another plop and another explosion, this time two yards to my left. Knowing that some people claimed it was possible to see a mortar bomb in flight I strained to watch the sky when I heard the next plop from the barrel, but this one at least ran its course invisibly before exploding in the circle round me. How long would it be, I wondered, before they hit the centre? Then a sixth bomb completed the perimeter of a fairly exact circle – but still failed to hit its target. Waiting for the next to fall on this sunlit hillside among the heather and grassy tufts, I vividly recalled the hours I had sometimes spent as a schoolboy resting on the slopes of Dartmoor, basking in the scent of heather, watching a cumulous cloud drift by, and listening to the song of the skylarks. And suddenly I realised no more bombs were coming: my enemy had used up his stock.

So I signalled to a stretcher-bearer to join me. Together we got our wounded man on to it and began to make a dash for the top of the slope. Unfortunately, worse was to come because we now got caught in the machine gun fire again, and a bullet hitting the aluminium stretcher broke into fragments, two of which hit me in the back on either side of the spinal cord, by a lucky chance becoming embedded in the muscle and just missing the vital structures by millimetres. The hot stab bowled me over momentarily, but scrambling up again I was delighted to see that our unit at the top of the slope was firing smoke bombs to cover our retreat to the woods above, though not in time to prevent a further blast from a machine gun hitting the wounded man on the stretcher again, this time in the back. Yet we got to the top, and that man, by now wounded three times, was taken back to a casualty clearing station that had been established – and survived. But to my great sorrow among the men killed in that action was one of my best friends, Lieutenant Peter Bucknall, together with many of his men. Two people who visited that hillside more than 30 years later have told me that the mortar bomb craters are still just visible on it.

That same evening in response to an order from General Urquhart, Freddie Gough had pushed ahead towards the Rhine bridge with a small detachment of the Reconnaissance Squadron. But owing to a breakdown in wireless communications neither he nor the rest of the squadron knew where the other was when he reached the bridge. He therefore stayed and fought with the small party that defended it until they were finally all killed or exhausted by their wounds, when he was taken prisoner. The main body of the squadron remained with most of the division in the region of Oosterbeek under the indomitable leadership of its second-in-command, David Allsop.

We spent the night sleeping fitfully in a ditch and the next morning advanced towards Arnhem again.* The enemy bombardment was intense all day and intermittent at night, which I spent in an individual slit trench thoughtfully cut in the sandy soil by someone else and left unoccupied. Uneasily dozing throughout the bombardment, I noticed on waking at dawn an object only a few inches from my head. It proved to be a German 105 mm shell lying over the edge of the trench. In the darkness and din it had landed without my seeing or hearing it, and had probably failed to explode owing to the nearly horizontal angle at which it came to rest.

By 19 September the weight of the daytime bombardment, as concentrated as it was continuous, had made any kind of communication between units intermittent, while radio messages back to England often failed to reach headquarters there. In consequence we were mortified to watch the RAF dropping stores and equipment on to territory they thought we occupied but which was now in German hands. These flights were unforgettable as much for the hope they brought us of more weapons and supplies as for the despair that seized us when we saw the planes fall in flames through the intense flak hurled up at them. In an effort to drop their loads in what they thought – unhappily often mistakenly – was the right place the pilots flew so low that they were easy targets. That afternoon many of us witnessed the heroic flight of one of the RAF's Dakotas that was hit and set on fire as it dropped the main part of its load, then, still burning, wheel slowly round and come over the same area again to drop the remainder, when the flames finally engulfed an entire wing and it crashed. The pilot, Flight Lieutenant David Lord, had told the crew to jump for it – and in fact one survived – but continued at the controls himself. He was awarded the Victoria Cross posthumously.

The metal fragments had now become extruded from my back, leaving some small trouble-free wounds. So on 20

* "Always get there an hour before the enemy" was the CO's maxim.

September I was ordered by the Assistant Director of Medical Services, Colonel Graeme Warrack, to leave my unit for an hour in order to examine some wounded German prisoners who were on mattresses in a hall. Wearing my Red Cross brassard as always, and accompanied by a Reconnaissance Squadron trooper armed with a submachine gun, I entered the room and went up to the nearest patient, a boy of about 17 in SS uniform. Despite bullet wounds in one thigh he scrambled painfully to his feet, stood to attention, and said in English, "Please do not shoot me." Inured as I was to the Germans' scant respect for the Red Cross on the first day, I was nevertheless taken aback by the thought that some Germans expected British medical officers to execute their wounded prisoners.

The next day the bombardment again built up in intensity. Almost without interruption the Germans poured in shells and mortar bombs, some of the latter being fired in simultaneous groups of nine from banks of barrels. The ground shook with the incessant explosions, while the trees in the woods and gardens round us were torn into fragments or blasted into grotesque angles as shells burst among their branches. On our side the noise was almost as deafening from the fire that we returned, though from smaller weapons, and from the blasts as our troops blew holes in the walls of buildings to get at the enemy. Yet this barrage of eruption was not entirely continuous. A lull in the bombardment, perhaps only for a few minutes, would startle us with its silence, as when the conversation suddenly drops at the dinner table, and we would make a dash down a street hitherto impassable or enter a house whose windows had just been blown out. The days were a kind of negative picture of ordinary life: instead of quiet punctuated by outbreaks of noise from the street we had perpetual noise punctuated by outbreaks of silence. But sometimes the silence was not complete. It might be broken by the rattle of machine gun fire in a neighbouring street or even by some rifle shots from a sniper holed up in a nearby house, his bullets whining past us.

These quiet intervals also allowed a moment for the fancy

to wander over better times and to encourage us with the immediate prospect of relief by the Second Army advancing up through Holland. A rumour went round for a day or so that their tanks could be heard rumbling and firing in the distance. We were in sight of salvation! But the little hope we felt in our hearts could not be expressed in anything more than a sceptical smile.

A house in which I had set up my aid post received a direct hit from a shell which exploded in the attic, blowing the thatched roof out sideways in either direction, so that the two halves then came together again and hung down like great straw curtains from the central beam. But, though that particular bombardment spared me, to my sorrow another shell falling beside the house killed the Roman Catholic padre, Father Benson, who had been of great help in the aid post as well as an infinitely stalwart companion.

During a surprising lull one afternoon I went out into the woods to see if I could contact my CO, David Allsop, for though my aid post actually came to form part of the line across which the fighting was taking place I wanted to find out more about my friends and comrades at different places in the perimeter. It was then I learnt that another friend had been killed, Lieutenant John Christie, in a brave attempt to save a special gun when his troop came under attack.

In another reconnaissance through the woods I came upon a glider pilot who after landing his glider had joined in the fighting with the rest of us, as indeed those pilots were trained to do. The poor fellow was alone in the woods, had lost touch with his unit, and was wandering about desperate for water because his lower jaw had been shot away and he was unable to drink anything. Raising his hand and throwing back his head in a drinking gesture, he made me understand what he wanted, for having no jaw he could not speak. So I entered a neighbouring house which its occupants had left untenanted for the time being and found a teapot in the kitchen, which I filled with water still available from the taps (the flow later ceased). By holding the spout to his throat I enabled him to drink through his wound and swallow the water down in gulps. The expression of blissful gratitude he turned on me haunts me to this day, a memory all the more penetrating as I suspect he failed to survive.

The following day I myself had a lucky escape again. While going from my aid post to another in the next road I was knocked to the ground by a shell exploding near by. It slightly concussed me, caused an eardrum to bleed, and left me spitting blood for a few hours. But again I had escaped serious injury and after 12 hours' rest was back on duty – though to just what duty would now be hard to say. My jeep with part of the medical stores had been taken for no doubt more urgent needs, and the water supply having failed we had to take buckets to a well behind a neighbouring house. The most efficacious remedy in the aid post now was a bottle of rum. I am sorry to say it belonged to the owners of the house, whom I never met. Shared out all round, it gave us a small tot each.

Two of the patients in my aid post were German soldiers. One of them, a man with a wounded hand, was short-sighted and wore thick glasses. On that account alone he was hardly fit for military service, and in addition he was of obviously poor physique. But despite his physical disadvantages he was an ardent soldier, insistent that Germany would win and that the Nazis would rule Europe. Filled to the eyebrows with their ideology, he was a weak and pathetic figure drawing strength from their brutal certitudes. To his detestable views he added a disagreeable demeanour, so that I found him a bit of a pain in the neck. Still, there he was, a patient, and he received fair treatment as well as everyone else.

In contrast his fellow German was quite frankly a deserter – and proud to be. Conscripted into the army that year, he was still only 17, and had had a strict Roman Catholic upbringing. Young as he was, he had seen through the whole myth of Nazism, its façade of self-righteous brutality, its depths where the human spirit had been chained up to await destruction. Germany he repeatedly declared to be "kaput", to the disgust of his fellow German. It astonished me that, though he was a mere boy, he should have been able to reject so decisively a regime that had poured a flood of propaganda over him all his short life. Its despotism, its vitality, its comradeship, its tinsel glory – he saw through it all. His religion had given him the strength to stand firmly for civilised values. But tragedy followed. Helping as an orderly in my aid post, he would sometimes of his own courageous volition go out to the surrounding battle zone and help bring in our wounded. One day he was himself badly hit while on one of these sorties and was taken through the lines to a hospital in German hands, where somebody would probably have identified him as a deserter, so outspoken had he been.

By 23 September nearly all the medical services were in enemy hands. Many of the wounded, if suffering from small or remediable conditions, were now sent either to my aid post or to that of the Border Regiment of the Airlanding Brigade, whole those severely wounded were passed through the lines in temporary truces to be admitted as prisoners to the hospitals controlled by the Germans but being run by British RAMC officers and men together with Dutch doctors.

The following day a fierce battle developed in a garden where D Troop of the squadron were fighting under the command of a great friend of mine, Captain John Park. The firing was heavy on both sides but every so often was interrupted by a mortar barrage directly on D Troop's position. Sergeant James Pyper, who was awarded a Military Medal, hearing the plop of mortar bombs fired, shouted "Down!" When the smoke cleared he found John and two other members of the squadron standing in the slit trench with their weapons still pointing at the enemy, but dead.[20]

The end was clearly approaching by 25 September, and an order came round that anyone fit to do so should rejoin his unit for an attempt that would be made to withdraw south across the Rhine. So once again in a sudden lull, induced this time by the RAF's rocket-firing Typhoons, I journeyed through the strangely silent woods – and how silent they seemed between bombardments – to obtain instructions from Divisional Headquarters. Should I stay with the wounded or go with the remnant of my unit? Seeing a slit trench with some earth-coloured soldiers standing in it, I walked over to ask them for directions, since I was uncertain of the exact whereabouts of the HQ. As I looked into the trench I saw that they were all dead, as though clay statues had been placed there.

Going on along the track I was taking I had a strange encounter with the living. In the otherwise deserted wood, from which all the birds had fled, was a wounded officer walking towards me, his left arm in a bloodstained sling. He came up: we greeted each other like two ghosts. It was my old boyhood friend Eric Bussell, who I knew was in the division though I had no idea where. He had been sent by one of the parachute brigades to take a message to Divisional HQ and was on his way back to his unit. We exchanged a few reminiscences. I never saw him again.

Eric was killed soon after the battle in circumstances that were never ascertained, possibly when trying to escape from a train transporting prisoners of war to Germany. His younger brother Bobby, with whom my brother and I had also enjoyed so many days of our boyhood in Torquay, had been killed some months earlier when a shell hit the tank he was commanding in Italy.

From Eric I learnt that I was on the right way, but he warned me to beware of snipers firing in the area of the Headquarters. He was right too; a bullet hit the wall as I made a dash for the entrance. An anxious time then followed, for now the decision had to be made whether I was to rejoin my unit to try to get away or to stay with such of the wounded as remained in our beleaguered perimeter. The ADMS had been captured down in Arnhem, so a senior combatant officer retired to discuss the care of the wounded with General Urquhart. After what seemed a long quarter of an hour he came out and ordered me to rejoin the squadron. One medical officer, the one attached to the Divisional Headquarters, was in fact ordered to remain. Apart from myself only two others were left within the British lines. During the withdrawal one was severely wounded and the other was taken prisoner. Thus I was the only medical officer to get back with the remnants of the division at the time.

That night the rain came down in torrents as we formed up in accordance with a skilfully prepared plan to walk silently

Author aged 6 (photograph by his mother)

Author's mother aged
68 (photograph by
author)

Author's father aged
84 (photograph by
author)

Ulric Nisbet in 1955
(photograph by
author)

Christine Nisbet in
1954 (photograph
by author)

"Respite" by Christine Nisbet (oil, 30" × 40")

Some survivors from the battle of Arnhem, morning of 28 September 1944 after night withdrawal over Rhine. Author on right (photograph by staff photographer of London *Daily Sketch*, who brought the bottle of whisky)

Author's half-brother
Alister (photographer
unknown)

Author's half-brother-
in-law Robert Scott
(photographer
unknown)

Author and Josephine in 1966 (photograph by author)

Lunch in a pub, about 1960. L to R: author's brother Godfrey, Martin Ware, Hugh Clegg, author (photograph by professional firm, untraced)

Francis Rose in 1956 in the English Lake District (photograph by author)

Peter James in 1980 at
Topsham (photograph
by author)

Author's daughters. In order of age: L, Louise, R, Katherine; centre,
Rosemary (photograph by author)

down to the north bank of the Rhine along tapes which had been laid in advance. Each man held the tail of the camouflage jacket of the man in front. To cover the withdrawal the Second Army's 25-pounder guns were fired in a deafening barrage by the Royal Artillery far to the south, in fact at the limit of their range, so that their shells came down just behind us and many burst on hitting the trees. South of the Rhine some detachments from the Second Army had set up Bren guns to fire continual streams of luminous bullets over to our side to mark the lanes we were to use when crossing the river. Our friends were also shelling and mortar bombing the German positions near us, and the Germans were shelling and bombing our positions, those of the Second Army over the river, and the lanes by which we were trying to get across. Through this storm of devastation a Canadian company was operating canvas boats with outboard motors, while we queued at the water's edge to await our turn to get on board one of them. In the first hour half the boats had been sunk. Yet by dawn a few were still coursing to and fro, when daylight made it impossible to continue the operation. All told 2163 members of the 1st Airborne Division out of nearly 10000 withdrew over the river that night, together with 160 members of the Polish Brigade who had fought beside us and 75 members of the Dorset Regiment who had come up through Holland and striven valiantly to extricate us.

The boat in which I crossed the Rhine, which is nearly half a mile wide there, was overloaded like all of them, the water being only an inch below the gunwale; fortunately the river was placid though swift-flowing. Some shells exploded in the vicinity, but fewer than I expected. Even so, I wondered whether we should get across through the guiding stars of Bren gun bullets that streaked in phosphorescent lines past us. At last the boat crunched on the south bank. The journey across had been worrying, as I cannot swim.

Taken back to Nijmegen that night in lorries, we slept fitfully for a few hours and then paraded in the morning to find out who was there and who not. Around midday a press photographer arrived, presented a group of us with a bottle of whisky, and took a photograph. As my uniform had been torn to shreds on barbed wire during the final journey to the banks of the Rhine at Arnhem, I had to appear with an army blanket over my underclothes. Next day in London the photograph appeared in several newspapers. A friend spotted it there and telephoned my wife to say she thought this might be a picture of me, but when they studied it neither could be sure.

Back in Nijmegen, Monty had arrived to give us a bracing speech of thanks, slightly irking our bedraggled remnant by wearing a maroon beret of the Airborne Forces, and we were then transported to Brussels for the flight home. Here I called at a bank (decently dressed once again) to draw out some money with which to buy a razor, comb, and washing kit. On handing me the notes over the counter the clerk uttered a phrase that always stuck in my mind: "Vour êtes parmi les heureux." All he meant was that I was among those fortunate to survive, but his use of the word "heureux" with its connotation of happiness, and its context here of such immense loss of friends and comrades, rang out like a stone falling through the empty caverns of my mind.

During the afternoon one of our sergeants who had survived the thick of the fighting took me aside, tears in his eyes and said, "I'm sorry to trouble you just at this time, sir, my nerves are all...I can't...well, I hope you don't mind..." Here at least was a "psychiatric" casualty easily cured, and over the next two days he recovered his composure. And composure was something we all of us needed, to mitigate or at least conceal the desolation we felt.

Late in the evening of 29 September we arrived back in the village of Ruskington, near Sleaford in Lincolnshire, where we had been based during the summer before flying to Arnhem. Ten lorries had taken us to the airfield on 17 September: two brought us back.

It was after drinking hours when we returned, but our favourite pub in the village, the "Shoulder of Mutton", opened up, and the villagers soon crowded in with us, their eyes sad with apprehension of what they feared we must tell them, for they knew us well and we had many friends among them. The tears streamed down their faces as we had to say that John was killed, Peter killed, Freddie a prisoner, Trevor missing,* Tony missing,* Dick killed, Jimmy missing, one after another, endlessly.

As I looked round at the miserable faces of our troopers and of our weeping friends from the village I was sadly conscious of their loss too, not indeed of their lives or liberty like the rest of the squadron, but of their war-shadowed youth, and some lines of Verlaine's hovered in my unspoken thoughts:

> Qu'as-tu fait, ô toi que voilà
> Pleurant sans cesse,
> Dis, qu'as-tu fait, toi que voilà
> De ta jeunesse?

A particular friend of mine was a girl of about 20 called Doris Sexton (can she still be alive, I wonder?) Seeing I was exhausted she said, "Come back to my house." She was no more than a friend, but the tenderness of her welcome, the solace of her understanding, gave me 10 hours' deep sleep – and then the first bath I had had for nearly a fortnight.

Next morning we could telephone home – and so the photograph really was of me. A day or two later we were given a week's leave.

* Killed by SS troops after the battle.

10 Into Norway

Laughter and cheers rang out in the town square of Newark-on-Trent as I walked towards it on 8 May 1945, VE Day. Celebrating the lifting of a frightful burden from their homeland, the people of Newark sang and danced in the streets. Memories of loss subdued my emotions, and I also turned over in my mind the question: where next? So I returned to the mess and found several officers there already discussing it.

The squadron had been reconstituted under the command of David Allsop after the Arnhem battle. Such a close-knit unit could never be the same after the catastrophic losses it suffered in so short a time, but the new officers and men were warmly welcomed. I know there was a slight feeling of division in the unit between the old lot and the much greater numbers of the new intake, but it was really negligible. When the division as a whole was reorganised I was offered transfer to a field ambulance and promotion to the rank of major, but I declined as I preferred to remain with the squadron, where despite everything life was always so witty and exhilarating. The commanding officer said he would be sorry to see me go, but the decision to stay was mine, not his.

Though VE Day had brought an end to the war for many people, it had not done so for us. It could only be a pause before the next operation got us airborne again, perhaps in Europe, perhaps in Japan. Rumour had it that despite the armistice on Lüneburg Heath the Germans would try to continue the war in the mountains of Scandinavia and Austria. Having already taken part in two invasions I felt a degree of professional curiosity as we discussed the possibilities before us. All of us were in our 20s, and warfare was the only occupation most of us had known in adult life except for my six months as a house surgeon. The war had become our life. It had brought us adventure, boredom, excitement, grief, and an unforgettable sense of trust and comradeship. In the continuity of this experience VE Day was but a ripple.

Ours was an unsettled existence, a life composed of order and anarchy, with its expectation of the unexpected, its realisation of the unimaginable. If a town stood in our way, bomb it; if a building, blow it up; if a man, kill him; if women and children... but there was a point at which people ceased to be enemies. *Dulce bellum inexpertis** (war is pleasant to people who have not experienced it).

The next day we had the answer to our question. Our squadron, together with the 1st SAS Squadron, was to fly into Norway to prevent the Germans from carrying on the war there in the mountains as they were threatening to do. Other airborne troops were flown to Denmark and Austria with the same object of seizing control before the Germans could establish redoubts there. So we collected our equipment, "stood to", and once again we were off.

We had a memorable flight through low cloud over the North Sea in a Douglas C46 with an American crew. The American air force had many admirable qualities, but accurate navigation was not one of them. So at one point, as we circled down and down through the cloud while the pilot sounded a horn as though we were driving round Piccadilly Circus, I wondered: how good is his altimeter? It proved to have been correctly set, since we came out of the cloud a few feet above the sea; the waves seemed about to lap over us. The pilot lifted us up rapidly again into the cloud, and we finally emerged from it to see the Norwegian coast lying sunlit ahead of us. In a few minutes we made a good landing at Stavanger. One plane of that flight did crash in the mountains, with all killed.

The Germans had about 200000 troops in Norway, mostly of poor quality. We were outnumbered more than 100 to one,

* Inscription on the tomb of Henry III in Westminster Abbey (1272). All but the last six letters of it have now disappeared under the erosion of time and the neglect of his countrymen.

but numbers counted for much less than the confidence that animated us and the dejection that weighed in the enemy's heart. The show of strength was enough. The German command there fell into line with the armistice agreement. Our task evolved into hunting down Gestapo agents and SS troops.

Now I had another odd experience: for the only time in the war I was taken prisoner by the Germans – if briefly. Our airfield was some miles south of Stavanger, and when we landed I wanted to go into the town to find out what medical facilities it had. To my surprise I saw a German staff car driving towards the town, so I stepped out and halted it. An officer and driver were inside. Accompanied by one of our unit's junior officers armed with an automatic pistol, I ordered the Germans to take us into Stavanger. They appeared to agree, but soon afterwards I realised that we had left what must be the correct road and were going uphill towards the mountains which lay inland but descended in a series of foothills towards the coast. After a quarter of an hour we arrived at a castle complete with drawbridge, portcullis, castellated walls, and surrounding ditch.* Passing over the drawbridge we entered a courtyard where a number of German soldiers stood with (it seemed unusual to me at the time) fixed bayonets on their rifles. I could do little but get out and demand to see the commanding officer. After a time he arrived and said, "You have no right to stop my vehicles." We argued – I certainly could do no more, confronted by about a dozen fixed bayonets on no doubt loaded rifles – and I pointed out to him that Germany had lost the war, signed an armistice, and was required to lay down her arms. He was reasonable in defeat, and I was probably unreasonable in victory. He instructed his driver to take me, my fellow officer, and the German officer into Stavanger.

When I had visited the hospital and spoken to some of the Norwegian doctors there, the Germans drove us back to our unit. As we stepped from the car the German officer stepped

* The castle was a modern one, made before the war by a film company. It was dismantled after the war.

out too, gave a smart salute, and clicked his heels. I returned the salute equally smartly. If war between armies was chaotic, peace between armies was structured.

Even in the relatively homogeneous population of Norway there were enemies of the Allies: had not their traitor Quisling already had his name used to denote collaborators everywhere? In North Africa we had had contending parties and factions among the French and the Arabs, some only too eager to betray us. In Holland a substantial part of the population in the east of the country favoured Germany, and we had problems at Arnhem identifying the occasional collaborator from the great majority of helpful Dutch, some of whom risked their lives and died for us. In Norway we again had this problem. One man who seemed eager to help our unit was declared by authoritative Norwegians to have been equally compliant with the Germans if not an outright traitor. The exact definition of relations between an occupied people and the occupying force was impossible for us, arriving suddenly from the sky, to interpret with the subtlety or even justice that the local population were apt to expect of us, so that we were exceedingly wary at first about using the services of people who offered them and sometimes caused offence by our coolness.

Even so, friends vastly outnumbered enemies in the Norwegian population. On our first Sunday there we were invited to attend a church service. As commanding officer David Allsop felt obliged to go. For the rest it was a voluntary parade, except that to me he said, "Come on, Doc, you support me." So accompanied by a few others of the squadron we presented ourselves at a small but beautiful church on the Sunday morning. True to the Reconnaissance Squadron's code we arrived early, and it was fortunate that we did so, because the church filled quickly to full capacity, with some standing at the back. Towards the end of the service, which was in the Norwegian Calvinist mode I think, the pastor came over to David and asked if he would address the congregation on the history of the war, as they had had no independent news of it for five years except from listening illegally to the BBC.* David nudged me and said, "Your job, Doc."

So after the service I stood at the east end of the nave for 20 minutes and summarised the course of the war from 1941 onwards, speaking slowly so that each of my sentences could be translated into Norwegian as I went along, though many of the congregation assured me afterwards in excellent English that the translation was unnecessary to them. The story I told was, I hope, objective: it was meant to be history, not propaganda. They received it with appreciation as well as astonishment because, apart from clandestine listening, all the news they had received for years had told of one German victory after another; with one exception: they had been confusedly aware that Stalingrad was a defeat for the German army. This occasion was, I imagine, the only time a Taoist had addressed a Calvinist congregation. I hope I succeeded in dispelling some of the gloom associated with that faith.

Norway's national day, 17 May, was the most joyful they had celebrated in the lifetime of anyone living, and to match it the weather then and throughout the summer was the most beautiful they could remember – lovely warm sun shone down day after day. Another officer from the squadron and I took one of our jeeps and went down to the main square in Stavanger, picked up some gorgeous girls, took them back to their home – and drank something like beer with their parents. In the succeeding weeks the squadron received much help from loyal Norwegians in unearthing Gestapo agents. At the billet of one of them I succumbed to temptation and made off with a wireless set.

At night we used to hear choirs of Russian prisoners of war singing melodious national songs in the camps they had built under German direction. The prisoners had been brought there for a purpose. German plans had been found in Oslo that set out in meticulous detail the employment of the prisoners for constructing defences in the far north along the common frontier between Norway and Russia. The Ger-

* What a great part that institution played in the second world war in contrast to its broadcasts during the war with Argentina!

mans' actuarial calculations had shown that the average time a prisoner worked on these defences without adequate clothing or food was six weeks. The Germans had therefore arranged for the Russians to be transported from the camps at a rate that would allow the vacancies from death to be filled constantly by living replacements. The mathematics were simple, the plan was scrupulously executed, the labour force remained approximately constant, the defences were laboriously constructed, and the prisoners died in orderly sequence.

One afternoon in early August I was sitting in a wood by Lake Mjøsa, north of Oslo, tuning in to the BBC news on the wireless set I had appropriated. The sun shone like silver knives down through the spruces, warming the forest floor where the carpet of dead needles was pierced by low shrubs, mosses, and tussocks of lichens. The radio squealed and crackled as I turned the knobs. Then the BBC announcer's voice came faintly into that woodland glade telling me that an American bomber had dropped an atomic bomb on the Japanese city Hiroshima, causing immense devastation. At first it was difficult to grasp the meaning of this new twist to the war, but two thoughts came into my mind. The first was, surely this is the end of warfare as I have known it. The next 40 years were to show that this hope was too sanguine. Following close on this was the thought that this must be that unbelievable, unimaginable event, the end of the war for me.

So when a second atom bomb, dropped on Nagasaki a few days later, actually brought an end to the war, VJ Day itself meant as little to me as VE Day had done: neither did more than add signatures to a history that our friends had made. Friends of my youth – so many killed. Life had to be lived, and I have put the shadows away from me, but the memory never. I felt then, and still feel, an immeasurable debt.

> Friends of my youth, a last adieu!
> haply some day we meet again;
> Yet ne'er the self-same men shall meet;
> the years shall make us other men.
> The light of morn has grown to noon,
> has paled to eve, and now farewell!
> Go, vanish from my life as dies
> the tinkling of the camel's bell. – SIR RICHARD BURTON.
> *The Kasidah*

PART 3

11 Mandarin and pugilist

"Dr Swinscow, will you come in please?"

I stood among the members of the journal committee of the British Medical Association. Seated round a square of tables, these middle-aged, grey-haired, busy-looking doctors flipping through their papers were scrutinising me with a polite brevity so that they should not make me feel uncomfortable from the beginning of their inquiry into my suitability for the post of subeditor of the *British Medical Journal*. The chairman introduced himself as Dr Carter, a handsome man with a tanned complexion and wavy silver-grey hair swept back from his forehead, and directed me to a chair.

"Please take a seat, Dr Swinscow, and tell us something about yourself."

Though I had been a member of the BMA for several years, I had never imagined until a few weeks previously that such a place as this building in Tavistock Square, London, this room, this committee existed. When I was in my last year at St Thomas's the consultant physician who was head of our teaching firm gave us some advice. It sounded age-old, uncontroversial, and was no doubt uttered by most if not all his fellow teachers to the students hoping shortly to be registered for independent practice.

"As soon as you qualify," he said, "join one of the medical defence societies – it doesn't matter which. And start taking one of the weekly medical journals. You probably know there are two of them, the *Lancet* and the *British Medical Journal*." He paused, lowered his voice a barely perceptible decibel as though making a token payment to a convention that the teacher who inspired our confidence by his impartiality, his scholarly judgment, must not transgress the bounds proper to his office and to the trust we reposed in him as the holder of it, and added, "you'll find the *Lancet* is pretty good."

His preference was probably shared by most of the teachers at St Thomas's for several reasons, among them one that was compelling: in the 1930s it gave week by week a more informed and more thorough account of clinical medicine than did the *BMJ*. It could do this for another reason that made it specially commendable to my teachers, namely, it had no obligation to fill many of its pages with reports of medicopolitical meetings and edicts, as the *BMJ* was required to do owing to its being published by an association that undertook much work of a political or official character on behalf of the profession, including doctors who did not belong to it. Thus to the St Thomas's teachers the *Lancet* appeared to be intellectually pure, politically free, as untainted by the commercial aspects of medicine as it was unrestricted in its medicopolitical allegiances, to be academically based, and, while not ignorant of the type of medicine practised by National Health Insurance doctors, at least unconcerned with reaches of medical practice that could only, if apologetically, be thought of as lower – but with the proviso that the feet are as necessary to the perfect functioning of the human body as are the arms.

In contrast the *BMJ* was seen as being directed largely to general practitioners; and none of our teachers expected their students to hold at that tender age the ambition of a career in general practice. The unfortunate people who finally slipped into and even became more or less reconciled to that fate were those who, in a phrase subsequently used by Lord Moran, had "fallen off the ladder". To these grievously situated doctors, sprawling in the mud of financial stringency and intellectual compromise, the *BMJ* bore weekly reports of negotiations on their behalf, as intricate as they were unending, together with original papers, teaching articles, and obituaries. This being the St Thomas's view (though for many years now I am happy to say it has been entirely different), I naturally accepted it and became a subscriber to the *Lancet*.

But after three years the professional and social ambitions which St Thomas's had presented to me seemed to have diminished in perspective against the rugged scenery that the tragedies and dramas of war had set around my medical work in the RAMC. I compared some of my *Lancets* with copies of the *BMJ* and concluded that the *BMJ* contained more articles of interest to someone in practice like myself, less medical politics than I had been led to suppose, and that the reputation it had acquired at St Thomas's was false. It was certainly outdated.

Whatever truth there may have been in the judgment passed on it when I was a student, the journal entered an altogether new phase during the war under the impact of Dr Hugh Clegg. Though he had been on the staff for some 10 years, latterly as deputy editor, it was during the war that, owing to the illness of the editor, Dr Gerald Horner, he gained effective control of the editing of the journal. The striking improvements he introduced were matched by a diminution, owing to the war, of medicopolitical reports, so that the journal was freer than it had formerly been to provide instruction and to publish current research without being swamped with reports of committee meetings, deputations, and negotiations. I consequently said farewell to the *Lancet* and joined the BMA so that I could obtain the *BMJ*.

It was as a member of the BMA therefore that I received a message one day in the spring of 1946 from a friend of ours called Rodger Winn whom my wife had met in London during the war. He told me of an advertisement in the *Times* for the post of subeditor on the *BMJ* and thought I might like to look at it. Rodger was the elder of two brothers, the younger being Godfrey the well known journalist, and was badly disabled by poliomyelitis contracted when he was a boy. Despite a school life in a wheel chair he became head boy of Oundle. By 1939 he was a successful barrister, and though he was able to stand with some effort in court he sometimes had to lean forward with his hands on a desk to relieve his all too feeble legs of the weight of his body.

Though his disabilities would ordinarily have debarred him from service in any of the armed forces, he managed to fulfil a boyhood ambition soon after the outbreak of war and get into the Royal Navy, where he built up an intelligence unit in the Admiralty that detected with uncanny skill the positions of enemy submarines. In fact so effectual was its work not merely in plotting the whereabouts of U-boats but in forecasting their future stations that in the end no large operation at sea and no sailing of any convoy took place without his scrutiny of the submarine threat to it. Offered at the end of the war a knighthood or a CB for his services, he chose the CB (he was later knighted on being made a judge).

Rodger's physical disabilities did not impede him from expressing himself with charm and aplomb. A pleasing voice, a ready memory for a good story, and a capacity to be both tactful and sensible were aspects of a man who was no obsessional academic but, rather, a forceful and dependable friend, so when he told us of the advertisement I followed his suggestion, applied for the post, and was glad to be able to include him among the referees who supplied testimonials on my behalf.

Since being demobilised in March 1946 and collecting my blue "demob" suit in which to enter a world still precariously at peace, I had thought about the lecture on army psychiatry by Dr E A Bennet that had so impressed me five years previously. I therefore got in touch with him and asked if he would give me an analysis that would help me to decide whether I was suited for a career in psychiatry, a thought that I had occasionally turned over in my mind. He agreed, we renewed our acquaintance, and I underwent a Jungian type of analysis. One of its requirements was that I should record my dreams, and for this purpose I kept a writing pad and pencil at the bedside so that I could jot them down on waking. Here an interesting characteristic of the human mind – or at least my mind – came to the fore. Whatever unconscious layer these dreams welled up from gradually began to resent my recording them, and perhaps also my subsequently discussing them with Bennet, so that I became aware on waking, just as I reached for my pencil, that against my will a part of my mind was clutching at the vision, dragging it away somewhere, covering it over hastily with oblivion. These are no metaphorical phrases: the memory I had of the dream on waking seemed to be roughly snatched away from my conscious attempt to recall it as though another part of my mind were contesting possession of it.

Not because of this analysis particularly but more because it seemed to have nothing further to offer to a person more interested in other things than his own ruminations, I terminated the analysis after 15 sessions; but my friendship with Eddie Bennet grew and deepened over the years, so that when he died in 1977 I was grateful to his widow for inviting me to give the address at his memorial service. This allowed me to bring our friendship to a conclusion, to draw the strands together in a patterned skein, for I believe that more than most people I have a deeply felt need to reach a final harmonious chord. This probably reflects my reaction to the discord in which I grew up.

> The perfect knot needs neither rope nor twine,
> Yet cannot be untied. – *Tao Te Ching*, Chapter 27

So I took the seat the chairman of the journal committee indicated. After I had outlined my experience, expressed the ambitions I hoped to fulfil in an occupation about which I knew almost nothing, and told the committee in response to a member's question that I should be glad to settle down after my wandering life, Dr Carter turned to me and with a moment's hesitation, but with a slightly impudent smile, said, "Do you agree with the politics of the BMA?"

Several members of the committee glanced about quickly to see how their colleagues were taking that one. Observing their expressions of amusement, embarrassment, or surprise I realised that what might have been a tricky question for a candidate to discuss with his prospective employers had equally perplexed the committee: they were as uneasy about its propriety as I was about finding an innocuous answer to it.

In the pause that followed, a member turned to Dr Carter and said, "But Mr Chairman, what exactly *are* the politics of the BMA?" He gave a nervous laugh, everyone chattered in a buzz of conflicting opinions, and I declared that I was "more or less in agreement with them". As I uttered the words I was momentarily stabbed by the doubt whether "politics" is a singlular or plural word, something I thought the committee would expect a potential editor ought to know. I need not have worried: in the BMA politics are plural.

Doubt and difficulty gave way to bonhomie, and I left the room in a hopeful frame of mind. Two days later I heard from Clegg that my appointment to the post would be recommended to the council of the BMA, who must make the final decision. On appearing before that body I was nervous and its members wanted to get on with more important business than questioning someone whose appointment to the most junior of posts had already been determined by the machine. They put a few desultory questions and then formally accepted me at a salary of £850 a year.

Sitting behind a desk piled high with papers, Dr Clegg had his hands folded on it as I entered his room on 1 August 1946. He was sitting placidly, his features in a benign but alert smile as though he were a Chinese mandarin, a little difficult to see clearly because of the windows behind him but presenting a picture of amiable repose. He rose and stretched out a hand to welcome me, suggesting we go round for some introductions. Never can a first impression have been more misleading.

By this time Clegg had been acting editor for several years while Gerald Horner, the titular editor, was due to retire at the end of 1946. For most of the war Clegg and his secretary had run the *BMJ* between them, though Horner always paid special regard to the obituaries. A felicitous style combined with a nicely balanced judgment made him an admired exponent of this branch of literature, but as an editor of a journal that was sometimes plunged into public contention and was behind the scenes within the BMA often subjected to the pressures of various groups of politically experienced members – and politics is after all to do with power – he was inclined to be too diffident, too compliant even, for a job that needed a more aggressive personality.

This I gradually learnt over the years from Clegg and other people who had known the journal in the 1930s, when it had sometimes been criticised to the verge of censure by BMA members, while many doctors who were not members, as I had learnt at St Thomas's Hospital, regarded it as being all too characteristic of the BMA, whose reputation evoked a distant little smile on their lips.

Horner had been brought on to the *BMJ* staff during the first world war, when the then editor, Dawson Williams, spotted him on the *Lancet* and persuaded him into the rival camp. It was a move that annoyed the *Lancet* more at the time than it probably did later. But if Horner was not entirely suited to editing the *BMJ* he was scrupulously honourable in his manner of dealing with all who came into contact with him, and he was in turn honoured by the medical profession in being elected a fellow of both the Royal College of Physicians and the Royal College of Surgeons.

Having little editorial responsibility left to him, he undertook to teach me the craft of subediting, preparing copy for the press, and writing news reports and short editorials. One day I took into his office my subedited version of a report of a General Medical Council session that Harry Cooper, our reporter had sent in. Horner scrutinised the text carefully. Finally he turned on me his eyes now sad with the worries of life and with their vision dimmed by partially detached retinas, and said in his slow, hesitant voice:

"Thank you, Dr Swinscow, but…there is just – one thing…I usually, well yes, I think it's better – if we put the…sordid *details*…of these cases…in *small type*."

If I now recall this colloquy with the sense of amusement I felt at the time I must in all fairness add that on thinking it over later in my apprenticeship I learnt to admire his kindly sympathy for the errant doctors who had fallen foul of the law or of the profession's ethical standards. As a journalist he knew he must report the facts, but as a fellow doctor he would refrain from exposing them too prominently. Though to many people Horner seemed to be a poor editor, he was also widely esteemed as a man in whom humanity and judicious balance were turned upon every problem – qualities that must be counted rare in successful journalists. To robust characters like Clegg, as to many others at that time in the association, he seemed to have been rather ineffectual in his conduct of the journal, an oarsman who was apt to lose control of his boat when the waves blew up. And yet...?

> Perfect activity leaves no track behind it;
> Perfect speech is like a jade-worker whose tool leaves no mark.
>   – *Tao Te Ching*, Chapter 27

The assistant editor was a man who had been on the staff before the war and recently returned from five years' service in the RAMC, almost the whole of which he had spent as medical officer in charge of workshops at Cairo. This was Dr Harvey Flack, an experienced journalist of 34, whose warmth of temperament made the newcomer feel at ease and made Flack himself a welcome guest in any company. A motor crash in Cairo had unfortunately damaged his face, leaving the bridge of his nose depressed, but an attractive voice and an alert, confident expression erased the disadvantage of his appearance and won an immediately friendly response from anyone to whom he spoke. Yet after only a few months I was to learn that his absence was likely to lead to a more united staff than his presence.

The other medical member of the staff was a second subeditor appointed at the same time as I had been. We two had been chosen out of 39 candidates and of those who were not chosen one was later appointed to the *BMJ* staff (Dr John Thompson) and one to the secretarial staff of the BMA, of which he ultimately became secretary (Dr Elston Grey-

Turner). My newly appointed colleague, Dr E G Murphy, was unusually well qualified in having an MSC degree in physiology and being a fellow of the Royal College of Surgeons of England. But only a few weeks were to pass before his ideas for editing the journal, which had all the novelty that a newcomer could give them, came into conflict with those of Hugh Clegg. Murphy had the conviction of youthful enthusiasm, Clegg the experience of some 15 years on the *BMJ*. Neither would yield. Murphy departed.

In his place John Thompson was appointed to a parallel post to mine, now designated assistant editor. He had come from being medical officer of health for the county of Dorset. Clegg was 47, Flack 34, Thompson 40, and I was 29. Like a ring of bells hanging silently these hollow facts give no prevision of the clangour and its reverberations that were to roll from them in future years. For fairly soon after the staff had been consolidated in this way Clegg came into my office one morning with a serious air and a surprising piece of information. Harvey Flack, he said, would never be editor. Clever journalist though he was, his talents were not suited to the *BMJ*. The next editor would probably be John Thompson. It seemed that I was being let into a confidence – "Don't spread this about," he added. Actually I was being let into a conspiracy – to edge Flack out of the *BMJ*.

By now I had come to see that my first impression of Clegg as something of a contemplative, slightly priestly figure, a father confessor to the profession's woes, needed modification. A more typical appearance was his challenging expression and stance. Of muscular build and a little below average height, with a broad intellectual forehead below thinning grey hair, his brown eyes gazed steadily ahead, while the set of his features and especially his firm mouth and jaw expressed determination. Yet he often broke into a smile which, though more likely to be ironic or even scornful than tender, could be surprisingly wistful. A keen boxer at school, he still seemed ready for a fight, whether in an office or committee room or even waiting to go into dinner. He once told me that the biggest regret of his life was having missed the experience that had dominated the lives of so many of us, active service in war. He had been just too young for the armed forces in the first world war and had been required to stay at home and run the *BMJ* in the second. Combative by nature, sceptical in outlook, he enjoyed the excitement of finding an issue on which to pick a quarrel, revelled in the fight that usually followed, and could rarely rest content with mere victory unless he could drive the lesson home to the end. Like the cavalry of old, he pursued the routed enemy with drawn sword.

Yet if that side of his character makes him sound unattractive, there were other sides to it that mitigated its harshness and won achievements to his credit, and to the lasting benefit of the *BMJ*, that would not have been attained without it. Despite an obsessional quality that gave drive to his pugnacity, he was not in the least secretive or defensive. To the contrary, he habitually declared his mind more openly than anyone else I have worked with. Though far senior to the assistant editors at that time, he often came into the office of one or other and discussed at length some idea or project he had in mind, rehearsing as it were the approach he would take in a committee or the argument he would deploy in a leading article. He was never too proud to learn from his juniors or so insensitive as to disregard criticism from readers. With his staff he was invariably frank, sometimes to the point of rudeness, but having been inured for so long to the candour of my mother I used to laugh at what my colleagues sometimes found more difficult to withstand. So when he told me of his plans for the future staffing structure of the journal I was grateful for his openness on a subject that must be of concern to subordinates but is apt to be avoided by their superiors until too late.

12 Pemmican fare

My acquiring a job allowed Josephine and me to look for better accommodation than the flat we then occupied in Hampstead. Both of us preferred the country to the town, and I wanted to be able to travel to a station in London from which I could easily walk to my office in BMA House. This meant living north of London so that I could travel to one of the termini on the Euston Road. Knowing nothing of that part of England, I bought 1-inch Ordnance Survey maps of the whole area from Essex in the east to Buckinghamshire in the west. The maps showed that the place fulfilling most exactly our requirements was Knebworth in Hertfordshire, a village with a railway station on a line that terminated at King's Cross. By a happy chance the first house that the agents offered us was in that village. When we came to inspect it we were struck above all else by a splendid blue-flowered hydrangea by the front door growing in alkaline soil only a couple of feet deep on chalk. (It had some alum put on it most years, but even so I have never again encountered a hydrangea so easily blued.) We told the owners, Gerald and May Addington, that we would probably accept their asking price but would like half an hour to think it over. On a stroll round the streets we agreed we must find the money somehow, so we returned to discuss the details. They were delighted we did so, for just after we had left to go on our meditative walk another couple had arrived and, hearing that we were probably going to buy the house, offered £500 more for it, which was 11 % of the price. To their eternal credit the Addingtons refused the offer until we returned to say whether we would accept their price. We did, and with these honourable people and their family we remained lifelong friends.

We managed to buy a second-hand staircarpet from one of the BMA secretaries, Leslie Potter, and to borrow an old threadbare drawing-room carpet from a sister of Josephine's. The bed, a table, and two wardrobes we bought on dockets – "Utility furniture" as it was called: we use the bed still. We could not of course afford a car, and postwar inflation took care that we remained poor.

During the winter of 1946–7, my probationary six months on the *BMJ*, I had an opportunity of seeing Hugh Clegg in action at his combative best. The weather was exceptionally severe in January and February. In the editor's office a candle dripped its wax down over the neck of a sherry bottle that stood on the table, while dense cloud covered London at midday and blanketed the room in dusk. The absence of gas, electricity, oil, and coal had resulted in its temperature falling to freezing, and we worked in overcoats and gloves. The Minister of Fuel and Power, Emanuel Shinwell, assured us that there would be no fuel crisis that winter, but many people felt this to be a statement of probability rather than of ascertained fact – and how right the sceptics were. By the middle of February widespread power cuts and "load shedding" had reduced most homes, factories, and offices to a cold and twilight existence. Crisis or no crisis, the government had to issue a succession of edicts designed to direct what power was available into the channels where it was most needed for the nation's wellbeing. Naturally many people differed on just where that wellbeing lay. But a moment came when the government decided that, without any serious impairment of the freedom of the press, the weekly periodicals should make their contribution to fuel saving by suspending publication for the time being. In retrospect it may seem rather a strangely trivial yet contentious sacrifice to order, but, strictly rationed as we still were in almost every walk of domestic and commercial life in the aftermath of the war, a ban of this type seemed more reasonable then than it would now.

Looking back at that fuel crisis and the production during it of the two smallest ever issues of the *BMJ*, we need to have the background in mind – a nation accustomed to hardship, to shortages, to the rationing of food, fuel, clothes, and furniture, to standing in queues, and, so much more than today, accustomed to getting government permission before taking action. But the last in particular was not something that appealed to Clegg.

In response to the government's decree to suspend publication we on the *BMJ* staff, with that hubris that is a constant source of annoyance to the laity, decided that medicine was too important to the community to have its most cherished journal (as we regarded it) swept from the scene for an unforeseeable number of weeks. Nor did we contemplate infringing the law in letter or spirit by using fuel in its production. But why not produce a journal without the use of fuel? And what exactly was the nature of the ban that lay on weekly periodicals? Clegg made a number of inquiries, the replies to which convinced him of two things: firstly, the government had no legal power to order the ban – or at least had not invoked such powers as it might be able legally to command; secondly, even if we used no fuel at all the mere publication of the *BMJ* would incur the displeasure of a body called the Periodical Trade Press and Weekly Newspaper Proprietors' Association (PPA), which was said to have entered into an agreement with the government to observe the ban. It is worth noting that the *BMJ* was not a member of the PPA, its application to join having been rejected in 1938.

Thus, determined not to allow the *BMJ* to vanish needlessly, Clegg called an editorial meeting round the candle in his room, and we began work on the issue dated 22 February 1947. Meanwhile he had obtained assurances from the secretary of the BMA that his staff would be available for cyclostyling the *BMJ* and dispatching it without the use of any fuel except candles. To make this possible the editor decided that the whole issue should be on a single sheet of foolscap paper, cyclostyled on both sides. We thereupon reduced news items to a line or so, letters to "Points," obituaries to name, age, and a sentence, and advertisements for hospital appointments (one of our most essential services) to much abbreviated but what we hoped were unambiguous announcements. Finally, a leading article drew attention to the fact that coal is a source of medicine as well as of power, for its constituents had given us carbolic acid, dyestuffs from which the sulphonamides had been synthesised, synthetic antimalarials, aspirin, and stilboestrol. The text of the whole issue was then carefully cut on a series of stencils, from these the cyclostyled sheets were printed, and some 62 000 copies were put into envelopes, addressed, and dispatched with the aid of the secretariat.

As the fuel crisis continued, it became apparent that another issue of the *BMJ* would be needed on the same lines. So for 1 March we prepared the second "pemmican" issue, as they were called – from the American Indian word for "a cake of dried and pounded meat mixed with currants for travellers in the Arctic" (the *Oxford English Dictionary's* definition). This time the leader was on "freedom to print". The theme touched on here was that "the freedom of the press is not a privilege of the newspaper but a fundamental liberty of the subject". Once again willing hands in the BMA secretariat cyclostyled and dispatched the entire issue without the use of fuel.

Thereafter the fuel crisis subsided, the weather improved, our feet warmed up, our breath was less cloudy on the air, and a shoal of congratulatory letters flooded in.

No doubt the episode was a small crackle in a lurid sky below which the world was trying to rebuild itself from the ruins of war, but to me Clegg's action on that occasion has always seemed to be as perspicacious as it was resolute. Nearly everyone accepted the need for rationing to continue after the war for a time, but the feeling was also strong that the government must govern under the law and that a vigilant press was needed to make sure it did so. The abuse of its powers by our own government seemed to us on the *BMJ* to contain a hint of all that we most detested. A reader today who thinks that must be an exaggerated view makes his judgment from a different perspective, for the most obvious threat to parliamentary democracy in this country now comes from individuals and organisations outside Parliament who attempt to destroy governments by extraparliamentary means. But in 1947 a vast web of wartime controls still persisted, on the whole with the nation's consent, and the slightest misuse of them by the government needed to be challenged.

Between the publication of the two pemmican issues of the *BMJ* during those ice-bound days my wife gave birth to our first baby—Louise.

13 Rancorous days

Sometimes on Tuesday afternoons in 1947 and early 1948 Clegg would come into my room with an air of moody consummation and say, "Well, I wonder how they'll take the leader this week." And he might add, "I've tried to give the troops a lead – but they probably won't take it." Military metaphors sprang to the lips readily in those days of strife over the coming National Health Service because we could take more comfort from the vision of a disciplined army on the march than from the somewhat bedraggled reality.

Rancour was the keynote of the debates on the NHS, both within the medical profession and between the profession and the government. The appointed day for it to start was 5 July 1948, and for about a year beforehand the columns of the *BMJ* had reflected the arguments going on all over the country. The doctors regarded Aneurin Bevan as vituperative and untrustworthy; he regarded them as confused and obstructive of the people's will. In retrospect it seems surprising that such bitter argument between profession and government should have bedevilled the discussion that preceded the introduction of a social measure which, in principle, the great majority of doctors favoured, the BMA had declared itself to support, the general public ardently desired, and the government was committed to introduce. But agreement on any point was accompanied by reservations, so that, though agreement in general might add up to unanimity of aim, the multiplicity of reservations promptly destroyed it.

The medical profession was very conscious of having spent several centuries evolving into a self-disciplining body whose members owed allegiance only to their patients, a relationship based on freedom, trust, and secrecy. To have a third party, the government, breaking into this privacy threatened to destroy medicine as a profession, so some doctors thought, unless many of the old traditional practices could be preserved as a framework in which the relationship between doctor and patient could retain its vitality. One of the "planks" of this platform, as it used to be referred to, was the right to buy and sell the goodwill of general practices. The doctors who owned practices were generally in favour of its retention and declared it to be nothing less than a safeguard of the profession's independence from state control. The many doctors demobilised from the armed forces who did not own practices were more apt to believe that the retention of this traditional commerce was a denial of individual freedom. Thus, as commonly happens in life, were self interest and philosophical principle confused.

Similar arguments in defence of tradition had attended the start of National Health Insurance in 1911, but the difference in 1948 was that the whole population would be covered, and almost all doctors would of necessity be drawn into the service, though the option to undertake private practice as a doctor or to receive private treatment as a patient was allowed. The doctors themselves were deeply divided on how to retain the best of the past and bring it into a world where everyone had become accustomed during the war to the planning of national resources for the benefit of the nation as a whole. Consultants differed from general practitioners, medical officers of health from both, the National Health Insurance ("panel") doctors differed from those in purely private general practice, politically right and left wing doctors had their separate platforms, the younger and the older doctors looked in different directions, and the many doctors who had served in the medical branches of the armed forces rejoined civilian life with attitudes that often diverged from those of their colleagues who had stayed at home.

Comprising at that time about two-thirds of all practising doctors, the BMA was, like the profession generally, composed of this explosive mixture. One of the main concerns of the *BMJ* was to prevent it from going up in smoke when Bevan applied a match to one or other fuse sticking out.

Looking at it from the other side we could only envy Bevan's operating, as it were, from interior lines of communication against our scattered forces. He knew the subject inside out, was the architect and executant of the scheme before us, and had no divisions within his own ranks to contend with. In fact he enjoyed the complete support of the government and the hopes of the general population. But there were weaknesses too, and the principal one may be put metaphorically: he could not practise medicine. In other words, it made no difference in the end what politicians said or did, it was the doctors who attended the sick and dying. They could only be won over, they could not be commanded, if the kind of health service that the government and nation wanted was to come into existence. A few doctors would have supported any type of service that Bevan might introduce, for the left wing of the Labour party, of which he was an ornament, had its admirers in the profession who were as dedicated to its policies as were its avowed politicians. But they could not have operated any kind of *national* health service. Though politicians can create peers to advance their policies in the House of Lords, they cannot create doctors to practise their policies at the bedside.

In addition to the conflicts of opinion in its own membership the BMA had to operate despite another impediment that is common in political bodies generally – members whose indifference at the time is followed by recrimination later. Many members who played no active part in the meetings, discussions, or correspondence, when they found agreement had been reached on a policy they disliked blamed "the BMA" for taking the wrong course. Consequently the executive body of the BMA, the council, had to reach out to a traditionally non-political mass of doctors, extract from them a multitude of contradictory opinions, juggle them into a coherent policy representing the majority view, and then persuade the members that this really was what the majority of them wanted. Against a decisive minister and a government with a large majority the BMA could sometimes only console itself with the reflection that, if incoherent, it was at least one of the most truly democratic of all our British institutions.*

In trying to interpret this turmoil to its readers the *BMJ* had an additional problem of a technical nature. The weekly issue appearing on Saturday (Friday in the London area) went to press on the Tuesday of the same week. But the council customarily met on Wednesdays. So providing a leading article on the Saturday embodying the wisdom of a council that had not met when we went to press put a premium on the journalist's life-saving resource, guesswork. Yet to have delayed until the following issue, 10 days after the council met, would have been to write history rather than journalism, so swiftly were events moving at that time. On at least one occasion the guess was so wrong that in the middle of Wednesday afternoon we had to stop the printing press, destroy the several thousand copies printed, and start again, necessitating a slight delay in bringing the tablets down from the mountain. On other occasions a minor error could be sidetracked by having the early copies sent overseas instead of to the London readers. Thus the editor did sometimes feel himself cast in the role of soothsayer rather than hero in this drama, and some of the leading articles contained passages whose ambiguity would have satisfied the Delphic oracle in her most hesitant mood. To readers asking for leadership – though in 20 different directions – as to a council calling upon the *BMJ* for clarion utterance, we sometimes appeared indecisive.

As well as these causes of reproach the journal was subject to another equally troublesome but less exposed to the daylight. We received many letters and a variety of public statements from doctors – often members of the BMA – who disagreed with BMA policies, though the exact nature of these policies was not always easy to determine despite constant communication with the secretariat. Editorial judgment had to be exercised on what we could find space to

---

* And was fond of recalling it had been singled out for praise by Sidney and Beatrice Webb for so being. But that was before it was fully realised that the Webbs were backing their social statistics with a warm admiration of Stalin's regime.

print – a by no means abnormal condition for editors to work under, but necessitating a degree of independence for the editor that some members of the BMA found difficult to understand. Thus the refusal to publish a letter because its theme was hackneyed or insulting would be regarded by its author as an attempt by the BMA and its journal to suppress dissident opinion. But the publishing of a letter expressing a dissident opinion would be regarded by BMA stalwarts as a betrayal of the association's cause by its own journal.

In walking over these coals of fire the editor had the support of a long tradition in the *BMJ* office that, so far as was reasonable, any member of the BMA had the right of entry to the journal's correspondence columns, and in this context "reasonable" did not mean conforming with BMA policy. It meant, for example that the letter should not be a long dreary rigmarole, rambling, rude, and repetitious, should not fly too obviously in the face of facts, and should have some relevance to the argument it was putting forward. But a substantial body of opinion in the association held that the *BMJ*, at least in those distressful times, should be in effect a propaganda organ. Not that the word "propaganda" itself was often heard then, because having started in the seventeenth century under respectable auspices in the Roman Catholic Church it had been usurped by the recently execrated and defeated dictators Mussolini and Hitler, and so had come to denote a very undemocratic manner of influencing people's opinions. No, Clegg's phrase was that "we can't allow these people to turn the *BMJ* into a parish pump gazette", and he never hesitated to express his dislike of the idea in terms that made its advocates squirm with shame or (if they were more resilient) resentment, for it must be admitted that many who might have conceded the substance of his argument were apt to be vexed by his manner of stating it. Our object on the *BMJ* was to make it not a house journal of the BMA but something worthy of the whole medical profession in this country and respected abroad as an ambassador of British medicine. And so far from being antipathetic to the association, this hope and ambition we had for its journal would bring the BMA itself renown as well as fulfilling its duty to find room within its fold for doctors of every persuasion.

Two themes ran through Clegg's thoughts in those days. The first was, to quote an oft repeated phrase of his, "the journal is bigger than the association." He meant this not in any parochial sense of defending his own territory but rather that it must appeal to a readership beyond the BMA itself and draw its picture of medicine week by week from research institutions, hospital wards, family doctors' surgeries, the benches of pathologists, chemists, and physicists, the bookshelves of historians, the machines of statisticians, and the newly invented ballpoint pens of lone, worried, frustrated, angry doctors. So that, while the editorial pronouncements on matters of BMA policy were restricted to the bounds of that policy, the rest of the journal was open to anyone who had something fresh to say.

The second theme was that the BMA must be held together. The recurring nightmare of both editor and secretary was that the BMA would split up into conflicting factions mainly composed of different branches of the profession. Neither had much confidence in the chairman of the council, Dr (ultimately Sir) Guy Dain, a general practitioner in Birmingham. Clegg came back to my office from seeing the secretary of the BMA, Charles Hill, one afternoon, stared out of the window at the sky, and said, "Charles has been telling me – after that speech of Dain's yesterday – 'Dain just doesn't understand what's going on.' Charles is right you know." It was a speech that both feared might be received with annoyance in some sections of the profession – though, to give Dain his due, what speech would not have been? But to Clegg anything that could possibly dissolve the ill-fitting joints in the BMA, whether the acid of acrimony or the oil of conciliation, was the most feared of all weapons to put in the hands of Bevan. If that happened, the battle would be irrevocably lost and Bevan would carry the day.

But I wonder now whether it would have been anything more than the day. Without a coherent and responsible BMA the NHS might never have got off the ground. For the BMA, in its medicopolitical experience over many years, in its opposition as much as its agreement, in its ability to solicit its members' views and to make decisions, was as necessary a part of Bevan's political life as the pebbles that a crocodile accumulates in its lower stomach to give it greater weight, more effective thrust, when plunging into the river.

Just as in the early stages of the war I had been reading the mediaeval legends of the Holy Grail and found there a set of poetic co-ordinates by which to map the turmoil of those days, so Clegg, by chance, I think, had lighted on the works of Lecky to give him philosophical nourishment during the health service debates. W E H Lecky (1838–1903) was a Member of Parliament for Dublin University in 1895–1902 and wrote works on English and Irish history, European history, and *Democracy and Liberty*. Probably he is a somewhat neglected author today, and I must admit with regret that I am among those who have read nothing by him. But from his writings Clegg derived the concept of democracy – or if not the concept at least the fire to warm his words – that he thought should operate in the BMA and feared might falter there. This was that, while the majority must prevail in the execution of a policy, otherwise there would be stalemate and chaos, in the evolution of policy every expression of opinion must have a fair outlet, and, equally important, the majority must not be allowed to trample over the minorities when putting the policy into effect.

Looking back at the editorials of that time when the health service was being brought on to the stage and for some years afterwards, mostly written by Clegg, I have had to admit to some doubt whether they directed events in any recognisable way. When they were published, Clegg in particular put his all into them – work in the daytime, reading in the train, cogitation at night, discussions in between – but in the end did they influence anyone? For such is the nature of editorials that at the time they change few minds, appeal to none except the converted, anger none except the unconvertible, bend thought no more convincingly than a telepathist bends a spoon. As historical records they have a place. Clegg and I used to wonder what effect they had on the present.

His own views on the proposed structure of the health service were as mixed as they were moderately held. Like almost everyone except for a few on the medical fringe he thought a nationwide service was needed, but with regard to the particular one presented to us he had some piecemeal reservations. His main concern again was that the BMA should be brought through this crisis in one piece. If it could remain a single, strong association, it would have the power to bend any health service into a framework where doctors could practise sound medicine. Clegg was not a man of firm political convictions at all; if anything, he could be described as a liberal, I suppose, but with a small "l". He would attack left, right, and centre impartially, and he rigorously excluded from the pages of the *BMJ* any hint of party politics. The British system of social classes, so fascinating to foreigners, hardly touched him, and I never heard him express a judgment in terms of social class. He almost belonged to that category of people who are at ease with all classes; almost, but not quite. Rather I would say of him that he was rarely at ease with people of any class – it didn't matter which.

Finding that they could not dictate to the editor what he should put in the *BMJ* or what he should exclude from it, some members of the association hoped they saw an opportunity to get rid of him. By telephone and letter and private word they had tried to control him during the storms, but to no avail. All right, he had rejected their friendly advice, betrayed the BMA to Bevan, compromised the entire medical profession: he must go. These indeed were the very words Clegg overheard being spoken by a prominent member of the association, Dr R P Liston, when walking along a corridor in BMA House one day. Liston was a general practitioner in Sevenoaks who also did some industrial medicine. Some months previously he had personally taken a paper up to Clegg's office and asked him to publish it. Clegg looked through it at Liston's request, saw that it was a "puff" for some proprietary product made by a firm that Liston was connected with, and handed it back. Refusing to take this decision unchallenged, Liston was rash enough to make some sort of veiled threat based on what he held to be his prominence in the affairs of the BMA. Clegg became annoyed, told him to leave the office immediately, and when Liston proved dilatory took him by the arm and propelled him to the door. "I personally threw him out," were Clegg's words to me when describing this episode. So when he heard Liston saying to a crony that the editor "must go", he took the threat seriously enough to prepare a memorandum in his defence if it should be needed. I assured him that if he were sacked I should go too, and in fact I took a small step in that possible direction by cancelling a financial commitment that I had entered into for the construction of a greenhouse at home. In the end the ambitions of Liston and his friends proved to be illusory, a wary truce between the editor and some sections of the BMA gave us more time to devote to editing the *BMJ*, and I was able to have my greenhouse constructed.

Clegg used to bewail having to spend so much time away from the practical work of editing so that he could combat by letter or committee memorandum the criticisms aimed at the journal, yet even as he spoke to me on such occasions his eye would glitter with momentary rage at the recollection of some insult, real or imagined, his face break into a smile at his reply, contemplated or dispatched. The material being prepared for the journal's pages took second place for a moment. I used to think he was never really happy unless every nerve and muscle was tense with confounding his opponents; he needed a quarrel to dispel the lassitude, the boredom of the daily round, and give a sharper edge to his life.*

Finally, after a great deal of shunting this way and that, the two halves of the train were hooked up and the National Health Service came into being on the appointed day to the tune of a conciliatory message to the medical profession from Aneurin Bevan. Clegg suggested to Bevan that he should make this gesture and Bevan did so in words whose contrast

* Here I am speaking of him as the colleague I worked with for many years. His life at home was notably more harmonious than what we saw at the office, and with his family we would see him express a quality that he kept concealed at work, namely tenderness.

with earlier diatribes was striking. Strangely enough for one so familiar with demagogy, Bevan never seemed to realise that very few doctors had any interest in politics; they felt themselves to be remote from the wrangles and ignorant of the issues, bewildered by "speakers from London" and plebiscite forms. Instead of trying to win their hearts, not in the sense of appealing to them over the heads of their appointed leaders but simply to have the good will of ordinary practising doctors, he was often abusive of the profession in tone and metaphor to such a general extent that, irrespective of his policies, he aroused widespread dislike among people who, if challenged to think about the matter, largely agreed with his plans. This I believe was the greatest single cause of the mistrust of the health service that doctors felt for years after it began. Though he was doubtless prodded beyond the bounds of patience at times by the obstruction, or inertia, or simple disarray of the doctors, he too often lost control of what can well be a politician's greatest asset, a persuasive tongue. His invective tainted an era.

If the disputes over the health service forced the *BMJ* into an indecisive role from time to time and gave its editor an unpopular image, Clegg himself thoroughly enjoyed the rough-and-tumble of it all. Having at first thought the service would provide for the medical profession a stable, equable way of life in which medical politics would gradually wither away, we began to learn that the exact reverse was the case: committee work proliferated, larger limousines carried more deputations here and there, legal advisers worked overtime, public relations officers never left the telephone except for another briefing, and relations between different groups of the profession attained a Byzantine complexity. Gone was the pastoral dream of the contented doctor practising medicine in a service whose regularity and harmony had freed him from the attentions of administrators and politicians. Instead BMA committees looked ever more hungrily for space in the *BMJ*, and the growing volume of work bred a new race of virtually whole-time medical politicians.

In 1952 the *BMJ* was lucky to be able to recruit to its staff a new assistant editor, Dr John Thwaites, a general practitioner who had sat on many of the BMA's committees, including the council, and so was familiar with the medicopolitical scene from the BMA's viewpoint. At the same time too Clegg asked me if I would like to go on a statistics course: "You seem to have got that sort of mind," he added ambiguously. The prospect delighted me for two reasons. The first related to the articles coming into the office for publication. Mainly owing to the work of Professor (later Sir Austin) Bradford Hill, a pioneer of whom it is not too much to say that he changed the character of medical research throughout the world, reports coming to us from the Medical Research Council had a statistical framework. Patients were being sorted, and the results of investigating and treating them analysed, by means of techniques based on probability theory. It is to the great credit of Clegg that he saw how medical research was about to be transformed by these methods and that he found space to publish papers employing them, for his doing so aroused hot opposition from many readers who wanted less abstruse fare. To have someone on the staff who could understand the jargon would clearly be useful.

The second reason for my welcoming this proposal was more personal. Having been on the *BMJ* staff for about six years instead of the two or three I had originally planned I found that, although the work was enjoyable, there was something lying deep in me that it did not satisfy. Two years later I was to discover my true vocation, but meanwhile I attended a course under Bradford Hill's direction at the London School of Hygiene and Tropical Medicine and received some formal teaching, for which I have been enduringly grateful to him. Like an aloe plant that spreads out its spiky leaves and some 25 years later produces a flower, I published some papers with a statistical background and then, after that interval, a little book on the subject.[21]

14 Storm in a pram

In their different ways the production of the pemmican issues of the *BMJ* and the editing of the journal during the health service debates showed Clegg at his most determined to defend a fundamental principle of democracy, the right to publish. In both cases he identified the need of the hour and met it. Now a less favourable picture of him must be drawn, for although, again, he correctly identified a need, in this case medical education of the general public, he failed to fulfil it in the way he wanted owing to two defects in his character: he could not delegate responsibility and he could not calm down ruffled tempers; on the contrary, he was more likely to inflame them. The reason he could not delegate responsibility was that, having determined a certain course should be followed, a desired goal reached, he could imagine no other way of striving towards that end than his own. Other people could not be trusted to step out of their slippered ease, to abjure compromise, to push on undeflected, to beat off diversionary attacks, to stifle their exhaustion as they approached the end of the battle, for in his make-up there was a distinct obsessional streak that never quite allowed him to believe other people could be as determined in their own way as he was in his or as effectual in achieving an objective that might be slightly different but was as estimable as what he had in mind.

As I have mentioned above, he told me after I had been about a year on the staff that Harvey Flack would never be editor owing to his unsuitability for the post. Some time later, early in 1948, he gave me a more positive reason for this decision. Flack would be made editor quite soon of a popular health magazine.

One day in 1949 Clegg came into my office and leant against the window, gazing at the plane trees (now alas cut down) for longer than usual.

"God, I'm so bored," he said, "but I'm thinking of giving up the editorship... well not leaving," he added. "Oh there's that creature Carter arriving." He was looking down into the car park and could see the chairman of the journal committee climbing out of his car after driving up from Bournemouth. "No, what I was thinking of – I'm tired of the detailed production every week, and I was thinking I'd be a kind of managing editor, like they have in the newspaper world, overseeing the *BMJ* and our other journals and giving general guidance. What do you think?"

It was characteristic of Clegg that, despite his high standing in the medical profession and an assured consciousness of his own talents, he should not be too proud to test this idea out on a colleague 17 years younger who had been on the staff a couple of years and was its most junior member. I told him I thought if he was bored with editing the *BMJ* he would soon be bored as managing editor of all our publications, having no specific role in the production of any of them.

It was partly the aftermath of the health service disputes that had induced this mood of relaxation. The continual tension had gone, but, more important, the deep fulfilment had not arrived. A shadow of some half-perceived longing lay near his heart, a shadow I did not clearly identify until the last year of his life and will depict more fully when I come to that. The dream of managing editorship soon faded or, perhaps I should say, became transmuted into a fresh preoccupation, namely, the popular health magazine of which he would be supervisory editor with Flack under him as executive editor.

The idea of educating the general public in the ways of healthy living had occurred to him early in the war, when the Ministry of Health was putting out advice of that kind ("Coughs and sneezes spread diseases") and the Ministry of Food was telling the population how to choose and cook such food as was available, thus providing an education of both contemporary and lasting benefit to the nation. Two strands came together in Clegg's mind: he himself had written the occasional pamphlet directed at lay people, and during the 1930s he became experienced at starting new journals covering special branches of medicine, thus bringing credit to the BMA as publisher. So, when the war ended and restrictions were eased, he turned again to his pet idea of a popular journal, written by doctors and bearing the authoritative imprint of the BMA, that would teach the public how to eat, work, sleep, and exercise in a healthy way, how to have lusty babies and "hopefully" (as they say nowadays) reach a dignified old age. Health, how to attain it, preserve it, live it, enjoy it, was to be the lesson of every page.

Soon after the health service was launched Clegg persuaded the council and journal committee of the BMA that the time had come to plan the publication of the new monthly magazine. Flack became its editor designate (substantive in 1950), and in due course a small editorial and business staff was engaged. Plans, appointments, and draft contracts wended their way through the BMA committees successfully, and hopes of making at least a small profit began to animate the venture, though it was thought of primarily as taking education to the public and in return bringing prestige to the association.

But relations between the supervisory and executive editors were more troubled. On a personal level neither of them fully understood or trusted the other. While admiring Flack's skill as a popular journalist Clegg considered that he needed supervision on any issue of importance, for he dwelt too much, in Clegg's view, on the pathological rather than the preventive aspects of disease, was too inclined to excite the morbid dreams of women who read his articles in the lay magazines then beginning to multiply as postwar restrictions were lifted, and was altogether too slapdash in his presentation of medical advice, too careless of the reservations needed and of the alarm that he might cause among hypochondriacs.

Flack for his part, while accepting in principle the aim of educating the public in healthy living, differed entirely from

Clegg on what constituted education, the public, and healthy living. From his already wide experience of writing for lay magazines Flack believed that education should consist of a simple message, several times repeated, without hesitation or qualification – so far as possible. The new journal, he believed, should contain the sort of popular articles that he wrote for the magazines, whereas Clegg had more in mind the instructional leaflets issued during the war. When it came to healthy living, Flack did not exclude, as Clegg would have done, the provision of information on the symptomatology and diagnosis of disease, details of treatment, descriptions of operations, and so on.

This discrepancy of view between the two editors reflected not the extreme poles but recognisable divergences in the profession as a whole – divergences which are as evident today as they were then. But Flack foresaw, which Clegg did not, that if the magazine was to succeed commercially it must swim with the tide of more open medical exposition and provide the kind of material that has since become commonplace, but was then an innovation, in magazines under lay control and in television programmes. There is certainly a substantial public who thrill nervously but pleasurably at the blood and guts of surgical operations just as there was two centuries ago among the throngs at public executions. Today they believe themselves to have derived intelligent understanding from the spectacle; their forebears believed they derived moral edification. Quite possibly both are right. But in trying to keep the new journal, now given the title *Family Doctor*, on the lines he had conceived – that is, teaching healthy living to the family – Clegg became during the planning of the first few numbers increasingly at odds with its editor and, not being a man given to compromise on an important issue, began to undertake some of the detailed editing himself.* After some months of disputes Harvey Flack confided to me that something must be done "to get Hugh off my back."

* Yet on minor issues he would often yield. It would have surprised his enemies to know that one of his favourite phrases was "Better turn the other cheek."

The journal committee was then responsible for the business administration of the *BMJ*, the specialist journals, and *Family Doctor*, but Carter (the chairman) and several other members regarded themselves as privileged to go beyond business matters and make suggestions to Clegg on how he should edit the *BMJ*. They naturally annoyed him greatly, for advice was being given by people who had neither the qualifications nor the authority to give it. Into committee meetings already made tense by this tactless interference the growing discord between Clegg and Flack brought further dissension and recrimination. Carter was an experienced committee man and at that time was probably a member of more committees at BMA House than any other person (apart from officers ex officio), but as a chairman he tended to identify himself too closely with some idea or other that took his fancy at the time. Though fair-minded in the way he approached a problem, he was apt to be injudicious in the way he disposed of it, and though himself urbane and even-tempered he was inclined to assume a role that caused annoyance to the staff.

Carter was never devious: Liston was. When trouble in the *Family Doctor* became evident, Liston recognised his opportunity of hitting back at Clegg. He was to be seen hurrying to and from the *Family Doctor* office, giving advice, being "briefed", playing the conspiratorial role with relish. Flack of course knew what sort of man he had as ally in his troubles and may be forgiven for making use of him. But the opposition to Clegg was not restricted to a tactless chairman and a trouble-making member of the committee. Several other members were disturbed by the conflicts between Clegg and Flack and in a perfectly honourable manner tried to resolve them.

The first number of *Family Doctor* appeared in April 1951. Clegg and Flack were by now hardly on speaking terms, and Flack was editing the journal so far as he could within his assignment without reference to Clegg. The final clash came with the September issue. An article appeared by a staff writer on the safety of prams, and it included the phrase "At least one pram-manufacturer fits a steadying arm..." On the opposite page was an advertisement for Pedigree prams, with a "non-tipping safety device" arrowed. There was obviously a tie-up between the article and the advertisement.

In the BMA's professional journals stringent precautions have always been taken to prevent any kind of connection between the editorial pages and the advertisement pages. No firm is allowed to place an advertisement in a particular issue of the journal because a scientific or clinical article mentions a product favourably (or unfavourably) in that issue. Lay periodicals, even esteemed ones, follow a different code of ethics and allow a connection between advertising and editorial matter, even to encourage one and arrange pages round it, so that one may for instance see an advertisement from a firm offering holidays on some sunny coast and on the opposite page an editorial article extolling the delights of the same coast as a place to take a holiday.

Owing to the discord between Clegg and Flack over editorial policy, Clegg was receiving only the necessary minimum of information about forthcoming issues. He therefore did not see any set of proofs showing the advertisement lying opposite the article. Owing to his growing distaste for the whole venture he no longer scanned through each issue of the magazine with eager attention when it appeared, so that he still remained unaware of the juxtaposition of article and advertisement even though it lay on his desk. And owing to – perhaps inattention, certainly impercipience, he landed in trouble.

The story moves to a meeting of the journal committee on 11 October. Liston then produced the September issue of *Family Doctor* and asked "through you, Mr Chairman," whether Flack was responsible for the pram advertisement and article facing each other. Flack accepted responsibility for the article but not for the advertisement. Liston then asked Flack if he was in control of *Family Doctor*, and Flack replied, "I am in control of the editorial side of *Family Doctor*." Liston suggested that Flack was not therefore in control of the magazine. Clegg pointed out that the circulation manager was responsible for advertisements and added that tie-ups of this kind should be watched. After some discussion the committee resolved to consider at its next meeting the position and responsibilities of the editor of *Family Doctor*, and it asked for memoranda from Clegg and Flack to be placed before it.

John Thompson and I were gossiping in his office after the meeting when Clegg came in.

"More blasted memoranda," were his opening words.

"Liston was in characteristic form," said John, and I added, "Yes, what are you going to do about his insinuation?"

"What do you mean, insinuation...?"

"Well, the pram – he's accusing you of..."

"My god! Of course..." We all fell silent while Clegg allowed the full force of the accusation made against him to build up in his mind, to understand the predicament in which Liston and Flack had caught him. Incredibly in one so sharp to spot hostile thrusts, whether against himself or the *BMJ*, Clegg had entirely failed to understand, what had been clear enough in the meeting to John and me and was what we were talking about when he came into the room, that Liston's question and Flack's disclaimer of responsibility for all but the "editorial side" of *Family Doctor* implied that divided responsibility could lead to grave error, and perhaps more – to a clear breach of the BMA's publishing ethics by the supervisory editor, Clegg. So it came about that Clegg's lack of consultation with Flack owing to their personal antipathy, his failure to scrutinise the proofs more closely, lack of enthusiasm to read the copy of *Family Doctor* that arrived on his desk, and now a too-trusting inattention in committee – all had combined to tie a weight round his neck that threatened to sink him. His features broke into a sardonic smile mixed with a determined frown. Now that he understood what had happened, now that he had clearly identified the enemy's position, he felt his energies released at the prospect of the coming struggle.

Clegg was a more sensitive person than he sometimes showed at the surface, and like most sensitive people he needed a righteous cause to put heart into the fight, even though he enjoyed the flow of adrenaline. And here he was, personally assailed, and certainly in the right on an unquestioned ethical principle fundamental to the BMA's repute. Yet as events were to show, his fate was what many a nation has suffered over the centuries: he was in the right, but was overborne; he won the battle, but lost the war.

Interviews with Flack and other members of the staff brought Clegg the facts. There had of course been a complete, planned link between the advertisement and the article. Memoranda from Clegg and Flack put before the committee at its next meeting showed that their editorial policies were in irreconcilable conflict. On the whole the committee did not take kindly to the practice of linking advertisements with editorial articles, and they acknowledged that Clegg was in no way blameworthy. But this was now a side issue. Flack had really fired the winning shot when he told the committee he was responsible only for the editorial side of the magazine. Obviously editorial responsibility needed to be clearly defined, every part of the magazine ought to be within the sphere of that responsibility, and one man should exercise it. Flack must be that man. So all connections between Clegg and *Family Doctor* were severed, Flack was put in sole charge, and a separate committee was set up to deal with its production.

Within the bounds of *Family Doctor* and its educational booklets, subsequently developed, Flack achieved his ambition of a successful editorship and enjoyed a job that came to an end too soon. A heavy smoker all his life, he died in 1966 aged 53, living out his last months with great courage. Clegg wrote his obituary in the *BMJ*; it was warm, magnanimous, just.

As in Clegg's view the flower had rotted on the stem he was glad to be rid of *Family Doctor*, and among its various lessons was this: if Flack was unsuited to work on the *BMJ* (which I think was a fair judgment), Clegg as supervisory editor of *Family Doctor* would have ruined its chances of success whoever had been editor. His talents did not lie in that direction. He was a leader, not a supervisor; and he lacked the common touch needed to appeal successfully to a lay readership wanting to have their fancy as well as their education brushed up.

One effect of the battles over *Family Doctor* had been to diminish for a good many months the attention that Clegg normally gave daily to the *BMJ*. Though the episode caused turbulence in the office, John Thompson and I felt the relief of being to some extent on our own. But while the main role of editing the journal fell temporarily on John as deputy, and he could enjoy the relaxation of being free of the editor's interruptions in the daytime, he often had to withstand Clegg's labyrinthine ruminations on the *Family Doctor* troubles far into the evening after the rest of us had gone home. John was a sympathetic listener, and over the years Clegg liked to unload his worries on to him. In the end this confessional relationship led to an anguished question being asked.

Meanwhile other doctors had been appointed to the staff of the *BMJ*. Gordon Ostlere, later to become a popular novelist under the name Richard Gordon, joined us in 1949 as an assistant editor but left after a year to devote his life to writing. Clegg was unhappy about this departure and asked me whether I thought his manner had offended Gordon. I told him I did not think it had, that Gordon wanted to concentrate on his writing. But this was the first intimation I received that Clegg realised he could be a difficult person to work with. He became increasingly candid about this as the years passed and more inured to causing offence to his staff.

After he left us Gordon liked to claim that he learnt to write fiction from being in charge of the journal's obituary columns. But his most lasting contribution to the *BMJ* was that he taught us to call our secretaries by their Christian names. Before he came they were Miss Smith and Miss Brown; by the time he left they were everything from Anne to Zena, and remained so ever after.

He was succeeded by two new assistant editors. John Crammer, who had been a brilliant biochemist at Cambridge, left us subsequently to become a successful psychiatrist.

Martin Ware came from the Medical Research Council's headquarters, where he had been editing their publications. A couple of years older than I, he was rather younger than Thompson. Coming into my room one day John Thompson said, "I've just seen a strange sight – Martin is crawling about on the floor of his office surrounded by filing cards." This was indeed something new in the office, where filing and indexing were in a primitive state, papers and journals were piled up all over the place, and editing the journal was more a question of inspiration than precedent. Card indexes began to appear, and they helped to bring some much needed order to our desks if not to our brains. Yet one or two famous pockets of untidiness remained. A pile of papers lay on a shelf in Clegg's room – "They've been there since before the war," he told me in a tone of sorrow mingled with pride. They must have gone by the time he left, I suppose. Certainly they are not there now.

Among the tasks I undertook then was to scrutinise continually about 100 journals to find subjects of importance for discussion in editorial articles, so that our readers could be kept informed of what was being published round the world. Before the war, according to Clegg, the editorials had been written by a small number of people with a ready pen and a broad general knowledge of medicine. His first priority when he became editor in 1947 was to improve the scientific standing of the journal. So Thompson and I persuaded experts in many different fields to draft leading articles on subjects we would select from the current journals, and then we often had to edit or rewrite them ourselves. All this, which seems so obvious and elementary now, was then a novelty in the *BMJ* office. Discoveries were being made everywhere – in endocrinology, virology, antibiotics, allergy, and many more branches of medicine. The expansion was exciting, and in the multiplication of new drugs posed all sorts of problems.

One of my jobs was to scrutinise advertisements to see that the claims made for a drug did not exceed judgments formed on it by trustworthy medical opinion (not always easy to identify). There were no government committees in those days to help, so I relied a great deal on experts in pharmacology and therapeutics, but disputes with manufacturers were fairly common. In order not to feel compromised in any way I never then held shares in a company manufacturing or marketing drugs. People who did made some hefty profits.

15 The gold-headed cane

At 10 o'clock on Monday 2 April 1956 Clegg came into my office bearing some sheets of typescript.

"Dougal, I've drafted a leader, did it yesterday evening over a bottle of claret, have a look at it – I want your free and unfettered... just tell me what you think. I'm not going to influence you by saying anything more now." He left with me the first draft of a leading article that was published in that week's issue of the *BMJ* under the heading "The gold-headed cane."[22]

When I took it back to him a quarter of an hour later I said, "You can't possibly publish that stuff about the College of Surgeons."

"Why not, what's wrong with it?"

"Well, it's not really true, I mean, you might be able to justify it in a way, but you exaggerate the defects you mention. I get the impression you've drifted on from the first part of the leader about the College of Physicians and not been able to stop."

"What about the rest of it?"

"Yes, with some toning down ("No, I'm not toning it down" – but he did) and tightening up here and there, then I think it would be all right." And my last words were, "Hugh, the claret *has* got into it a bit, but I should go ahead." He did. I read the final version in the early copies of the *BMJ* on Wednesday morning.

This leader caused a more tumultuous quarrel between the editor and his employers, the council of the BMA, than any other episode during his tenure of the post. Yet in the end it brought greater definition, stability, and authority to the journal, and to the association a sharper awareness of its democratic conscience and its corporate power.

In its original form the text was a rambling criticism of the Royal College of Physicians of London and the Royal College of Surgeons of England. These two London-based colleges, with their distinct and cherished histories stretching back over the centuries and their contemporary authority extending throughout the medical profession, were in Clegg's view tangled up in a web of traditions, out of touch with the younger men and women then toughening the scientific rigour of medical practice, and failing to support those workers in research who were stepping forward faster than had ever been known before. To add insult to injury the leader accused the College of Physicians in particular of drawing too great a proportion of its income from examination fees – in a nutshell, the old sitting on the backs of the young.

In addition to criticisms of the College of Physicians' outlook and policies the leader was also hostile to the continuance of Sir Russell (later Lord) Brain as president, for to some extent Clegg identified the failings of the college with lethargic leadership from its president. It was here that I suggested some toning down, but Clegg was never very successful at separating the man from the office, and a text that was intended to exhort the college to find a new president appeared to some readers, including Brain himself, to be a wounding personal attack. Clegg had not intended it to be taken that way. He had formerly had a high regard for Brain when he was elected president six years previously, regarding him as a decent (to use one of Clegg's favourite epithets about doctors) and straightforward physician in contrast to his predecessor, Lord Moran, whose great gifts of drive, advocacy, and clarity of expression many people had come to distrust as having been diverted into medicopolitical opportunism. (The book he wrote later on Winston Churchill, whose personal physician he had been, earned him the execration of the Churchill family and the reprobation of many doctors.) But, if originally a welcome breath of fresh air in the college, Brain had gradually, in Clegg's view, failed to prevent it from sinking into the immobility of Old Cathay. From this the leading article was intended to shake it.

Though he expected an artillery barrage from Brain and his friends in the college (of which Clegg had been a fellow since 1944), the first shots came from an unexpected quarter, the BMA itself. The chairman of the BMA council, who at that time was Dr E A Gregg, a general practitioner in north London, telephoned to express his sense of outrage, and he was quickly followed on the telephone or in writing by several other members of the council. One or two were rash enough to ask Clegg what he meant by publishing a leader expressing policy contrary to that of the BMA, whereupon he asked them to read it again and they would find there was nothing in it contrary to any BMA policy as laid down by the only body competent to make it, namely the representative body. This body meets annually or, for special occasions, more frequently.

Technically Clegg was correct: there was nothing contrary to any declared BMA policy in it. The real nature of his offence was that behind the scenes at that time a closer relationship was being sought between the BMA and the royal colleges, so that just when the officers of the College of Physicians might have expected a delicately phrased welcome to a new era of cordiality they received what appeared to be an officially inspired and insulting lecture on how to put their house in order. Clegg knew of the prevailing desire in some BMA circles to improve relations with the colleges but not of any particularly sensitive discussions at that time. Had he done so he might have delayed publication of the leader; or he might not, for he regarded it as attacking not the college itself but a small group of people whose running of the college he opposed and whose closer relationship with the BMA he distrusted. His immediate reward came with the congratulations he received from some of the younger members and fellows of the college soon after the leader appeared.

What influence the leader had on the college's adminis- tration can never be known, for its admirers claimed it hastened the changes they sought, while its critics replied that it delayed, if anything, the changes that were coming anyway. Nor could the younger physicians speak out so boldly for reform as their elders for fear of prejudicing their future: this anxiety was privately expressed to us by several. So for some while conflicting but not always outspoken partisans took the field.

In the BMA itself, clearly defined battle lines were quickly drawn up. Here at last was the opportunity, his critics in the council and some of the committees believed, to bring their recalcitrant editor to heel. Indeed "Will nobody rid me of this turbulent editor?" would have been the cry but for the objection to it, already noted, that nothing in the article was contrary to BMA policy. It had sailed against the warm breezes the BMA was blowing towards the Royal Colleges – but that was all: an embarrassment but not a casus belli. And when its chief target, Sir Russell Brain, replied to it in an angry but dignified letter[23] a week later in the *BMJ* he reinforced that impediment: "But the main trend of the leader is the clear implication…that the B.M.A. should occupy a position of exclusive privilege and power in medicine." So the leader was a blow struck on behalf of the BMA!

On 2 May the BMA council was due to meet and would undoubtedly discuss the position of the editor and the purport of the leader. Clegg therefore spent some time preparing a written defence, and unwilling to risk its being leaked in the office worked on the text in the evenings at home. There his wife typed it out for him, copies were made, and when the members of the council entered their chamber on 2 May each found a copy on his seat. Clegg would have preferred them to have more time to study it thoroughly, as it ran to several pages, but the need for secrecy and the constitutional problems of addressing every member of the council in the end dictated this procedure. Though Clegg had friends in the council who spoke on his behalf, the general opinion was against him, and a majority passed a motion stating that "Council wishes to dissociate itself from the publication of the leading article…of which article the

Council had no prior knowledge, the article being the entire responsibility of the Editor, according to the usual practice."[24]

In itself this fell short of what some members wanted and left Clegg's position unchanged. But it sounded "reveille" rather than "last post" to the army of critics gathering together on the surrounding hills. What they wanted was to forge some mechanism by which the editor – and so the *BMJ* – could be brought under the control of the council, presumably through a special committee, enabling the leading articles to be vetted and if necessary altered or excluded if they did not conform to what the council considered to be BMA policy.

Constitutionally the representative body, normally meeting annually, determines the policy of the BMA, and the council is its executive, seeing that the policy is put into effect, filling the broad sketch of the scene with the detailed brushwork, turning ideas, wishes, and opinions into negotiations, demands, treaties. So that to speak of what the council "considered" to be BMA policy may seem to be the words of a hostile critic throwing doubt on the capacity of the council to determine fairly or accurately the requirements of the representative body. But in practice the most effective way, perhaps the only way, of gaining acceptance of a policy may necessitate its presentation in a form that some of its proponents think objectionable; negotiation may require some give and take and to reach a conclusion some compromise. In addition many problems need to be resolved, between meetings of the representative body, by decisions and actions that the council must take. Just as a member of the journal committee during my interview for the post of subeditor, had asked the chairman, "What exactly *are* the politics of the BMA?", so in the *BMJ* we often asked ourselves the slightly more pertinent question, "What exactly is the *policy* of the BMA?" We would consult the secretary or expert members of his staff, but often enough the answer came, "There is none," or "We are not quite sure ourselves."

Thus we were, as so often in Clegg's day, at the heart of democracy. And it was democracy that Clegg was in love with despite being an autocrat to his finger tips. He strove all the time to understand her will, to encourage and cherish her, to introduce her to the uncomprehending, to defend her against the malevolent, and in response to her behests to check the digressions to which his own inner feelings tempted him. What *is* the will of the people? How is it to be ascertained, interpreted, executed? This question that the twentieth century has come to ponder so deeply ran like an electric current through the BMA – energising here, lighting up there, giving a shock in that chamber, blowing a fuse in this. And it was because Clegg recognised the importance of it, not merely to the wellbeing of the BMA but to the enhancement of the human spirit, that working with him was, despite the storm clouds, so often an exhilarating battle over issues that really mattered far beyond the cloisters of the BMA itself.

Clearly no editor could remain in office and retain his self-respect under the sort of regime that the more extreme critics of the leading article would like to impose. They of course knew that, and they hoped that introducing the controls they had in mind would lead to Clegg's resignation – as it indeed would have done, immediately. Foreseeing these possible consequences I discussed with him what I should do. It was then he told me that any outside restriction placed on his editorial judgments would lead to his resignation, but he urged me not to follow him for two reasons. The first was the practical one that I had a wife and now three young children to support. The second was that the article was much more his personal responsibility than many of the leaders we published: I had not been familiar with the detailed background to his thoughts on the college's development. The implication that I had simply followed him in blind but loyal ignorance was not true enough for me to accept. So I told him that what I would do was to look around for another job and go when I could get it. He again pressed me not to go at all, but he knew that I could no more have accepted the dictates of a supervisory committee than he could.

Two months later the great day came, a day we had looked forward to with anxiety about its outcome mingled with the excitement of landing on a dangerous shore, forming up, advancing inland, engaging the enemy. But what would life be without the thrill of such anxieties? That year the representative body held its annual meeting at Brighton, and the Winchester division was to lead the attack on the *BMJ*. This division had for some years been one of the journal's chief critics and in consequence some animosity had grown up between several of its leading members and Clegg. One of its main objections had been what it regarded as the disproportionately small space and little emphasis devoted to medical politics and the affairs of the BMA – not only the business at headquarters but the activities out in the divisions also. I believe there was something in this criticism, but it was not one that Clegg would accept at that stage because of his desire to build up the scientific and clinical reputation of the journal, with which I entirely concurred. But on one occasion a leading member of the Winchester division had written a long and detailed letter to Clegg not for publication but offering advice on the editing of the journal, and with that insouciance of which he was sometimes a master Clegg allowed the letter to sink to the bottom of one of the many piles of papers in his room and then forgot about it. The result was that a deputation including the writer of the letter attended a meeting of the journal committee to air their criticisms in person and at the same time to launch a complaint against the editor. The writer of it repeatedly banged the table with his fist in so histrionic a fashion while castigating the editor's failure even to acknowledge, let alone reply to, the letter, that John Thompson and I could only smile irreverently at this demonstration of nature once again imitating art.

Clegg was apt to treat his critics with more disdain than their genuinely held opinions should have allowed him to do, but if he regarded a view or an argument as, at least by his standards, unworthy of being taken seriously, he was not averse to withering the advocate rather than the argument.

In July at the annual meeting a motion from the Winchester division was moved, "That this Representative Body instructs the Council to take steps to ensure that leading articles in the *BMJ* reflect the policy of the Association." In view of its previous contacts with the *BMJ* it came as no surprise to us on the staff that it should be the Winchester division that put forward this motion. But a BMA division, like many a political body, is apt to be a large vehicle with a small motor, and we had reason to believe that our opponents were a few zealots rather than the general body of practising doctors in the Winchester area or anywhere else. Even so, the course of the debate astonished us. One after another the representatives went up to the platform and urged their colleagues to reject the motion. A deep distrust of the council as supervisor of the *BMJ* became evident, and as opposition from successive speakers piled up against the motion so the faces of the Winchester representatives and their sympathisers in the council became ever more glum. There were calls from the floor of the meeting to end the talk and have a vote, but the chairman rightly allowed more speakers to debate this issue of such importance to the BMA as well as to the running of its journal. Finally the motion was put to the meeting. It was rejected by an "overwhelming majority".[25]

When devising the form of its motion the Winchester division doubtless found itself in the same difficulty as the council had earlier, for, while the motion was concerned with trying to ensure that the *BMJ*'s leading articles reflected the policy of the association, the article in question was not contrary to any identifiable policy. Several speakers made this point, but in their disquiet about the possibility of the council by some device supervising the editing of the journal they went much further. They recognised the *BMJ* for what it is, a broadly based medical journal attempting to serve the needs of the whole profession composed of doctors with innumerably varied interests, and not merely responsible to the exactions of the council and the main committees, not restricting the published letters from its readers to those that were uncritical of official policy, but reaching out to the many members of the association who played no part in its medicopolitical struggles, and directed by an editor who was independent of the factions of the day, for as medical men and women they were specially aware that today's truth is often tomorrow's error.

The vote was an incontestable defeat for the Winchester division. Their teeth were drawn and scattered to the winds. And in the council it extinguished completely the fires being lit to incinerate the editor. For Clegg it was a personal triumph. But its importance for the BMA was greater, for it ratified and established for the future the *BMJ*'s independence from the council's interfering with the day-to-day editing. Of course the editor is subject to the council: it appoints him, employs him, pensions him, and can sack him. But it cannot tell him how to do his job.

We on the journal saw the debate above all as a victory for the BMA, the *real* BMA in all the wayward complexity that doctors can bring to any organisation they create. It was an affirmation of strength in heterogeneity.

People turning back to read the article today are inclined to wonder what all the fuss was about. The claret has flowed under the bridge. Though the results were far-reaching, the thing itself is largely forgotten as a little local rumpus:

> These things seem small and undistinguishable,
> Like far-off mountains turned into clouds. – SHAKESPEARE.
> *A Midsummer-Night's Dream*, IV, i

When he retired 10 years later the BMA awarded Clegg its gold medal.

16 Succession to tragedy

> *Antonio* Necessity compels me:
>   Make scrutiny throughout the passages
>   Of your own life, you'll find it impossible
>   To fly your fate.
> *Echo*   O, fly your fate!
> *Delio*   Hark: the dead stones seem to have pity on you
>   And give you good counsel. – WEBSTER.
>   *The Duchess of Malfi.* V, iii

John Thompson was sitting at his desk looking through some journals, his pale, lined face patiently inquisitive of my interrupting him as I came through the door.

"If you're busy...?" I said, "only a gossip..."

"Come in."

The April sun was casting a patch on his desk like a glass of moselle, and a smile flitted over his face as he put down the journal, marked his place in the pages, and asked by his expression rather than by any words what was on my mind. With his unruffled manner, courtesy, and readiness to listen, John was a natural confidant, accustomed to having members of the staff, whether senior or junior, come to him for advice or explanation, offering a receptive, attentive ear, giving them at least sympathy if he could do no more than suggest acceptance of the inevitable.

His position as deputy put him next in line for the editorship. It was now 1962. Clegg was due to retire in three years, and I wondered if John was making any plans for the future – indeed if Clegg was too.

"He's going as late as he can," said John. "Are you free for lunch today? I'll tell you all about it."

"He's been considering the three of us," John said, "you,

Martin Ware, and me. And it's Martin he's going to recommend to the council to succeed him."

Despite his being deputy, John in Clegg's view was unsuitable – or so he had led John to believe – in that he was too pliant, too accommodating: "You can't say no, that's your trouble," had been Clegg's phrase to John, and I too had heard him complain in these terms of some decision that John had taken. Clegg regarded "saying no" as one of the most important qualifications of an editor and was apt to bring out this phrase in conversations on the craft of editing.

As well as being a skilful writer John could judge the character of people and the quality of their work with discernment, knew the idiosyncrasies of many of our leader writers and reviewers, and could weigh them up with a cool judgment. But was he too well balanced? Too indecisive from seeing all sides of every question?

"And you won't be editor," John declared, "because Hugh thinks you're too tied to your outside interests."

This conversation, though not a turning point in my life, since that had already been taken, confirmed my intention to continue along the path I had started on some years earlier and now, as one range of hills when climbed discloses another, and then another beyond, continued to traverse in my quest for the meaning – of which I have always been so consciously a seeker – the meaning of our existence.

"I don't think Hugh is right," John was saying to me through my thoughts of wandering over the hills. "I'm sure I could do it perfectly well."

"I'm sure you could too."

"As Hugh has taken this line," he went on, "I'm thinking of trying to whip up some support for myself in the council – I've got some friends there, you know; they might back me."

A few days later Clegg came into my office, sat in the chair facing my desk instead of pacing up and down as he usually did, and said, "Dougal, as you know, I depart in three years' time. I've been thinking about the succession, the next editor. It's a rotten job in some ways. It would kill you – it's nearly killed me. I thought I should tell you I'm recommending that Martin should succeed me."

His expression suggested he had made this announcement more abruptly than on reflection he thought quite appropriate. Thoughts seemed to be trapped behind his tense but determined gaze, pushing here and there, worrying to find an outlet. What could be added? What toned down? What explicated (to use one of his favourite words)? What words could he find that would be kindly in case my feelings should be hurt, fair to Martin, straightforward as an expression of his decision that would not shame him as boss, and explanatory so that we should continue working as friendly colleagues?

"Martin will be all right," he went on, "he's got a lot of sense you know. If you and the others help him at first, he'll find his feet. He can be very firm...I hope you'll support him."

Clegg could not shake off the impression he was giving of being slightly defensive about his choice, in fact of being dissatisfied with the field from which he had to choose. I wondered what he would say if I asked him why he was not recommending John Thompson, but a tactful impulse kept me silent. "You've got your botanical interests." He had walked over towards the window and was staring out across the plane trees, over the roof tops to the ridge of Hampstead Heath on the skyline. He had uttered the last words with – was it disappointment, rebuke, envy?

Some months later Clegg was talking to our business manager about the decisions he had been taking over the editorial succession.

"Martin will be easy for you to work with. I've decided on him."

"What about Dougal?"

"Oh well, I didn't want too clever a chap to succeed me," was his reply, as the business manager told me long afterwards.

But like many remarks made in the course of conversation this should not be taken literally as though it disclosed his real thoughts on me and Ware. It was in the first place a pleasantry, not seriously intended to be either laudatory or disparaging, for two deeply rooted attitudes lay behind it. The fact is that no conceivable field of candidates for the post would have been entirely satisfactory to Clegg. He had been on the staff for over 30 years, for most of that time as editor de facto. From this great experience combined with a strong personality he had derived a confidence that no other person could make a deep impression upon. That is not to say his mind was closed to change: on the contrary, to the end he was eagerly receptive of new proposals, alert to developments in the medical scene, and ready with his pen to comment on them. But he found it difficult to imagine that other people could fill a post as effectively as he did if their conception of the task differed from his own. He would have had little confidence in any successor, and indeed caused Ware many difficulties after the transference of power.

Nor was this all that underlay his words. The implication that I was "too clever" derived from the chagrin he felt that I had put myself out of the running by devoting my spare energies to interests other than the *BMJ*, and, perhaps above all, that I had found my deepest satisfaction in them, for as had been evident to me ever since he proposed, back in 1949, giving up the editorship in favour of a managing or supervisory role, he did not find, any more than I did, that journalism offered a satisfying life. It was a profession, and diverting, engaging, demanding – but distracting, yes, all the time distracting one from the reality that lies between birth and death. Gazing out of the window, as so often, in my office one day he said, perhaps in response to the shadow of a passing cloud, "Well Dougal, what is the meaning of life?"

"I don't know, but sometimes, I think I may be getting nearer to it."

"I used to think that, but now I seem to be further off than ever."

Each of us knew we were talking about something of serious importance to us, and it was occasional glimpses of this kind, and the silences that fell between them, which made me realise that despite the multitude of differences between us there was also a kinship.

Like many people who carry on working at the same job Clegg came to regret he had developed no interests outside his work and that he had continued in his post till the last moment. After he retired I was having lunch with him one day and we were talking over old times – laughing at the controversies, the mistakes, the failures, the victories. But the gleam of former triumphs faded when he looked at me sadly and said, "I should have retired earlier, I stayed too long." He had become imprisoned in his own image of himself as editor, and to his discomfiture it was a prison cell with a small window from which he could look out over the trees and the roof tops and the ridge of hills to the sky beyond.

The two other explanations he had given for not recommending me, namely that my heart would not be in the job and that its responsibilities would crush me, were different aspects of the same judgment he had formed of me, for by now I was leading two lives, though I never allowed my botanical studies to interfere with my editorial work, which indeed I continued to enjoy at a practical level. In my heart I felt that for the succession to pass to Ware was the right decision for the journal and the best one for me. But John Thompson was deeply disappointed. It removed from him, while it gave to me, the opportunity of fulfilling our ambitions. Perhaps wisely, he did not seek allies in the council to contest it.

A few weeks later John became ill and was away from the office for a time. Clegg then told me something of his history, of an inborn physical frailty and of a liability since his undergraduate days to fall victim, though only at long intervals, to attacks of depression. Though he had received treatment for it, he could not bring himself to take the disease seriously enough; partly from his own choice the treatment he did have was not so thorough as it might have been. With his equable temperament and complete absence of "neurotic" anxieties John had seemed to be the best balanced mentally of any of us, so that this disclosure was a sad shock. He returned to the office for a week or so, but felt too unwell, too haunted by what he himself recognised as being a completely irrational sense that his life was no longer worth living, too worn out to continue until he had had more time to recover in the company of his wife, as tenderly sympathetic to him as she was hospitable to us who knew them both.

The BMA's annual meeting was held a couple of months later at Oxford. One of the virtues that the annual meetings held for the staff was that we could meet the younger specialists who came to read papers. Though the days had long passed when original work was published for the first time at such meetings, to have the opportunity of talking to people who were at least reviewing original work which they had carried out was an education we enjoyed all the more for being able to take it over a dry martini. And it was of benefit to the *BMJ* too when we could watch new ideas in the making and get to know the doctors who were turning the old ideas into new ones or at least replacing old fashions by new. All this would have been a diversion for John, and he had declared in several letters how much he looked forward to coming. Had he been able to face the exertion of the day's routine he might have found there some lifting of the spirits, at least a bannister rail to hold on to as he walked slowly upstairs. But his hopes were destroyed by the continuance of his illness.

I was sitting in a room near the conference hall one morning when Clegg came up to me and said quietly, "John died yesterday. I didn't want to spoil the dinner, so I didn't tell you last night." He turned and went back to the meeting. There was no need for him to say what must have happened.

This tragedy struck to the core of our working lives, for the "family" of our office, our relationships and daily collaboration in a common effort, moulded us into a shared pattern of slots and joints and interfaces forming reciprocal obligations. Could we somehow have stretched out a hand to stop the boat from tipping over?

A few weeks later Clegg said to me, "Do you think I pestered him too much?"

Clegg had known from the time Thompson joined the staff that he had suffered a depressive attack at Cambridge, and he had been worrying about this history in the context of his own forceful, sometimes moody, personality in contrast to the gentle patience with which John Thompson would listen to his tirades at all hours of the day against the *BMJ*'s enemies or provide a sympathetic audience to Clegg's rambling development of a theme – or a long succession of themes – in what was effectually a rehearsal for the next leading article. I admired Clegg for asking the question. Certainly he would not have ventured to do so if he had expected me to say yes, but he probably risked it on other people too, for he addressed himself to personal relationships in a manner both frank and courageous. No doubt he hoped desperately – and equally needed – to be given reassurance, but though he could be confident that no reply I gave would be such as to devastate his peace of mind, he must have felt that he was staring over the edge of a dangerous cliff.

The history and character of Thompson's illness, so far as I knew them, seemed to me to signify a depressive tendency of endogenous type, and I told Clegg that I didn't think the working conditions in the office had any part in it. If anything the affliction seemed to an important extent to be biochemical in origin, perhaps linked to an endocrine defect from which John suffered.

Indeed, are these biochemical tides that rule us all, causing changes of mood, good days and bad days, sudden bursts of exhilaration or fits of the shivers, are they much influenced at all by the morning's post, the importunity of a colleague, or the failure to meet a deadline? To some extent there must be an interaction, but the chemical groundswell has always seemed to me to be perceptible. I now understood at least one reason why Clegg had not recommended Thompson to succeed him as editor: his health was too uncertain. And when a friend of John's remarked to me some time later, "He was passed over, wasn't he?" I could only say that the same thought had crossed my mind. While the decision was understandable against the history of John's susceptibility to depression, to which the burden of editorship would have added a strain that might have brought him to the same breaking point, yet in destroying his ambition it spared him no anguish. Either course threatened to head him for catastrophe. Whichever way he went, a tragic end seemed to be his fate.

17 A last look back

What's gone and what's past help
Should be past grief. – SHAKESPEARE. *The Winter's Tale*, III, ii

Many years later I received a letter from Clegg. "Do come and see me one of these days when you visit London." He was living in retirement in Fulham, and now he was nearly 80 I decided after several pleas from him that friendly relations must be restored.

When he retired nearly 15 years previously at the end of 1965 on having reached (in fact passed) his 65th birthday, he came into my office for a final handshake. In the gloom of the December evening outside, even the lights within seemed to shine dim and yellow over a parting which, as the memories of my working under him ebbed and flowed and ebbed away, left a residue of sadness. For 18 years of my life he had been my mentor, boss, colleague, friend. Now I had to admit to myself as the end came that despite all the turmoil of working with him the best years of my life on the *BMJ* were probably going too. Having stood up to his rudeness, laughed at his wit, enjoyed his leadership, and tried to play a part in the rebirth of the *BMJ* he wrought after the war, I felt sorry to lose a colleague whom, whether we agreed or disagreed, I never ceased to respect. He was courageous, humane, surprising still – all qualities that rose to my mind as I said goodbye. Which of us is not a mixture of good, bad, and indifferent? But to a greater degree than most of us he was unafraid of scrutiny.

As the years of his retirement passed he grew for a time to hate me, at least professionally. Having obtained a part-time job with the Royal Society of Medicine to run an office providing information to medical people visiting this country and to members of our own profession going abroad, he at the same time conceived the idea of starting a new journal. This was to go to doctors practising in tropical countries and keep them up-to-date by providing review articles, series of refresher courses, and notes on current medicine. I used to have lunch with him occasionally to discuss this project and in fact at one of them suggested the title which he adopted when it came into being, namely *Tropical Doctor*. But none of us on the editorial or business staffs of the *BMJ* were keen to follow him in a plan that was dear to his heart, and that was for the *BMJ* to publish it.

Part of his proposal was that he should have an office, secretary, and so on at BMA House. Here lay the source of what we believed would be unmanageable contention. And from a financial point of view the business manager had serious doubts about the benefits such a journal could bring to the BMA's finances. But in reality this was, what Clegg himself understood it to be, a conflict stemming from the personalities of the disputants, especially between Clegg, all his aggression released again into channels that his enthusiasm for this journal had undammed, and Martin Ware, the *BMJ*'s editor, who in stark contrast to Clegg, did not revel in controversy, even though when an important principle was at stake he was prepared to make a stand. Not only would Clegg have been a nuisance to members of the editorial staff if our business department had taken this journal on, the journal itself did not seem likely to be readily accommodated among those we already published.

Believing me, correctly, to be one of the opponents of his plans, he severed relations and tried to convince Ware – but without avail – that my views should be disregarded. So this quarrel dragged on till he found a publisher in the Royal Society of Medicine, and then his anger gradually died away. For he and I were old comrades in arms and had memories of standing together in the past that blanketed the flames of the recent skirmish. Memory is a great stabiliser.

So I finally arrived at his house for lunch. After a delicious meal with a bottle of claret, his wife Kira, as charming as ever, allowed us to depart to the drawing room to indulge ourselves in reminiscence. I had myself retired now, as I had declined the editorship of the *BMJ* when Ware went, for I preferred to devote more time to botany, and he asked me how my studies of the lichens were progressing, and added, "I stayed too long."

"I know. You told me that some years ago. It influenced me a lot to retire at 60."

"Yes, I should have gone at 60. I wasted too much of my life on that place."

"But what would you have done?"

"Oh well, there are always things to do." He looked at me reflectively. "I do envy you. You found the right life. I'd like to have done something practical with my hands as well as at a desk. You told me once how you enjoyed your microscopy."

Still with a touch of the benign mandarin he seemed when I had first met him 34 years ago, he recalled a career that he had occasionally hinted to me over the years was in some ways unsatisfying. Justifiably proud of what he had accomplished, he seemed to feel at the same time that the accomplishment itself neither won the public recognition it deserved nor fulfilled his deepest longings. On his retirement he had been appointed CBE, an honour (if that is what it was) that fell short of the knighthood he felt to be his due. And indeed it was not really an honour: it was a conventional award too inappropriate to be classed as an honour, approved by uneasy officials who believed anything less would expose them and the system to the criticism of people they depended upon.

Clegg was a non-conformist who never fitted neatly into the postwar years of the welfare state; he saw its hypocrisies more clearly than its ideals. And he was a maverick who lambasted the wielders of power, whoever they might be, over the medical profession – governments of all political complexions, Whitehall ministries, royal colleges, and (more privately) the BMA. It was the independence of his opinions from contemporary fashion and do-gooding clichés that underpinned his strength as an editor and his unpopularity in official circles. He was an uncomfortable man to have around. That he received a crown honour at all was surprising. That he accepted it was, as I remarked when congratulating him, in a way an acknowledgment of defeat. He agreed.

Nor in the last resort did he feel satisfied with what he himself regarded as his best and most enduring achievement, the transforming of the *BMJ* from something near his bête noire, a house magazine, into a journal of world repute and the founding of a number of specialist medical journals of the highest scientific standards. A champion all his life of scientific and scholarly learning, he felt he had turned aside from some lasting accomplishment in that field that lay within him. He looked now at the completed monument, at which he had carved and hammered and chipped and chiselled, often with furious energy, and was disappointed with its final appearance as a memorial to his endeavours.

Unquiet of gesture in the sunlit room, he finished his cup of coffee and then said with an air of amusement that lay beyond regret, "I put too much into the *BMJ*."

He seemed to feel that the name he would leave behind him lacked, not distinction, but definition, lacked a permanence that would show posterity an image of the real man, that it was – as a friend said of Oscar Wilde's – writ in hot water. And now it was trickling away.

"You were wise to get out," were his final words, "do look us up again."

PART 4

18 A parting

In the poorer countries literally unnumbered throngs of children press eagerly on resources that cannot satisfy them with work, food, water, or even a standard of health that makes life something less than misery. In the richer countries growing multitudes of old people struggle along with failing joints, hearts, lungs, kidneys, brains. More disturbing than ever is the thought that one of the criteria by which a civilisation should be judged is the care it devotes to its helpless people. So in 1948, foreseeing this expansion all too clearly, I began to work on the care of my aging parents.

In that year my father became 80 and my mother 59. By a lucky chance an elderly widower living in the house next to ours at Knebworth spoke of selling up and spending the rest of his days in a nearby hotel. So I encouraged this plan with hints of the trouble-free Nirvana that would await him there, looked after by the staff yet still able to meet his friends, enjoying a quietly reflective existence yet free when the spirit moved him to buy some grapes from the greengrocer's down the road. After some anxious hesitation he made the decision, sold his house to my parents, and moved into the hotel.

With the house my parents were fortunate to be able to take over a living-in maid called May. She had been there for many years and was by then middle-aged; in fact the house was home to her. Wild and stocky in appearance, with scattered brown hair and an expression that flitted through gleams of humour, determination, and abstraction, her forthright thoughts more often concealed behind a confident reserve than expressed in the ambiguities of which she was a master, May bustled to and fro tripping over the pekingese or clattering plates down on the table.

Though rambling in conversation she was shrewder than a brief acquaintance would disclose. But her observations were so often hedged about with qualifications and equivocal phrases that she might have been a politician of a later age speaking blandly into the TV camera. Coming in from the garden, for instance, she would reply to my mother's question, "What's it like out there, May?" with almost invariably the same phrase, "It's not very hot, m'm, not very cold neither." This formula was a great favourite of May's and could be adapted to any number of qualities, such as, "It's not very dark, not very light neither," or "It's not very sweet, not very sour neither."

My mother, who was fairly readily exasperated, would express her annoyance at these quibbles (as she saw them) by saying, "You *are* a fool, May."

"Yes m'm, yes m'm," May would respond in her squeaky voice and continue her dusting with a placidity that remained unshaken by my mother's impatience and equally unruffled by any incertitudes in her own mind. For May's equivocation sprang not from doubt but rather from philosophic calm, though her philosophy owed more to her temperament than to reason. Nothing to her was ever excessively hot or cold, blinding light or dark, distastefully sweet or sour. Life ran along comfortably between the extremes, kept to its middle way with the equilibrium a Taoist could only envy. But it must be admitted that her philosophy owed some of the stability with which it endowed her to the ease with which she unquestioningly jumped to conclusions. But then, is this not a solace to us all? If my mother were to ask her, for example, where the dog had got to, May would reply in some such words as, "He's in the garden, yes m'm, I saw him on the stairs." Or of me she might say to my mother, "Mister Douglas left this book here, m'm."

"Is it really his, May?"

"Yes, m'm, I saw him looking at it."

Only when I grew up did it seem strange that I was always known to my parents' maids as "Master Douglas" in childhood and "Mister Douglas" from the age of 16, for of course the name Douglas was never used in the family, only

Dougal. As I came to realise, in this way the difference between family and servants was symbolised. ("Among sensible people there should be no objection to the word 'servant.' It is merely a noun, a name to denote people in a certain occupation, just as brokers, salesmen, housewives, denote certain people in other occupations."[26]) A barrier lay between us, but it was not as between superior and inferior classes of people so much as the kind of boundary that a botanist would see separating two species in a genus. Each species has its particular ecological niche to which it is adapted, and breeding between the species would be an irregular event, contrary to the usual course of nature, yet, if it did occur, sometimes giving rise to progeny all the more successful for having hybrid vigour. Obligations lay on employers as much as on servants, but unfortunately they were often not fulfilled on either side: though in my own experience they certainly were in some families, the two communities living in perfect symbiosis and mutual happiness.

Irritating May must sometimes have been, and my mother, never clearly aware of how rude she herself could be, did on occasions allow a lifetime's ill-controlled impatience to burst its banks once again and declare, "You really are a lout, May," to which May, completely unperturbed, would once again reply, "Yes m'm, yes m'm," with a distant smile and the brisk, high-pitched voice of a nun whose imagination is filled with the symbols of her faith. In fact she did not seem to accept that such insults could be directed at her personally, but rather it was as though my mother were addressing not an actual person but a neoplatonic idea of servants in general, so that May's apparent affirmation, with her "yes m'm," of my mother's rebuke had more substance of concession in it than might have been expected, for May half agreed with the message my mother was putting across while having the capacity to disregard entirely the terms in which my mother clothed it. But later she might waddle over to Josephine next door and say to her, with a note of admiration in her voice, "The missus *was* in a track today."

In her impenetrable way May was devoted to my mother,

as were innumerable people whom the boldness of her attack and the candour of her no-nonsense judgment, so far from offending, actually delighted because of their forthright delivery. "She speaks her mind", "You know where you are with her" – conventional but heartfelt phrases were the refuge of friends too swiftly outpaced to make a studied retort, too dextrously battered to recover their balance when assailed. So that when the time came – some 20 years later – for her to die at the age of 81, many friends recalled with affection someone who had stood up to life, a character, a "fine old lady". For though the skittles fell with a clatter as her comments bowled her friends over, she possessed as a complement to her vehement frankness an impulsively generous spirit that did over the years retain for her at least some friends among the trail of reeling figures she left behind her in life's course. She had only to make a small profit on the Stock Exchange on her very few securities for her to insist on sharing it with Josephine and me by a gift of money. To my brother she was as generous as to me. During the war she supported by letters and parcels of food and woollen clothing for several years a British soldier from the east end of London who was a prisoner in a German camp. They met for the first time when he was released after the war. Quickly establishing himself in the grey market of dockets and coupons, he was able to repay her kindness on several occasions with a pile of coal or a chicken, and they became warm friends. Many charities appealed to her – never in vain – and in her younger days she had been an active worker for the Poppy Day appeals, founded as they had been by cousin Douglas Haig. Christmas and birthdays were occasions she never failed to cheer with extravagant presents, and at these festivities May shared in her generosity like everyone else.

"She's a good old thing," my mother would say when buying a handsome present for her. My father was benignly disposed but more cautious as the celebrations became closer and more jovial.

"I'm just pouring out a glass of port for May," my mother remarked one Christmas.

"Oh no," my father quickly interrupted, "port, don't give her that, Nellie, it makes the servants savage."

Wayward in her judgments of people my mother may have been, impulsive in her expression of them, she poured out her spirit equally in crushing their self-esteem by the sharpness of her tongue and in winning their hearts by the generosity of her gifts. Ordinary, quiet affection she found more difficult to express (her father had seen to that): it was all imaginative censure mingled with unstinting donation.

The violent quarrels that once divided my parents were now buried; the dead leaves of autumn had been heaped over them. Indeed the reality that had once divided them now in the memory united them, the memory, with all its ups and downs, of a shared life. My mother would speak in terms of amused contempt to my father, and he would reciprocate with the confident indifference of one who has come to terms with life, who has ridden over some difficult country – whether unscathed or not no longer mattered – and reached a peaceful grove, who sees that there is not much further to go to the journey's end.

In his last years as we were living next door to each other I got to know him if not more intimately at least with less constraint. He would lay down his newspaper or detective story and we would have a chat about matters of local interest or the current news. He still studied the stock market, but the stockbroker in whose judgment he had formerly reposed such trust, not altogether justified by the decline of his fortune, had by now breathed his last in the arms of Bacchus. The political news always held some interest for my father, but, if in one of my conversations with him I tried to find out what he really thought, he would quickly wrap himself up in an overcoat of clichés as though going off for a walk on his own, utter some conventional criticism of this or that public figure, and then mentally slip away.

One March day in 1953 he was in bed with a chest

infection, and the district nurse had just left after giving him an injection of penicillin. I went over to see how he was getting on. We were talking of the coming spring when a pause fell in the conversation and he said, "I really think my time has come." His voice was matter-of-fact, his expression not so much resigned as calmly assured. Behind the clouds of convention that had begun to surround him far back in the nineteenth century, through which I had rarely been able to glimpse the real man who, despite the remoteness, had always been to me a loving father, I now for a moment saw clearly a flash of blue sky.

Next year in the same month he again fell ill with pneumonia, and as my mother went down with an attack of influenza at the same time a nurse was brought in to supplement the care that Josephine and May were devoting to the couple. Before going to work one morning I called in to have a word with my father especially, for he was clearly very ill.

In the afternoon Josephine was doing some washing in the kitchen of our house next door when she looked up and saw May gesticulating through the window. Her dress and hair were slightly dishevelled as usual, while her generally rather impassive features were animated if not by a lively expression at least by a hint of agitation. As she opened the window Josephine heard her say breathlessly, "The old gentleman's a-going and the missus won't get up." They hurried next door together, to find my father still conscious but sinking, my mother too enfeebled to leave her bed, and the nurse attending to everything that lay within her province. But what really mattered was beyond it: my father taking leave of a life whose sorrows had imprisoned him in a little room that few people had entered since the Edwardian age, my mother preoccupied with the weakness caused by her own illness, the tumult of their marriage coming to an end in fulfilment of the vow they originally made in a Teignmouth church – till death us do part.

19 Two half-brothers

Towards the end of 1954 I was in my *BMJ* office when a call came through from my half-brother Alister. It was the first time he had ever telephoned me there. He asked to come and see me as he was in London for a few days and would like to take the opportunity for a brief chat. He sounded slightly mysterious, but in fact the mystery only began with his visit.

On entering the room half an hour later he greeted me warmly, bronzed and urbane in his middle age (20 years older than I, he was now 57), and mentioned how sad he felt at having been in America when our father died earlier in the year.

"There's something I'd like you to know," he added, "now that Pa has gone." He paused for a moment, turned his pale blue eyes on me with a solemnity that I mistakenly thought reflected the recollection of his absence from the beside as his father, who loved him above everyone, lay dying. "I work for the Secret Intelligence Service. I wanted you to know." After looking at me intently for a moment, "Does that surprise you?" he asked.

"Yes, it certainly does – I had no idea – congratulations – no idea you had such an unusual job."

He seemed pleased. "Well, I can't tell you what I do, but now that Pa has died – I should – nobody else knows in the family – I should feel happier with you knowing about it. Keep it under your hat." I was taken aback and could only drag out a stiff compliment. A few minutes later he departed.

To my regret I realised I could never confront my mother with this proof that Alister was not so idle as she liked to declare, not after all the fugitive image of manhood that she used to conjure up to tease my father with, but a man whose occupation had the specially honourable quality she would have admired, that he was serving his country. Though to him personally my mother had always been amiable in conversation, never less than generous – as he was hereditarily mean – when presents were exchanged at Christmas or birthdays, and hospitable if he stayed in the house, the idea of him rather than the man himself was repugnant to her, so that for as long as I could remember he had been, if not exactly a cause of bickering between my parents, rather a rag-and-paper guy that she would throw on the fire of a quarrel to make the flames leap up. Known in the family circle as Mac, he was 18 when my mother married my father in 1915, and it was out of her knowledge of him at that time that she in later years generated the venom with which she would utter her favourite epithet about him – "yellow". "To be quite frank, Mac is yellow right through." Out of politeness and out of disbelief aroused by her vehemence, out of sympathy for my beleaguered father, I used to protest, "Oh no, he can't be as bad as you say."

When he left Charterhouse in 1915 Alister should, in my mother's estimation, have followed his many contemporaries out to the Western Front, where his cousin Ulric Nisbet, after leaving Marlborough, had already seen active service and been wounded and her own cousin Dougal, whose name she perpetuated in my nickname, was to be killed in the trenches the following year. Instead, Alister elected to obtain a commission in the regular army. This meant that he went to Sandhurst for about 18 months, and it was not till 1917 that he reached France with a commission as second lieutenant in the Gloucestershire Regiment.

There he saw little actual fighting because early on his unit suffered a gas attack, and Alister, according to his own account, was incapacitated by inhaling some gas. It sounds ungenerous to speak of "his own account" as though in telling of it he might be embroidering the truth, but my mother never believed it because, according to her, he showed no signs of ill health when he returned to England except for an occasional cough, "obviously put on" she would say. Soon afterwards he relinquished his commission and was granted 100% disability pension. Though Alister's description of his gassing made him a heroic figure to my father and an object of contempt to my mother, my father was after all his father and my mother his stepmother.

Quite early in my youth I realised I had to make this distinction when trying to weigh up the substance of the quarrels between them if Alister was dragged on to the stage, and I was sometimes torn in two by having to compare the judgment made by my mother, who was close to my heart but biased against Alister, with the judgment made by my father, an unyielding partisan of Alister but to me a more distant parent. Ascertaining the truth as the wild elephants with their emotional charges and trumpetings trampled over it was often beyond me when I was a boy.

Alister was a handsome young man, as many photographs of him show, with a distinct resemblance to the matinée idol Owen Nares – tall, with dark hair, twinkling blue eyes, and a boyish expression. With good looks and an easy affability he also enjoyed a facility in light conversation that made him an attractive host and indispensable guest with a large circle of friends. In the 1920s he put these qualities to professional use by working as a kind of contact man for an insurance company – a type of job that is said to have now died out in the insurance world.

Repeatedly crossing the Atlantic to and from New York on business, always first class in one of the large liners, he met and after a six-year engagement married Madeleine du Parcq, daughter of a New York jeweller who had emigrated there from the Channel Islands. Despite, or perhaps because of, their prolonged courtship, the marriage was ideally happy, though childless. Even by the custom of that time the engagement was rather long, partly owing to the deeply cautious temperament Alister had inherited from our father, partly because Madeleine's father regarded Alister as being socially too frivolous, as holding a job that demanded no more than the exercise of a frothy charm, and as generally lacking the solidity that he deemed desirable for his only daughter's suitor. He felt that Madeleine, who taught dancing in New York, needed a steady, ambitious professional man to add weight to her own somewhat airy character. But in the end the fact that they matched each other perfectly was more important than that the qualities of one should counter-balance the defects of the other, and fortunately six years of mutual devotion led to the dissolution of the anxieties that had made Alister hesitate and the scruples that had made Madeleine's father withhold his assent. They were married in 1931 and were parted only by her death nearly 50 years later.

At the age of about 40 Alister retired after having, as he told me, made enough to live on, though the inheritance of a fortune from his mother must also have contributed to his independence. The trips continued to Long Island, where they had an apartment, to Nice, to Lausanne, to London to stay at the Dorchester Hotel, or to visit my parents. When in this country they drove everywhere in a 1930 open Rolls-Royce that Alister had bought in 1933.

When the second world war broke out they were staying in the south of France and from there travelled back to England to a hotel in Torquay. Where next? was the question now, for shipping of all kinds was scarce and requisitioned. A doctor in Torquay was approached, listened attentively to the long history of chest troubles from gassing in the previous war and a recent history of possible duodenal ulcer, and wrote out a recommendation that Alister should go abroad that winter "either to the south of France or Italy" (this was the period of the "phoney war") "and later to California, USA," and that his wife should accompany him to look after him.* In fulfilment of this recommendation they got berths to New York and arrived there on 8 April 1940. For the next five years Alister flew the British flag to good effect in Long Island as chairman of a British war relief society that he formed, winning the compliments of both Americans and Britons out there and being awarded a congressional medal for his work. For a short time after the war he carried on this work in London from an office in Regent Street.

When the Regent Street office closed, he and Madeleine

* Copy among Alister's papers.

continued their peripatetic life between Long Island and Europe, and in due course to his own substantial means was added a fortune inherited by Madeleine from her parents. Sometimes he would tell me that his work required him to visit New York or Geneva or London, and he hinted one day that his recruitment into the Secret Service had been while he was running his office in New York during the war. I asked him if he had ever been vetted for the work – this was long after the numerous traitors had been exposed – and he said, "Well, it was pretty easy in those days – they just sat you in a chair talking to an officer, and another would creep up behind you and say in a loud voice, 'ach zo!' If you turned round too quickly, you were under suspicion." The story certainly had a ring of truth that is lacking from many others told of the intelligence services.

Some 20 years later, when Alister was about 77 and my mother was long since dead, I asked him whether he still worked for MI6. He corrected me; it was MI5 he had worked for, but he had now retired. The correction seemed odd to me, for the term he had originally used, the Secret Intelligence Service, normally implied MI6.

He and his wife had settled in Torquay and from there they continued to make frequent trips abroad and to spend most of the summer in Switzerland. It was a pleasure to visit them, as we often did from our home near Exeter, for Alister was always cheerful company, an ever amusing companion in a light-hearted way. He had his pride too. Though he had resigned his commission in the army 60 years before as a lieutenant after two years' service, he was known in all the local shops except one as Captain Swinscow; the exception was the chemist's, where he was Colonel Swinscow. Speaking to a shop assistant or a servant Madeleine would always refer to him as The Captain. When they visited my parents' house at Knebworth, for instance, she would say to May laying the tea, "The Captain will be here in a few minutes"; or in the Torquay restaurant where we sometimes had lunch, "Could The Captain have a bit more cream please?" Nobody in the family, even my father, went along with this little foible. We accepted it with complaisance except my mother, who would express her exasperation by saying, "Mac a captain! – I could always outshoot him with a revolver."

Yet was it a myth? As we gradually discovered, myth and reality formed swirling patterns in Alister's accounts of himself; looking over the bridge into the river of his life Alister would show us the water eddying this way and that before it finally plunged over the weir.

For several years he devotedly cared for Madeleine before she died in 1978, and then later he asked Josephine and me to help him go through his papers. One room in his flat at Torquay was filled with 17 large trunks and suitcases which he had retrieved from stores in different parts of the country, though about half a dozen of them travelled round with him till the end. The boxes filled the entire floor of the room and were piled on top of one another. The keys for many had long been lost and we had to break into them.

Here we came upon the collections of a lifetime. Old clothes going back to the 1920s – or even before: a Sandhurst blazer was stored there – many pairs of shoes, some new, some worn out; scores of matchboxes, envelopes, sheets of writing paper from hotel bedrooms collected from the 1920s onwards, and pile upon pile of letters from hotel managers, travel agents, and shipping lines. His entire travelling life seemed to be memorialised in the boxes, though among them was hardly a single personal letter. Even so, when he actually looked on the contents of his boxes, to gaze on them with the eye of memory, Alister could not find it in his heart to throw much away. We had to put most of it back.

Then at the age of 87 he died suddenly during an afternoon rest with friends. Once again we had to go through the 17 trunks and suitcases with their old straps and layers of ships' labels. This time we uncovered a remarkable way of life. For among the piles of travel letters and receipts from hotels and shipping lines were numerous receipts from auctioneers in Torquay, London, and Geneva recording sale after sale of furniture, silver, Madeleine's jewellery, even such personal possessions as cuff links, a pocket watch, a signet ring. We had sometimes wondered idly in recent years what had happened to his furniture and once asked him about a table we coveted. "Oh, it's in my bedroom." he replied – but it was already sold. Not only was it the household property that had gone; there was virtually nothing in the bank either. In fact he had too little left to support himself for another year. Yet only the week before he died he had stayed for five days at the Dorchester Hotel, accommodating there also for a couple of nights, in a perfectly proper manner, a young woman who had long been a friend of his, and run up a bill of £800. It crossed my mind to wonder whether, knowing he had reached the end of his resources, he felt that he had reached the end of his life also, but inquiries of his friends convinced me that such a thought was not in his mind at all.

What we had released from the boxes was the detritus of a lifelong fantasy. All his life he spent large sums on preserving these papers in store rooms such as those of the Dorchester, Harrods, and one at Torquay, though he would always take a few suitcases round with him when travelling: they contained just the same type of papers – hotel and travel receipts. First class accommodation in hotels, ships, and trains – and even by Concorde latterly – travelling from nothing to nothing but thoroughly enjoying the saloons and cabins and captain's tables on the way, letting me into the secret that he was working for military intelligence, telling a friend of my younger brother's that he was president of the English branch of an American bank, where he was no more than a customer, accumulating on the way piles of hotel stationery and booklets of matches advertising the delights of their lakeside position or mountain view – all this had been done, not on the income, but on the capital of the two fortunes he had inherited. For, incredibly, instead of living on the large income they could have yielded he simply spent the capital year after year, and when that began to be alarmingly low he had to resort to selling off his personal possessions to sustain to the very end the life he had become habituated to. I could not help feeling touched and sad at the anxiety he must have felt as the paper life expanded out of control and bankruptcy came ever nearer.

Buried in the litter was a document he had carefully preserved for nearly 70 years, a copy of the army medical board's findings on 7 January 1918. Stating him to be "permanently unfit for any further military service", the board found him to be suffering from "Inflammation of the Naso-Pharynx". A common cold? No mention of gas, no record of lung disease. How was it done? No doubt the temporary major RAMC who presided over the board saw a young regular officer who had "done his bit" and understandably paid more attention to his patient's history than to the results of the inexact diagnostic techniques available at that time. In later life Alister was inclined to be a little dramatic, giving a puff or two when his gassing was mentioned, and subsequent medical boards were never so harsh as to find any disparity between the symptoms and the physical signs in a former regular officer with that history. All I could think was, perhaps there is something in it, but, as we have seen, my mother was less restrained.

Was he really in the intelligence service? I never questioned his assertion for many years, but in the end I felt some misgivings. If he had devoted all those years to it, what sort of intelligence could he have passed to his seniors? And if he was not in it? Either way it was a romance of the kind he enjoyed, with his 1930 Rolls, his 1920s clothes, invariable Old Carthusian tie, the broad-ribboned trilby from St James's ("They have my head measurements," he told me), his fund of gentle stories about America in the 1920s and 30s ("In Chicago a chap I annoyed stared at me and said 'Are you bughouse?' 'No I'm Swinscow'"), when in London having tea at the "In and Out" club, his lifelong first class travelling on errands, whether commercial or military that were at once confidential, uncommitted, elusive, accompanied by half a dozen suitcases plastered with the labels of a lifetime's cabins and hotels and packed with letters and receipts from travel agents and managers deriving from previous trips. "The Captain" must be laughing in whatever haven has received him, while my mother is probably saying with glee, "Quite frankly, I never believed a word he said." Refusing to be drawn, my father would merely grunt, "You don't know anything about it, Nellie." And he would have been right. None of us really know.

What seemed so transparent in life became enigmatic in death. But through it all ran an endearing thread: his devotion to his wife throughout their life together, whether travelling or for the time being settled, in war and in peace, and in the twilight between them, when she was a young dancing teacher in New York and when she was dying in Torquay. Nor have I ever ceased to be grateful to him for coming up to my bedroom when I was aged 6 and telling me about aeroplanes, in 1923 as this would have been. We used to laugh in later life when recalling this "talk about aeroplanes". But it planted in my imagination the romance of flying and in the end parachuting, which was not so much a choice as a destiny.

Just as I had half-sibs older than me from my father's first marriage, so did Josephine from her mother's first marriage, which had ended with the death of her first husband in early middle age. One of Josephine's half-brothers was Brigadier Robert Scott, born in 1898. His service in the second world war had been mainly in India and Burma, so that our paths had not crossed in the various countries we each had served in. Retired from the army, in which he had held a regular commission, he was secretary of the Rye golf club, and as he was to be passing our house one day in 1955 on his way back to Rye from visiting a friend he telephoned to say he would call in.

The chugging of the motorcycle and sidecar that he always rode heralded his approach up the drive, and in a moment he was off it and into our house. Our third daughter, Rosemary, had been born recently, and he congratulated Josephine on the event, adding, "But three girls — what a ballsup!"

"That's just what it isn't," she rejoined. Unmarried himself, he had a breezy indifference to the intricacies of domestic life.

Well over six feet in height and heavily built, Robert had a weather-beaten, pleasantly ugly face, greying brown hair, an alert expression, and an easy, massive presence. He came in and shook me warmly by the hand.

"How are you? Bored with peace?"

"Glad to settle down really."

He brooded for a moment on this remark and then his face lit up.

"My god! I envy you having been at Arnhem. That was quite a crisp party."

In exact contrast to my own half-brother Alister, Robert had spent his life seeking out and pushing into "crisp parties". In 1915 at the age of 17 he had added a year and got himself into the army. From Sandhurst he was commissioned into the Norfolk Regiment (later Royal Norfolk). With only slightly better fortune than befell so many millions on the Western Front he was severely wounded in an attack on an enemy position and at first thought to have been killed, but his batman saved his life by gallantly picking him up in the exploding mud off "no man's land" and carrying him back to the regiment's lines. In this, the first of many close encounters with one enemy or another, he lost his right eye and suffered fractures of a leg and arm. But back in uniform he saw the war out, learning to use his left eye to shoot with specially modified rifles. Then as hostilities in Europe came to an end he scanned the horizon for something more exciting than barrack square soldiering in Britain. So the 20 years of broken peace between the wars found him serving successively in the Sudan Camel Corps, the Cairo Police, and the Palestine Police before Germany again pushed Europe over the rim of a volcano in 1939 and thereby opened the way to the life he liked best – warfare.

Though he had to kick his heels in India for a time, his spirits rose again when the advance into Burma began. Commanding the Norfolks in 1944 during the battle for Kohima, he was in his element leading a reconnaissance against a complex bunker system the Japanese were holding with machine guns. Here his majestic size and bellowing voice terrified the enemy as much as they inspired his own men, with the result that the Norfolks cleared the position of its defenders and radioed their victory to brigade headquarters before they had received from HQ the fire plan they were supposed to follow. Recommended for the VC, Robert was awarded the DSO for his exploits.

Though modest in his recollecting of the battles and skirmishes he had fought in – and he was the last person to take to fighting them again with spoons on the dining room table – Robert had clearly enjoyed them all enormously. He was a warrior who took pride in his conduct of the hunt, stalking his prey, laying plans to outwit him through the valleys, disposing his troops and guns behind the ridges, concealing them in a wood here, leading them up a defile there, firing, charging, killing in a final clash between "them" and "us". This is not to say that he enjoyed killing people any more than, for example, a deer stalker enjoys the actual killing of a stag. But when the prey is regarded as legitimate the hunter or warrior fells free to take a judicious delight not merely in the accomplishment of a task well done but in the test itself, the chase, the risk, the exhaustion, the outwitting, the held breath, the trophy. It was a life which, though remote from my capacity or predilection, I could enjoy the telling and thrill vicariously to the adventure of, for sometimes in the peaceful pursuit of lichens I felt a similar sense of endeavour and elation, perhaps (as I relate below) when scrambling about in the mountains of southern Uganda or crossing its arid ridges in the north into the Sudan.

To Robert active service was his whole life. Win or lose, it gave fulfilment:

> To hunger and not have, yet hope on for, to storm and strive and
> Be at every assault fresh foiled, worse flung, deeper disappointed,
> The turmoil and the torment, it has, I swear, a sweetness,
> Keeps a kind of joy in it, a zest, an edge, an ecstasy,
> Next after sweet success... – GERARD MANLEY HOPKINS.
> *St Winefred's Well*

As human types these two half-brothers were in many ways opposite and complementary, the more notably so for having some features in common. Both started adult life from Sandhurst with a regular commission in the army. Both were unreflective men who neither repined over the past nor mistrusted the future, and both seemed to have attained a philosophic contentment with their fate, a balanced sense of harmony with their worlds, though perhaps in opposite pans of the scales. But where Robert was bold Alister was timorous, where Robert sought risk Alister withdrew, where Robert found his life's fulfilment in violent action, in storming redoubts among the whistling and crashing of shells, Alister found his in the shelter of his gentle affability, in captivating the hearts of his friends with charm; where Robert revelled on the fields of strife, Alister turned away even from controversial opinions.

In contrast to the two fortunes that came Alister's way only an army salary sustained Robert. With one eye and battered limbs, sometimes hungry in dangerous places and in tatters where the bullets whined, he nevertheless attained a fullness of life that eludes many who step more carefully.

> To remain whole, be twisted!
> To become straight, let yourself be bent.
> To become full, be hollow.
> Be tattered that you may be renewed.
> Those that have little may get more,
> Those that have much are but perplexed. – *Tao Te Ching*,
> Chapter 22

PART 5

20 Individual lives

Whenever I hear an old record of Fritz Kreisler playing one of those airs that seem to bring a haunting significance to the minutes while we listen to them, I am reminded of my mother's appreciative attention to that music when I was a boy, for then the emotional turmoil was stilled and we could share something without reservation or anxiety – it was the harmony of an aesthetic pleasure that came from outside the lives of both of us. Yet perhaps it is not my mother who fixes my attention now: rather with the egoism of recollection it is of myself, of the boy that I was, that I recall an image of peaceful awakening through the certitude of Kreisler's tone, so exact, so sure yet so tender – an awakening to the sun's bright and linear shafts gleaming through woodland in spring. The emphatic chords of which he was such a master, the hint here and there that we might succeed in lingering in the transfiguration despite the rectitude of his timing, made me thrill as though a woman's call on a hillside had arrested my steps for a moment and then beckoned me on. Now the old records rasp and rustle over the tune, and the blemishes accumulated year after year on the vulcanite in themselves lend an antiquity, a distance, to the violin that breaks free of them so sweetly, its notes scratched over by the same years that overlie my recollection of the day when I first heard them on a gramophone with its hand-wound motor and steel needles in the drawing-room of my home at Torquay.

So too when I see fern fronds unfolding in the spring, waving this way and that in the breeze, or pattering up and down under the impact of rain drops, my thoughts go back to the fascination I first felt for them when I was a boy of 9 or 10 and noticed them in the valleys round Dartmoor. Their delicacy of form and graceful stance, combined with a resilience that withstands the buffeting of the weather, remind me of the tunes, strictly yet tenderly evocative, that Kreisler bowed from his violin into the recesses of my brain. And just as the gothic architecture of a church sets it apart from the houses that cluster round it, giving it by contrast of style an air not simply of a past age, but rather of a vanished, even an alien, culture closer to the Incas than to today's accountants and footballers, so the gothic tracery of a fern marks it out from the flowering plants of hedge bank or woodland floor and harks back to a much earlier stage in the evolution of plants.

One day in 1952 I read with delighted surprise a short note that reported the finding at Dungeness in Kent of a single plant of the fern species *Dryopteris cristata*, in which I was interested at that time. Drainage of fields and fens had made a species that was once widespread in eastern to midland England now restricted to a few survivors in damp places remote from the mechanised farming that was well on the way to changing the countryside into something like a factory floor. But Dungeness? That seemed rather far from its stronghold in East Anglia despite a few outliers in central England.

The note was signed F Rose.[27] The name meant nothing to me, so on finding that he was a lecturer in the botany department of Bedford College in London I wrote and asked him whether the Dungeness plant had been well enough developed for him to be sure of its identification. To this somewhat impertinent inquiry his reply was an invitation to visit him at his department. Crossing Regent's Park to the college I felt apprehensive about questioning a person I had never met to dispel doubts I probably ought not to be entertaining, and as I went down some steps to where his office lay my intrusion seemed increasingly hard to defend.

Entering his room I saw a man in his early 30s, of medium height and robust build, with a sallow but weather-beaten complexion, who from his untidy brown hair to his casual tweed jacket appeared as someone who knew the countryside and did not bother much about urban vanities. He laid his pipe on the table and rose to shake my hand with an unassuming politeness, a humility far removed from servility, an air of at once encouragement and patience that suggested it was he rather than I who had most to learn from our meeting.

"I'm glad you could come along," he said. "Here's a frond from that fern, I'd be grateful for your opinion," and he laid before me a herbarium sheet with a frond on it that was unquestionably identified correctly.

He was pleased to be able to describe to an enthusiast, even though an amateur, the unusual locality where he had found the plant and to discuss the ecology of the species. Encouraging me to add my views to his greater experience of this peculiar plant he drew away, by the enthusiasm with which he described his studies of it, a curtain from a scene which I recognised as irresistibly attractive. When he ended our talk by suggesting that we might spend a weekend in Kent looking for ferns and invited me to stay with him and his family at East Malling I warmly accepted. This meeting with Francis Rose altered the whole course of my life.

He that enlarges his curiosity after the works of nature demonstrably multiplies the inlets to happiness. – SAMUEL JOHNSON[28]

The study of plants in their natural habitats was opened up to me under Francis's guidance: the trees, shrubs, herbs, ferns, mosses, liverworts – the multiplicity of forms that had evolved with their specialised lifestyles, their modes of germination, nutrition and growth, reproduction and decay, and their relationships to each other. All these unfolded before me under the tuition and demonstration with which Francis enlivened our – not "rambles", no, our minutely planned excursions to localities where unusual plants held out, still defying the catastrophe of man. Sometimes one or all of his three sons might join us (a daughter was born subsequently), while his wife tolerated our return with muddy boots and wet clothes without fuss ("I knew I was going to marry her the first time I saw her," Francis told me).

Francis would sometimes join me in Hertfordshire to look for mosses in that county, then little known to him. Having collected some on his first visit in the autumn of 1952 he turned to me with a hopeful smile and said, "They're really rather fascinating, you know."

"Yes," I replied, "I think I'll take up mosses."

Until that day I had hardly been aware of their individuality or the striking differences between the various species, as a traveller to an unfamiliar country in Asia or Africa might think everyone there looks very much alike. But now I had seen under the hand lens and microscope the beauty peculiar to each kind and in the field the variety of habitats for which each species had a predilection. Even so, I began to wonder how I could possibly enter into what seemed at first so recondite a study. But from this moment the study of mosses and liverworts (constituting the bryophytes) became absorbing, and over the next five years I spent many spare hours walking over what was then a more rural county than it is today.

> Colour washed cottages reed-thatched
> And weather-boarded water mills,
> Flint churches, brick and plaster patched
> On mildly undistinguished hills –
>
> They still are there. But now the shire
> Suffers a devastating change,
> Its gentle landscape strung with wire,
> Old places looking ill and strange.
>
> – JOHN BETJEMAN. *Hertfordshire*

In the summer I might combine a trek over the hills with a family picnic. But the best seasons to hunt for bryophytes in such a dry county as Hertfordshire were often winter and spring, when Francis would sometimes come over for the weekend. In the 1950s the oak and hornbeam woods in the south, with damp patches and old tree stumps, contained some rare species, while the chalk hills in the north had shady banks that sparkled under the winter mists with their mossy emeralds in the turf.

Francis was always reluctant to leave the field till light had failed completely, so that on one occasion we were continuing to hunt in the turf on hands and knees while striking a series of matches to illuminate it. In our duffle coats and kneeling posture, our slow progression and intent gaze, we must have appeared to the occupants of the cars that passed by on the road below more like penitential monks from the fourteenth century than professional men of the twentieth, and I suppose we were as wrapt in the contemplation of nature as they had been in their devotion to a sacred vision. The results of these excursions, to which Francis made a valuable contribution, were reported in 1959.[29]

Francis was not then, as he has never been, a scientist whose only understanding of the universe is derived from the application of the scientific method. Like the illuminators of mediaeval manuscripts, decorating the margins with intricate wreaths of vegetation or the forms of half-animal, half-demon creatures, he enjoyed the quirks as well as studying the forms of nature around him. And his companionship was all the more sympathetic because we shared the view that, though scientific study leads us through successive approximations ever closer to one kind of understanding of the universe, there are other ways, other modes of thought, that also lead us to an understanding no less valid despite being insusceptible to rational testing. So that it was not simply in the guise of scientist that Francis or I studied the bryophytes: in the minds of both of us was also an aesthetic quest for harmony between man and nature and a philosophic quest for an understanding of the relation between our lives and those of the plants we were peering at by the flare and flicker of successive matches.* Two ways to truth, equally valid even though immiscible.

> To understand others is to have knowledge;
> To understand oneself is to be illumined. – *Tao Te Ching*,
> Chapter 33

Among various trips we made was one to the English Lake District in 1956. In a wood near Ullswater one afternoon the

* Back in 1939 I heard on the radio a woman being interviewed on her 100th birthday. She was asked what she thought was the most remarkable invention in her lifetime, which spanned the most stupendous technological advances the world had ever seen. She replied: "Matches."

rain was unceasing as we scrambled from one boulder to another, trying to pick out interesting liverworts here and there and examine their leaves through hand lenses covered in droplets which were impossible to wipe away in the all-pervading wetness. As we clambered slowly from one hummock to another, feeling for a foothold on the slippery rocks and clutching at wet branches for support, we discussed the policy of the Roman Catholic Church on contraception. A profuse beard now added to the rusticity of Francis's tanned features and harmonised with his jovial expression, rough tweeds, and pockets from which fragments of plants were hanging to suggest the reincarnation of a "green man" from the forests of pre-Christian Britain. But in fact he had been born and brought up a Catholic and still honoured his religion, so that an interlude from plant hunting was a necessity on Sundays to allow him to go to church. That rite had been observed in the morning, and now here we were in the pouring rain locked in argument, he defending a policy that I was criticising on the traditional grounds that it was preventing the teaching of birth control to people who both wanted and needed to practise it to preserve their own health and self-respect and to keep man's breeding within limits that the earth could tolerate. Shivering with the rain running down our necks we exchanged with assurance the time-honoured platitudes in the language of biological statistics, Francis courteous as ever while standing by his principles. But a year or two later I learnt that he had given up his religion, passing from a well-tended garden into a wilderness of barren earth, as it may seem at first before the new crop germinates and unfolds its green shoots. The biological arguments had proved to be too strong. I was worried lest my influence had destroyed his faith. Had I been too persuasive? Not, I knew, by any subtlety of argument or originality of proof – it was all old stuff – but simply as a respected friend who might say, "Would you like to read this book – it seemed quite good to me?" And you hand over a book that, not all at once perhaps but over a year or so's reflection, reduces to a dusty heap something that took an age to build.

But it was not only that. The mortar between the bricks was already crumbling. Francis knew that spirit and reason offer two routes to different kinds of truth and that, in Jung's words, "Science must serve; it errs when it usurps the throne".[30] They need not meet in a clash of armour on a churned-up battlefield as they were apt to do in the nineteenth century, yet the Roman church had now made the mistake of fighting just this sort of battle. To people like him, sensitive to the longings of the human spirit and responsive to the Christian revelation, the church in its pronouncements on contraception seemed to have lost its way in a labyrinth of mediaeval pseudoscience. In its emphasis on physiological rather than spiritual exhortation, in the sophistical compromises of its arguments, it simply opposed sound biology not with divine guidance but with faulty biology. And that is what drove many of the flock from the fold.

On my many field trips with Francis I learnt in finer weather than hampered us at Ullswater a great deal about plants in general, but he was not my only teacher. Belonging as I did to several botanical societies, I was often deeply grateful for the help that more expert members would generously give to novices like myself. At that time the British Bryological Society in particular was to me almost an educational academy, and I have often been struck by the lack of any barriers between professionals and amateurs in the biological sciences in this country. So that when someone asked me once what I thought was the qualification most necessary for an amateur botanist, I replied, after thinking for a moment about my own experience, "To have the right friends."

When I later obtained from London University various degrees in botany, a subject in which I have never been anything but an amateur, people have sometimes said to me, "You're not a *real* amateur." Yet I certainly am, and I decline to have my amateur status snatched from me. The amateur botanist or zoologist who nevertheless produces serious work is a member of a flourishing race in Great

Britain. We are sometimes thought of as peculiar to this country. Certainly we are relatively more numerous here than anywhere else, and we play a part in the wings where academic biology holds the centre of the stage. So when asked to write on this subject a few years ago[31] I opened the *Oxford English Dictionary* to see how it defined the term amateur and found "One who is fond of a thing". Obviously a professional can be fond of his subject as well, so the second definition given by the dictionary fits the case more precisely: "One who practises a thing as a pastime". No doubt amateurs themselves may sometimes feel reluctant to acknowledge a status that has given rise to the adjective "amateurish", meaning (to quote the *OED* again) "Having the faults of amateurs' work, unskilful in execution". Struggling to cast off that slur and win our laurels we do on occasion feel the elation of having gained the respect of professional workers and are encouraged to believe that in practising – indeed enjoying – our pastime we have succeeded in making some lasting contribution to knowledge of the universe in which individually we have so brief a journey.

For amateur botanists – and the same must be true of zoologists – the mainspring of their often arduous devotion to scientific research is a love of nature. By studying the lives of plants and their genetic and social relationships we amateurs learn something about the human condition and open a window into our own souls. Contemplation of the almost infinite variety of pattern in nature, whether the pattern is of structure or development or behaviour, disrupts the conventional modes of thought in which we tend to take shelter as we grow older, keeps alive a youthful sense of wonder at the fullness of life, and continues as the years pass to stretch the imagination out to barely perceived visions where hill meets sky.

But as an amateur I could never have turned to any branch of zoology that entailed killing the animals I was studying. For a time I became interested in spiders and had to kill several in the course of work, but the look of abhorrence on my 6-year-old daughter's face so faithfully reflected my own revulsion that I abandoned the project immediately. Though in no way an anti-vivisectionist I know that I could never have carried out experiments on animals myself, grateful as I am for the benefits brought to us by the physiologists and pharmacologists who do not have these qualms. Nor am I alone in the medical profession in having these reservations, as I have found.

Many years ago, for instance, a paper submitted to the *BMJ* described some work on rats – not the most appealing of animals – whose manner of death seemed to me to be unnecessarily harsh. The editor, Clegg, agreed with me, and we decided to obtain the opinion of an expert adviser experienced in animal experiments. When sending him the paper I was careful to phrase the question in completely neutral terms. He also thought the method of killing them was offensive, so we rejected the paper. The adviser was the Nobel prize winner P B Medawar.

On its own this experience proves nothing more than that people are occasionally deemed to have overstepped an arguable mark. Yet several members of the medical profession (all as it happens consultants associated with teaching hospitals) have over the years expressed to me their doubts whether enough care was being taken to find alternatives to experiments or tests on animals. And not necessarily alternatives: one of these critics said to me he believed too much of the research on animals in his specialty should never have been started, so trivial or pointless were its aims. Another contended there was an undeclared scale of prestige relating to the complexity of the animal that a research worker needed, and was permitted, to use for his work. From mouse to monkey, as it were, his reputation could rise in accordance with the type of animals he required for his research.

There are of course legal restrictions on vivisection, and their observance is carefully monitored. Nobody who has seen what is permitted in other countries, among them the USA, could regard Britain as generally lax or callous in its control of such work. Indeed there have always been people here who claim that research is impeded by an excessive concern for animal welfare at the expense of the welfare of man – or for that matter the welfare of animals, which also benefit from the results of such work. And, though an estimate of the amount of benefit to be expected from any particular investigation is often attempted in individual cases before the experiment is begun, no rational conclusion to an argument can reach conjunction with an ethical conclusion that may be held on the value of an animal's life. The two are incommensurable and can only be balanced against each other in the last resort by a decision that combines both rational and irrational judgments. My own belief is that mankind presumes too much on behalf of science.

In a small way the terminology that has become fashionable in scientific papers reflects some of the uneasiness that scientists have come to feel about experiments on animals. It began in the USA but is now current in Britain. Thus at the end of an experiment the animal is reported in today's jargon not to have been "killed" but to have been "sacrificed", as though it were offered up on the altar to science by the high priest in his laboratory robes. And the research is described as having been carried out not on "animals" as such but on an "animal model", so that the reality of a sentient creature gives way to the myth of an insensible automaton as the object on which the experiment is performed. No wonder that people who were once called "patients" are now often termed "subjects" in medical papers reporting on their diseases.

For different reasons a greater solicitude for the welfare of plants is also beginning to show like a new moon above the horizon just as man is slashing the forests from the face of the earth. When I was a boy playing golf with my mother and some of her friends at Torquay, someone would occasionally bring along a trowel to dig up a plant from the rough ground to take back to their garden. From the limestone promontory it might be a white rock rose, *Helianthemum apenninum*, a species that is very rare in Britain though more widespread on the European continent, and a comfortable bed would be found for it at home among the limestone of the rock garden, where in a year or two it would inexplicably expire. Or some orchid would be borne away from a picnic site around

Dartmoor and planted with loving care in the herbaceous border, where it would rarely be seen again after flowering once. What in retrospect is seen to be shameful vandalism certainly did not appear so at the time. Keen gardeners were digging up plants all over the country because nature seemed inexhaustible, capable of infinite replenishment, and in fact a cruse from which man could draw endless refreshment for his own pleasure.

Natural and laudable "curiosity after the works of nature" can, like most human impulses, be put to harmful purposes, and when it has been sated by the study of common species it seeks more obsessionally the rare ones, so that the love of nature, like other loves, has its perversions, among them the "safari" trade in the shooting of wild birds and mammals for their skins, the robbing of birds' nests for rare eggs, and the gathering of large populations of orchids in some tropical countries for the greenhouses of unscrupulous gardeners. To this debasement of a natural instinct to enjoy the beauty of the world's wild life must be added the unconcern with which whole habitats may be destroyed in the name of "development". Even the prestige of science itself is called upon to justify – as well as to conceal – the collecting of plants and animals that ought never to have been taken. A flagrant example is the insistence of several nations on a right to kill whales for "scientific study" as a means of evading an international agreement banning their being killed for commercial purposes.

If any life is to be preserved on this planet apart from the creatures that serve man's needs and comfort, a knowledge of the individuality of each plant or animal may help to stay the "abhorrèd shears". This lesson was taught me when I was resting on a bank in the Lake District during a second visit, in 1957. A young man walking by stopped to ask what I was looking at under a hand lens. My reply, mosses, puzzled him. "But I always thought moss was just moss." I explained that there are different kinds and showed him several of the common species around me. "So I must be careful where I go," he said; "incidentally there are a lot on the lawn at home." What had previously appeared to him as an undifferentiated carpet became, when looked at closely, a garden party of individuals with the sun glittering through their translucent leaves, their stems and branches jutting out in assertive Anglo-Saxon attitudes.

To see that each organism is an individual and each group of them a community with its own complex associations, and not just a blur of unrecognisable faces in a crowd, a patch of slime at the edge of a pond, a stretch of turf to be walked over, is the first step to preserving it from needless destruction.* And the protection of other forms of life now ranks second only to the preservation of the human species itself from extinction by, paradoxically, our contrasting powers of procreation and destruction. The stimulus to my understanding that every creature, whether plant or animal, is a distinct life I owe to Francis Rose.

I delight in the study of natural history because it establishes a sense of kinship with creation. No longer solitary and puzzled, I feel restored to the sea of genes that everywhere casts up living organisms in all their variety of form and function. In analysing their relationships I unconsciously count myself and my friends among them, finding a harmony between us in the matrix of our genetic concordance.

* Exeter University has the right idea. Notices on its campus lawns warn anyone tempted to walk on them: "Your feet are killing me."

21 The right friends

In 1958, on 1 February, 24 of my botanical friends and acquaintances met at my invitation in the boardroom of the Natural History Museum in London. By general consent I took the chair, and by the unanimous resolution of everyone present we established the British Lichen Society.

It had all started in the previous autumn. For some years I had been interested in the lichens that I noticed when out collecting or photographing bryophytes or pteridophytes (ferns, horsetails, and allied plants). And when I was walking through Borrowdale in the Lake District on 10 October 1957 the thought suddenly came to me that I must take these fungus-like plants more seriously than I had done previously. Everywhere they formed their crusts and cups and beards, plastering the surface of the surrounding rocks and trees with their rococo decoration, yet of their real nature I knew very little: here was something to be explored.

As I have mentioned above, an amateur who wants to do scientific work in addition to enjoying the observation of nature in all her oddity needs to have the right friends. Intellectual isolation is a desert where he soon loses his way, where ideas become sparser and drier, break up into fragments, and finally peter out in the sand. Having been a member for several years of the British Pteridological Society (the oldest society in the world devoted to ferns and allied plants) and of the British Bryological Society, I had quickly learnt from corresponding with their members or attending their meetings how generous the experts can be in guiding the novice and how warmly even a busy professional botanist will generally welcome the inquiries of the serious amateur. I had received nothing but kindness as well as enlightenment from the members of these two societies. But when it came to lichens the study of their taxonomy, ecology and physiology had fallen into neglect in Great Britain despite the exceptionally rich variety of species to be found in these islands.

Arthur Wade, a professional botanist at the National Museum of Wales, Cardiff, had almost alone taken a scientific interest in these plants and played a part in a small club for the exchange of information and specimens. It was mainly composed of a few amateurs. In fact at that time it was probably an amateur, Ursula Duncan, who after Wade had the most knowledge of British lichens.

One of the leading amateur botanists of her day (she died in 1985 aged 74) Ursula, who was unmarried, lived with her mother on the family farm which she ran near Arbroath in the east of Scotland. She combined an exceptionally wide knowledge of plants in the field with a strict devotion to duty and keen sense of fun. Rather Scandinavian in appearance, with pale handsome features, brown hair that had a glint of red, and an athletic figure that gave her day-long energy when out in the hills, she was proud of her Lowland Scots attachment to education and work. I was rash enough once to say how I had enjoyed staying among Highlanders in the west of Scotland.

"Yes," she replied briskly, "but we call them *dozy*," and I felt slightly admonished by her disdain. But it was an admonishment that she at the same time knew would not hurt my feelings – something she would have been most scrupulous to avoid when speaking to anyone – because she was aware that the Scots blood in my own veins derived like her own from the eastern Lowlands.

By sheer force of character Ursula had succeeded in living to the full the life that circumstances had given her, a life in which the river of her energy seemed to have become all the more forceful owing to the high banks that restricted its course. One day we were eating our sandwich lunch in the upper reaches of Glen Clova, with the wind blowing over the boulders among which we sat for shelter, and we talked about the effect of the war on our lives. She surprised me by saying that it was the happiest time in her life until then, when she had been in her early 30s, because of the freedom it gave her from her home circle.

"I was frightened of my father," she added. "In the war I went to Inverness and worked in the army censorship department. It was the first time I really stood on my own feet."

Her father had been a distinguished naval officer, and as he died in 1943 I never knew him. To what extent he deserved the tremulous respect his elder daughter felt for him I never inquired further: myth and reality are apt to be confused in any family – indeed the myth may actually be the reality.

"And the trouble is, you see," she went on, "I'm a bit frightened of men. They worry me. I like things neatly organised."

"But you're not frightened of me?"

"Oh no, that's different. We're botanists – I mean that's what interests us." Her gaze drifted down the steep slopes of the valley to the River South Esk far below. "Well, time for some more collecting." And she wrapped up her sandwich paper and pushed an apple core under a rock: "I don't think we do any harm with apple remains, do you? But orange peel is different – it doesn't belong. I bury that."

In her dress and demeanour she followed a mode that without being old-fashioned was conservative. She always wore a skirt and gumboots (now know as wellingtons), never trousers or even walking boots, and if the rough weather that so often sweeps over the Scottish hills caught up her skirt she would push the hem down with a wry apology for the wind's indelicacy. She was herself conscious also of following a more formal, perhaps a stricter, code than most of her botanical companions did. When at home she would go to church on Sunday mornings. "They expect it of me here," she told me. Did God expect it too, I wondered. But I would never have dared to touch such a sensitive spot in her soul as her deepest religious beliefs, and there were some aspects of human conduct too on which her reserve would have been absolute. Though I never heard her speak about the Christian faith, it must have been an unquestioned foundation to her life.

No self-indulgence of any kind found a place in the hurrying minutes of her day. One evening we returned to her car after having been out all day in the Perthshire hills, and she was looking tired.

"I'll drive us home, if you like," I said.

"Well, if you wouldn't mind."

"Have you got a headache – would you like an aspirin?"

"Oh no, I'm *quite* all right, thank you." And after a pause she added with an emphasis at once defiant and amused, "No aspirin or alcohol has *ever* passed my lips."

She uttered these words with a smile, perfectly well aware that some people might think them priggish, but knowing me well enough to be sure that I should not mistake her meaning.

Since childhood Ursula had been an accomplished pianist and when they were girls she and her younger sister would play duets for the entertainment of visitors. She did not go to school but received her education from a governess, and the first academic qualification she obtained was in music, the LRAM. When her father died she had to leave the freedom of the censorship office at Inverness to run the family farm of 500 acres, with a manager in charge of the detailed work. A hankering for a more formal academic education led her after the war to enrol as an external student of London University, with the result that she graduated BA in classics at the age of 42 and proceeded to the MA four years later.

Meanwhile she had become one of the most skilful field botanists in Scotland, able to identify species through the whole range of flowering plants, including the grasses and sedges, down to mosses and liverworts, and to discuss from intimate practical experience their distribution and habitats. Being specially expert on some genera of mosses she served as adviser on them to members of the British Bryological Society, and any inquirer, whether novice or old hand, unfailingly received a prompt and instructive reply on specimens sent for her opinion. From the bryophytes she moved on to lichens, and while the academic study of them lay in the doldrums in this country her enthusiasm ensured

224

that she was among the few people who knew at least something about this intricate group of plants.

As though all this was not enough, she had no sooner obtained the MA in classics than she enrolled for a PHD and spent several years in the 1950s writing a thesis on Paracelsus. But here for reasons which, as I have mentioned, may hamper the amateur she met disappointment: it was not accepted. Lacking as she did close connections with academic scholars in her subject, she could not obtain the kind of guidance that comes not so much from formal instruction as from casual conversation, a suggestion in passing to look up some particular reference or the criticism that somebody else has already had that idea. To determine just where the limits lie between knowledge and ignorance and to detect a place on the boundary where a step into the darkness may be worthwhile presented difficulties to her working in such isolation. So far as her classical studies were concerned she lacked the "right friends".

Not only she but everyone who knew her was delighted when later on her botanical work won her the recognition she deserved from the Linnean Society with the award of its Bloomer medal and from Dundee University with the conferment of an honorary doctorate.

Her family home was built in 1801 of old red sandstone taken from a quarry later made into an attractive feature of the garden. Though the house sheltered them from storm and snow with solid ease, Ursula and her mother endured much the same temperatures within as did its first occupants. To stay there in spring or autumn (winter I never attempted) gave occasion to admire the fortitude with which the mother carried on with her beautiful silk needlework pictures during her 80s without having to wear glasses while the daughter brought her herbarium sheets out successively to dry them before a small electric fire – a routine she was compelled to follow through many of the cold, damp months of the year. When Josephine was with me there during an autumn visit she managed surreptitiously to slip a log on to the embers in the drawing-room grate one evening while Ursula's mother was out of the room, but such luxuries were hard-won, for

Ursula had accustomed herself to the cold while her mother was oblivious of it.

Yet the chilly though well furnished rooms seemed to be the natural concomitant of Ursula's entire devotion to her studies, to reflect an unconcern with the ordinary comforts of home which, if they had usurped her attention or soothed her senses, could only have distracted her from more important occupations. Whether she was supervising the farm, which she did every day with skill and enjoyment, or reading the Latin and Greek classics, or writing a guide to the lichens of Great Britain (on which she published an admirable volume), she contrived a disciplined schedule to make room for it all.

Though her riches were of the intellect rather than the imagination, her enthusiasm lit up the vision of her friends and students – some of whom from Dundee University came under her tuition. She taught them not merely the methods but the joy of botanising in the damp, moss-filled gullies of the hills and on the windswept ridges, or the excitement of discriminating with the aid of hand lens and microscope between the infinitude of forms in which the world's genes express themselves. If her mode of life had a touch of the ascetic, this quality reflected not a dour religious mortification but her desire to pack every moment of it with enjoyment, whether fulfilling her duty to the farm or pursuing her intellectual interests. The rigour of her self-discipline followed on from the home discipline which she declared had been the context of her childhood. From obedience to that code she drew the strength of will that guided her through adult life or occasionally roused her to astringent comment on the less exacting standards of her friends.

For instance, when we were going over some specimens one evening I suggested she send a particularly puzzling one to a friend for his opinion.

"No, I shall never get a reply from him," she replied, "*that man lacks drive.*" She spoke with regret, but the fact that he was undoubtedly busy with studies of his own could not mitigate the scorn she also felt for someone's lacking a quality that she herself possessed so abundantly – a quality, incidentally, with which she imbued the very words as she uttered them. She was expressing too her underlying anxiety that she suffered from the isolation in both human and geographical terms, the inability to obtain advice or information by just dropping into the room next door or at the most by taking a short train journey. It was all so far away. She wanted to get things done, to see the flower set seed.

It was to avoid this kind of isolation that I conceived the idea of starting a lichen society when I was walking through Borrowdale on that autumn day in 1957. The time was more propitious than I then realised, because when I returned home and began to make inquiries I found that the Natural History Museum had appointed a recently graduated botanist, Peter James, to take charge of its collections, though he still had to complete his national service in the army before taking up his post.

During November that year I wrote first to about a dozen botanists, amateur as well as professional, without whose support the founding of a society could hardly be attempted. They urged me to go on with the project, and so I then wrote to another 50 who I thought might support the scheme. Rather to my surprise almost all replied favourably. So it came about that 25 of us gathered in London a few months later and formed the British Lichen Society.

Having taken the precaution beforehand of finding people who would be willing to serve as officers of the society, I presented these victims to the meeting and saw them duly elected, so that we started off with a team to manage its business. What did take me by surprise was the eagerness of the meeting to start publishing a journal, not in a year's time when we had expanded (as I hoped) but as soon as a printer could be found. So having already offered them a potential editor in Peter James, and their having agreed to his suggestion that when a journal did appear it should be entitled the *Lichenologist*, I did not feel I could delay trying to start one.

The funds that our small society could raise and the number of copies of the journal we should need to have printed would both have been unattractive to a conventional printer. In the upshot two issues appeared in the next 13 months. This was made possible by my good fortune in having at that time a secretary, Miss Gillian Lambert (later Mrs Dent), who was skilful, quick at her work, and to my eternal gratitude willing to devote her spare time after office hours to the production of the new journal. While I entered into negotiations with a local firm for the use of a photolithography machine, articles poured in for publication. Miss Lambert had to type every article out twice, first on to paper sheets of page size and then, after arranging the typed sheets in the order required to make the "book", a second time in that order on to large aluminium sheets. From these the pages were printed, and the first issue appeared on 1 November 1958. The second issue was produced in the same way four months later, but by the time the third issue became due we had accumulated enough funds to move over to conventional printing.

Now 30 years later the society is a flourishing international body with over 500 members from countries all over the world – in Europe, Asia, Africa, Australasia, and the Americas. Its quarterly journal, the only scientific journal devoted to lichenology, reflects the international composition of the society.

The society came at the right time partly because its foundation coincided with the appointment of a full-time botanist in charge of the lichens at the Natural History Museum. But it owes its success also to the resurgence during the 1960s of lichen studies in the universities of many countries. New methods of chemical analysis (and many species have a complex chemistry) were developed mainly by Chicita Culberson at Duke University in the USA, and these methods, especially thin-layer chromatography, combined with a much closer microscopical study of their anatomy to revolutionise the taxonomy of lichens, one of the main problems of which is their consisting of a fungus in symbiosis with an alga. The complexities of that symbiosis were at the same time attacked by Sir David Smith, FRS, at Bristol and Oxford.

The new research techniques enable species to be identified and plants determined much more exactly than hitherto, so that natural habitats such as woodland and exposed rocks or semi-natural habitats such as neglected churchyards and old walls can be understood in more precise and more comprehensive biological terms. And since lichens are exceedingly sensitive to air polluted by industrial or agricultural chemicals they have been extensively studied as measures of the effect of man's activities on the natural environment.

When he completed his national service Peter James took up his post at the Natural History Museum in 1958. In June of that year he and I visited north-west Scotland and made a large collection of lichens. One of our problems was to dry them, so that we were alarmed when the waitress in our hotel at Inchnadamph came to our table at dinner one evening and said to Peter, "I'm sorry to have to tell you that your specimens have fallen into the soup." She had the tact to speak low so that the other guests should not be alarmed by the knowledge that a quantity of lichens placed on the rack above the kitchen stove to dry had slipped off into a cooking-pot below – fortunately in their packets, so that the specimens themselves were undamaged when retrieved from the soup. The collections we made on that trip all ended up in the museum, Peter's going there immediately as of duty, mine following later as a gift. Surprisingly this was the first substantial collection of lichens from the British Isles to have been added to the herbarium this century. A collection at Kew made in earlier years by W Watson, of Somerset, was subsequently transferred to the Natural History Museum.

When I first met him Peter was still in his 20s, rather a tall young man whose expression, studious in repose, readily broke into a smile. Now, with the passing years and retirement in sight, a beard that sprouted on an expedition to South America has been allowed to remain, the brown hair is streaked with grey, and the studious expression has taken on a judicious cast as well. But he has always been the welcoming host at the museum. To a visitor arriving at his department his opening words would be, "Now, is there anything I can get you?" An expert in a key position, his friendly help to visitors, amateur and professional alike, has been an unobtrusive, unsung benefit to the British Lichen Society as well as to lichenology more generally. The touchstone by which a scientist's reputation is apt to be judged is the papers he has published. It is a matter of publish or perish. Peter has of course made a reputation in that way, but for him more than most scientists it is necessary to look beyond the publications to the man himself for a true measure of the impetus he has given to botany.

As well as exerting a diffuse but none the less positive influence in this way on lichenology Peter has a love of the arts, especially music and the theatre, that makes him a cultivated host over dinner (which as an expert cook he may have prepared) and one of those rare professional men who can entertain his guests without ever mentioning his work. Despite an alert sense of humour, often witty in its expression, and a sociable disposition, fate has decreed that he remain a bachelor. A slight formality in his manner (as Ursula Duncan also possessed) perhaps reflected in his youth the wariness that a traveller feels as he steps up to the customs barrier at a foreign airport; now in middle age it has evolved into an expression of innate courtesy. Through the facilities he provided at the museum he enabled me to discover some of nature's secrets – to use a conventional phrase, though the "secrets" are simply things of which man was ignorant, such as distinct kinds of organisms, previously misunderstood genetic relationships, unrecorded modes of life, overlooked anatomical structures.

When I was travelling in Uganda with an African friend – a botanist called Katende, of whom more will be said below – we could see through a bank of papyrus the waters of Lake Victoria.

"We sometimes laugh at the way you English say you 'discovered' this lake," he said. "We knew all the time it was here."

Perhaps with a whiff of sophistry I defended our "discovery" by saying that it was like discovering a new species of plant – which was something he would delight in doing as a botanist. It is there all the time, but what we mean by "discovering" it is that we recognise its existence in a way that allows our knowledge of it to be incorporated into a science that we are building up – botany in the case of the plant, geography in the case of the lake. Thus we come to understand the relationships of the plant to others like it and unlike it, and of the lake to the River Nile that flows from it and far to the north determines the whole life and economy of Egypt.

In this sense "discovering" has been the scientific side of the quest that has led me through life, and it is complementary to the mystical journey towards an understanding of its meaning.

PART 6

22 Fear of blood

Distance, farawayness, this is the gaze of Africa. To go anywhere you travel hundreds of miles. To get a response you signal across a gulf.

We were standing on the terrace in our host's garden, my wife and I, in November 1967, looking out over the Johannesburg suburbs below us, where the sky seemed to have come down and spread over the gardens and streets filled with jacaranda trees in flower. Every shade of blue from silvery to ultramarine shimmered among the houses as a faint breeze disturbed the flowers. We had struck the right moment to see them, to enjoy the contrast they provided to the city centre with its modern office blocks of concrete and glass devoted to the wellbeing of financiers like any modern city in Europe or America.

Africa is a continent where the extreme is the norm. Tragedy and farce equally abound, and the commonplace is always out of place. Few people of any prominence there, black or white, display the virtues of the middle way – dispassionate judgment, compromise in debate, gentleness in action. And over much of the continent hangs the curse of disease caused by organisms against which man has never developed effective antibodies – malaria, bilharzia, sleeping sickness, river blindness, and many more – a biochemical failure all the more extraordinary for his ancestors having evolved in that continent.

My devotion to Africa began in an unpropitious place – the Republic of South Africa. I visited it on behalf of the *BMJ* for three weeks in 1967 and again for two weeks plus a week in South-West Africa, now known as Namibia, in 1969. My valuable spouse, as Boswell used to call his wife, came too. In contrast to many students of those countries whose knowledge of them derives from visits as brief as mine or from the imagination alone, I have no solution to their political, social, and racial problems – that is, no solution likely to influence the people who hold power. What I did learn is the familiar lesson that the traveller who enters an alien society and observes it for a short time is like a goldfish darting to swallow one crumb of food after another. What comes to his attention is only a succession of fragments of greater or less palatability. To make an impartial observation under the conditions of scientific study is difficult enough, because what we record has been filtered through a network of preconceptions, expectations, prejudices, misunderstandings, and wish-fulfilments. Hence the elaborate precautions we take to exclude possible sources of error when doing research. But how much harder it is for the visitor to make a clear, true, unbiased observation of the society he moves among not as an anthropologist but rather as a guest. When he tries to get below the surface of a people who are geographically remote, historically divergent, and politically estranged, he is apt to find he is peering from the prison of his own past.

> Home is where one starts from. As we grow older
> The world becomes stranger, the pattern more complicated
> Of dead and living. Not the intense moment
> Isolated, with no before and after,
> But a lifetime burning in every moment
> And not the lifetime of one man only
> But of old stones that cannot be deciphered. – T S ELIOT. *East Coker*

Down the road from our hotel on the day after we arrived members of the South African Scottish Regiment, resplendent in bonnet and kilt, were marching up and down to the bagpipes in celebration of Armistice Day and in honour of their comrades who had died in two world wars fighting as our allies. Stepping into Joubert Park, Josephine and I were startled to see some of the public seats with plaques on them proclaiming them to be for "Europeans only". They have since been removed. But their presence and subsequent removal epitomise a whole philosophy. Dating from some decades previously, the term "European" denoted a racial rather than a geographical category and included, for example, Americans, Australians, and New Zealanders – provided they were white. But the time came when the Boers ruling the country wanted to emphasise that they were no longer "Boers", that is, farmers of Dutch extraction, but historical inhabitants of South Africa, in fact "Afrikaners."

So a distinction that once underwent a transition from geographical fact to racial euphemism underwent a further transition. The abolition of some of the laws of "petty apartheid" and the removal of this particular racial barrier left the plaques bearing their primary geographical meaning once again – and this was now an embarrassment. For the Afrikaner no longer thinks of himself as a European any more than an Englishman thinks of himself as a Norman, let alone an Angle. And away went the plaques. Though the removal of some of the restrictions that went under the heading of petty apartheid, restrictions which exacerbated race relations while adding little or nothing to the declared aim of apartheid to impose "separate development" on the races, might have been interpreted as a softening of the policy, it was nothing of the kind: in fact by refining it the changes made apartheid more rigorous in its aim and more indisputable in its enforcement.

Coming down in the lift in the hotel I found myself alone with the black lift attendant, so I asked him more by way of conversation than anything how he liked his life. Presumably my question was one that only a person recognisably a foreigner would have asked, for without a moment's delay to consider whether I could be a South African who might take offence at any trace of insubordination in his reply he produced from his pocket what looked like a booklet: "We have to carry these," he said. It was a pass that he had to possess in order to have the privilege of working there ferrying white people up and down in the lift all day. As he spoke his glance betrayed a glimpse of the resentment he must have felt at having to submit to a law that did not constrain everyone alike, while a shadow of habitual diffidence passed for a moment anxiously across his face.

For him apartheid could be thought of as a chronic disability, a paralysed limb that hampered him at every step as he dragged it through life, but the story of a 16-year-old schoolgirl reported in the papers while we were out there showed it could also be an acute catastrophe. She and her family lived in Cape Province, where she attended a school for white pupils. They moved to the Transvaal, and on her applying to enter a school for white pupils there she was rejected on the grounds of being black. From the girl's appearance in newspaper photographs it was evident that she had some Negro genes in her make-up. But how many? Here some trickly arithmetic was required. Inquiries in Cape Province had shown that her black ancestors were remote enough for her to be classified as white. In the Transvaal the same data put her in the black category. The social tragedy that this entailed for her is hard to imagine outside the psychotic delusions that govern South Africa, where the bus you take or the queue you stand in, the beach you lie on or the restaurant you enter, the place you live or the job you hold may depend on the "colour" of your skin – a colour that is interpreted differently from one province to another.

Passing from tragedy to farce, I hailed a taxi in Cape Town one day to take me to the foot of Table Mountain. On top of the cab was an unambiguous declaration: "Whites only". It was driven by a coal-black driver. He welcomed me with a broad grin and was eager for conversation, so I told him I had recently seen an article in a newspaper announcing that the Japanese were to be regarded as "honorary whites" while the Chinese were classified as "blacks". He doubled up with laughter over the steering wheel and finally contained himself enough to say, "Yes, yes, I've heard that too."

"So," I said, "if one or other stood at the kerb and hailed your taxi, as I've just done, how would you know whether you could pick him up? How would you tell the difference?"

"Well, I don't know, I don't know any difference between them. They look alike to me."

"But what would you do?"

He chuckled away to himself and at the passing traffic. "I think I'd pick him up just the same." And he slapped the gear lever to emphasise his independence. "Yes, I wouldn't worry. They'd be all the same to me."

Just as on a summer's evening one may see a cloud of gnats like a dark curtain across the lawn, so apartheid is not a solid barrier so much as a constantly flickering swarm of prohibitions whose force and direction change in small ways from time to time but whose overall form is constant. Conditions change. Restrictions are removed, others imposed, some relaxed, others tightened. But the laughter has become more subdued with the passing years.

The secret police keep an eye on everything, and an ear at every aperture, in their unobtrusive surveillance, so that in our hotel bedroom, for instance, I never discussed with Josephine the opinions of anyone I had met during the day. Bugs could be lurking in the telephone or the light switch. And I was amused to see that an official of the South African Government, married to a friend of ours, took the same view. On coming up to our bedroom and observing a decorative fabric plaque on the wall he made a face at it and pressed his finger to his lips.

For a white visitor to the country this kind of charade is an easy game to play, but for a native with a conscience, whatever his colour or creed, a moment's relaxation on a sunny terrace may be noted, an innocent blunder reported, a single slip fatal. And the dreamer wakes in the early hours with a sense of guilt.

Visiting Groote Schuur Hospital on the outskirts of Cape Town one day, I was taken down to a basement office and introduced to a doctor who had been isolated from his colleagues by a compulsory banning order. This was Dr Raymond (Bill) Hoffenberg. Stepping ashore at Cape Town after visiting, by permission, a student imprisoned on Robben Island for political dissidence, Hoffenberg had been stopped by the police, searched, and found to be carrying mail from a student in the island prison. Though the letters were inoffensive in themselves, the clandestine carrying of them was an offence.

Bill Hoffenberg was a well known and popular doctor, a member of the staff of Cape Town's leading hospital, a man whose political opinions were known to be humane and liberal but not violent or offensive, nor had he ever been implicated in any revolutionary activity. Yet his arrest was not the result of a random search, as I learnt several years later from an official of the Medical Association of South Africa. What had first attracted the attention of the secret police was a letter from Hoffenberg that the *BMJ* had published in 1962, some five years before his arrest.[32] In that letter he did no more than describe the political disabilities hampering any non-white student who wanted to study medicine in South Africa and advocate support of a committee that was working to alleviate them. Doubtless the moderation of his language was as irksome as his proposal was unwelcome to the Afrikaner government, and an informer in South Africa scanning the *BMJ* for material that might incriminate South Africans had put the police on the alert. From that moment they were watching his mail, listening to his telephone calls, observing his movements, casting an eye on his friends, introducing a "trusted" doctor or other professional person into his acquaintance.

In the upshot he was given the option: submit to restrictions here that will make a normal professional life impossible, or leave the country with your family for ever. Despite being a man of established attainment and popular with staff and students, he would have found that a tourniquet had been twisted round his life had he stayed. Deservedly he had friends in Britain. Before graduating in medicine he had served with the Allied forces for three years during the war in North Africa and Italy. His capabilities after he graduated in 1948 became well known in the British Medical Research Council and elsewhere in this country, so that a vacancy was found for him here when in 1968 he was driven to choose for his family as well as himself exile from their native country, thus like many a refugee bringing great gifts that have enriched the country of his adoption. In a few years his talents found their reward when he was appointed professor of medicine at Birmingham in 1972, elected president of the Royal College of Physicians of London in 1983, knighted in 1984, and installed president of Wolfson College, Oxford, in 1985. It is certainly an uncompromising political vision that drives out of the country people of such exceptional ability (and there are many more besides Hoffenberg) while at the same time herding into tattered areas of scrubland much of the rest of the population.

The secret police are the zealous, skilful, and unrelenting agents of a society that must do much more than protect its stability; it needs also to protect a myth. The Afrikaner people, that is, Boers of Dutch extraction, live in the exhilaration and the faith that they are building a nation. This myth – I use the word simply in a psychological, not a pejorative, sense – dominates their thinking and energises them with an undeviating belief in their destiny. Questions about their country light up the shining eye of the enthusiast who knows that the truth is in him, criticisms evoke an uncomprehending stare because they can only be based on mistaken premises. Thus the beauty of the countryside is a matter not so much of aesthetics as of pride. And, though the old Calvinist traditions taken to the country by early Scottish and Dutch settlers still lie in the depths, anchors in a turbulent sea, the Afrikaners today look in quite a different direction, more towards the innovative, anything-is-possible attitudes of the USA than to the hesitant impulses springing from old traditions in Europe; their eyes are on the Americans who, like the Boers themselves, threw off the colonial yoke and made a country in their own image.

Since the Afrikaner population is matched by about the same number of white people of non-Boer stock, and greatly outnumbered by people of the non-white races, the Afrikaners must spend a disproportionate amount of time and intellectual activity in simply maintaining power, though less time than might be imagined. For the sad admission was made to me several times by people of British origin: so long as the Afrikaners keep the country stable, "we shall go along with them." A defensive uncertainty mingles with the confidence that accompanies the remnants of frontier life.

"It's not like Europe, you know. We couldn't give everyone the vote – we'd be swamped."

The towering offices, the fine villas with their beautiful gardens, the highways and street avenues, the brilliant colour of native and exotic flowers, the night air heavy with the scent of frangipani and datura – it is an extraordinary offshoot of Europe, but of a Europe of the imagination rather than the reality, where Keats's "beaker full of the warm South" might have been poured. For the white people food is plentiful, servants are responsive, labour is available, sport is sacred. But the labouring hands that made it are now hammering at the gates. The visitor too may look in on the scene, see the Afrikaners cultivating their country, expanding their language – indeed consciously building it up into a flexible modern language capable of scientific recording and literary expression – moulding their future, guarding the laager, while all the time they live and move and think and dream in a hall of mirrors, seeing only endless reflections of themselves.

Yet the myth is also derided. Telling in a quiet way were the few words uttered by a medical professor when he showed me round his department. After the tour he took me back to his office so that I could collect my briefcase, and I mentioned I thought of visiting the Transkei. This must be the most irregularly shaped country known to the world's atlases; moreover it has changed its shape from time to time. Within its bounds the black people are given the opportunity to enjoy "separate development". There was a moment's pause as he looked at me; an expression of doubt as though he were seeking the right phrase crossed his features, while his eyes, thought directed at mine, seemed to be turned inwards to a distant past where life may have been harsher but was perhaps more honourable than his present existence allowed, where bonds of a common understanding joined mankind, and the compromises that united and the ambitions that divided were less hurtful to a sensitive man. He wanted to be sure that I too, a visiting European whose civilisation had its own values, should not lose touch with them. But could he trust me? Would I, whether from malevolence or inadvertence, or worse still from well-meaning conviction, betray him? As he handed me the briefcase while other members of the staff drank tea in an adjoining room he said in a low voice, "I shouldn't bother. It's all a sham."

So in a few hastily breathed words (how true they were I shall never know) he sought to enlist me, or perhaps I should say passed me a coded message to ponder, in the struggle to preserve humane values in a country that by legal statute often subverted them, in a conflict where as a teacher of the young he had to regard his every action and utterance as under surveillance. His intent gaze as we said goodbye has remained with me over the years.

Home. Where is home? "Home is where one starts from." South Africa is a country where many people are unsure of their home. To the Afrikaners the Republic itself is inalienably their home, declared to be so with a vehemence that seals every chink in the wall. But to many descendants of British stock home in the deeply emotional sense is still England, or more probably Scotland. Though born in South Africa they yet look upon it as a domicile rather than home. It is a country that arouses their pride, allows them a comfortable life, gives them professional opportunity, commands their loyalty, but in their heart comes second to a dream, a dream of "England" as it used to be in the old days. And every so often they feel sad that the dream now lies in fragments, some of them fading in the memory, some of them disbelieved, all irrecoverable in the stark sunshine of the Boer myth.

Two greetings with which I was received by native South Africans:

From a woman of British stock: "How nice to meet someone from dear old England."

From an Afrikaner: "Do you recall the Anglo-Boer war?"

South Africa is a land without a nation but filled with people of many races. In time I believe mankind will look back on his "races" as a transition phase in the evolution of the species. The slight biological differences between them – skin colour, hair texture, facial features, frequency of blood groups, and so on – no doubt developed as the species dispersed over the earth and the people in small local populations became bound to each other by cultural affinity, so that the ability to transmit culture within the local population from one generation to the next gradually established barriers, cultural as well as geographical, to interbreeding. As cultures became more elaborate and more self-defensive, the barriers rose. But now, as the falling of the geographical barriers increasingly offers hope to some and alarm to others, the cultural bonds that have held inbreeding populations together are weakening too; though, as the past dissolves and the future develops, the hiccups in history's metabolism often cause strange contortions.

"Do you mean you can't transfuse blood from a black donor into a white patient?" I asked a doctor showing me round Groote Schuur Hospital at Cape Town.

"Yes, I know it sounds absurd to you, and of course it is, but no white person would allow it. We have to go along with what they want."

And he was speaking for many of the whites of British origin as well as Afrikaners. While such grotesque biological antipathies as fear of blood and scorn of pigmentation abound, the way is blocked towards the creation of a living community whose destiny all its people may feel they share.

23 Floral interlude

The society and the flora of South Africa have something in common: both have evolved in an unusual degree of isolation from the rest of the world. The unique restrictions of apartheid governing that society and peculiar to it are matched by the high proportion of plant species unique to the region, surrounded as it is by geographical barriers of the oceans to the east, the south, and the west and the vast arid lands to the north. But in contrast to the denial of life that permeates the Boer culture the flora offers in its strangeness and beauty an affirmation of life that is a joy to the aesthetic as much as the scientific eye of the observer. Its proteas, heathers, pelargoniums, the bizarre forms of the succulents and the flowers of many liliaceous species are to be seen in abundance at the wayside, while the Compositae, with their variety of daisy-like flowers of every hue from scarlet through yellow to blue, carpet the land in the early summer and are represented by many genera familiar in British gardens such as *Helichrysum*, *Gazania*, *Mesembrianthemum* (in its broad sense), and *Felicia*.

Kirstenbosch must be one of the most attractive botanic gardens in the world owing to the beauty of its setting on the slopes of Table Mountain and the variety of species grown there, reflecting as they do the richness of the native flora and the surrounding region. In the Cape peninsular alone, a tooth-shaped projection seven miles wide at the top and about 20 miles long, more species of flowering plants grow than in the whole of the British Isles. In the drier regions the succulents are especially remarkable, and trying to find cover among the thorny agaves must have been an unpleasant novelty for soldiers in the Boer war.

To see the succulents at their best (and weirdest) I visited South-West Africa, now known as Namibia, for a week's exploring of the plant life in the subdesert between Swakopmund on the coast and Brandberg to its north-east inland, the highest mountain in that region.

Swakopmund itself was built as a holiday town by the Germans before they were dispossessed of their colony in 1917. The River Swakop, at whose mouth it lies, carries water only intermittently. Its bed is usually dry sand and boulders, affording here and there some level ground over which my guide and I took a Landrover. The tree-lined avenues of the town, the grass lawns, and the beds of flowering plants decorating the sea front with its holiday houses and palms are a testimony to the joy its early settlers must have eagerly sought there, for rain has never fallen on it: the trees, grass, and flowers, the leafy shade and the herbaceous splendour, the cool lawns and the neat hedges – all owe their existence to artificial watering, not just in a dry season but every month, every week, every day. Across one corner of a lawn I noticed the grass lying black on the soil because the spray from a hose had just failed to reach it. But so far from this town being a sunny if waterless haven along the shore of a glittering blue sea, it lies under a perpetually leaden sky and is often submerged in fog. The town is in fact a dingy flower on a stalk – a stalk of pipes bringing down from the inland hills some of the water that falls on them from time to time in storms.

North of Swakopmund a road runs parallel to the coast. It appears to be made of asphalt but was in fact constructed by the Germans of salt before the first world war. Since rain has never fallen to dissolve it, the surface remains hard and permanent. Between it and the Atlantic lies a strip of land a few miles wide where flowering plants with woody or succulent stems bearing sparse leaves grow in the sand despite their habitat being one of the few absolute deserts in the world. The water they need comes in the form of mist blown in from the cold Benguela current in the Atlantic by perpetual on-shore winds from the west. As the mist is blown further inland it rises to form clouds, and when these are driven up high enough by the hot land below they are precipitated as infrequent heavy rainstorms. Carpeting the sand by the coast are several species of lichens, and protruding from the surface in the old days before radio communications could summon help were the skeletons of men who had struggled in search of water after being shipwrecked in the dunes, for the combination of the continuous westerly winds, dense banks of fog, and shifting sand below the surface of the sea was often lethal. In fact when I was there a 15 000-ton ship was lying trapped in the sand and had been abandoned.

Inland grows one of the most fascinating floras to be seen anywhere. Species of *Hoodia* and *Stapelia* with brilliantly coloured flowers smelling of carrion and measuring up to 20 cm across on succulent stems like knobbly green fingers stood in the sand or lurked in the shelter of shrubs. Lithops plants imitating pebbles were half hidden among the rocks. The trees were mostly acacias armed with myriads of hooked thorns on their whip-like branches, swaying and curling at the slightest touch to embrace an animal or man and trap him in the burning sun, thus destroying a marauder's appetite for its leaves. And among these were scattered trees of *Aloe dichotoma* with tufts of sword-like leaves on stark, smooth trunks of battleship grey.

Most astonishing of all, like great bundles of green rags a couple of metres across and a metre high were the plants of *Welwitschia bainesii*, ranging in age from young seedlings to antiques 2000 years old. From a central plate on the ground the plant produces just two ribbon-like leaves. These slowly extend from the centre and rot off at the periphery, at the same time splitting into shreds, so that a heap of green leathery ribbons gradually builds up over the years and even the centuries. The flowers on the male plants are like small cones with bright orange anthers; the female cones have green overlapping scales on which a species of beetle lives that has no other known habitat. When the first discovered specimens of this plant reached Joseph Hooker[33] at Kew, he declared it to be "out of all question the most wonderful plant ever brought to this country – and the very ugliest,"[33] while F O Bower thought it "the most remarkable of all gymnospermic plants" (that is, with cone-like flowers).[34] The life of its discoverer was equally remarkable.[35] After adventures that took him from his native Austria to Portugal, and from there to Angola, and finally to England, he lies buried in Kensal Green cemetery in north London.

24 An impulsive decision

From the deserts of Namibia to the swamps of Uganda: Josephine and I were staying for a week in February 1969 in the guest house on the campus of Makerere University College, as it then was (later an independent university) while I met some of the doctors. After that she was to fly home and I to spend a week of my annual holiday collecting lichens.

The campus is beautifully laid out with flowering trees in which the frogs and insects trilled and whistled and rattled and cackled all night in an endlessly varying cacophony. To step on to the veranda and walk out into the woodland listening to the shrieks and cross-calls from the impatient creatures there calling for a mate is to be drawn into a world which demands acceptance of its precious variety, of its confident assertion, and of the trust it reposes in our benevolence. But to try to reach any particular call is like trying to reach a rainbow. Eyes anxiously watch you in the night. As you approach, mouths cease to hoik, throats to whistle, legs to scrape, wing cases to drum; the orchestra ahead lays down its instruments while behind you it strikes up again, so that your course through the bush is always towards its music but never reaching it. How old-fashioned Conrad's traders and Graham Greene's officials seem to today's biologist working in the tropics! Europeans in fear of their own unconscious for too long debased the validity of alien cultures and made a nightmare out of the fountain of tropical life.

Josephine and I were fortunate to be able to hire a car from one of the medical units and drive 150 miles north to the Murchison Falls on the Nile. To enliven the journey along a road so bumpy that our small car sometimes skidded across it over the ruts, we picked up a succession of "hitch-hikers" along the way. These were people who were enjoying the old Ugandan custom of travelling from one place to another, for most of the people who live anywhere near a road treat it more as a theatre than a highway, a theatre where they meet their friends, who often live some distance away, exchange their views on the comedy and drama of life, and enjoy the pleasures of companionship. They walk up and down or take a bus to the next village or pile on to a passing vehicle if the driver is willing to stop. Falling in with this custom we took ten or twelve groups of travellers varying distances along the way to a market or friends. They were often talkative, though rarely in a language we could understand; some spoke a few words of English; most gestured, seized our hands, touched our shoulders to attract attention, and spent much of their time waving to friends they passed. One man took off his shoes as a mark of respect in the back of the car; another offered me his pipe to smoke, and, on my declining it, politely put it in his pocket, where it smouldered till dying out. Many of the women were gorgeously dressed in the style of the English 1890s, a style that has persisted ever since it was introduced by the first Englishwomen to enter the country. The dresses were made up on the innumerable Singer sewing machines being operated in the shelter of huts along the roadside.

As we approached the Nile, which we were soon to cross by ferry to Paraa Lodge, we were stopped and the car was searched for tse-tse flies at a control point, the official sweeping through the car with a little net to the accompaniment of an invocation to any flies to come out and be caught – "tse-tse-tse-tse-tse…" The sleeping sickness (trypanosomiasis) that they carry is still commonly lethal to man for lack of an effectual remedy that is harmless and easily administered in a poor population. Ugandans believe the disease was brought into their country from West Africa by H M Stanley's expedition up the Congo River in 1887–9 to rescue Emin Pasha. It is certainly widespread in East and Central Africa today, existing in several forms that affect man and other mammalian species differently, and since it commonly shows a recrudescence in the wake of social disturbance it must have spread during the warfare in Uganda in recent years.

A boat trip on the Nile next day upstream to the Murchison Falls took us past basking crocodiles, a monitor lizard that feeds on their eggs, hippos plunging about in the river, fish eagles flying overhead from tree to tree, and the occasional elephant on its banks. Murchison was president of the Royal Geographical Society when Samuel Baker and his wife reached the falls on 3 April 1864. The scene before them was probably not much different from what we saw except that gun, snare, and chemical have reduced the crowds of crocodiles to a remnant. Can anything natural be saved? No doubt the warfare of the past few years has finished off most of the remaining animals.

"That is the place to go." Kåre Lye and I were looking at a map of southern Uganda. Josephine had flown back home, and I had decided to spend my week's holiday visiting the mountains in the south to collect lichens there. I had laid the plans for this holiday in advance by writing at the suggestion of Francis Rose to Kåre, who was a Norwegian postgraduate student of botany making a special study of the sedges of Uganda. The head of the department at that time was also a Norwegian, Professor S Manum, who was primarily a geologist but had botanical interests. Kåre and I discussed with him our scheme for going into the southern mountains for a week and received his enthusiastic support. Kåre also had the loan of a car, a Fiat estate model, so we were keen to get away in it. Before leaving Manum's office I noticed a large safe and asked him if he kept his specimens in it.

"Oh no, that's full of exam questions – they're far more likely to be stolen."

It seems they were mostly of the multiple-choice variety and that only a limited number of questions in that form can be devised on any particular subject. They therefore had to be used repeatedly over the years – presumably at irregular intervals, like the steps out of the dungeon in a mediaeval castle – so that if they became common property on the campus the whole exam system would break down.

Can any treasure hunt have a more exciting prelude than the study of a map before going on a botanical expedition? – a scrutiny that builds up in the imagination the mountains and rivers its lines hint at, clothing them with forests and rocks, lighting up the scene with the ripples of a lake lapping at trees covered in lichens, interpreting its contours as a shady valley green with mosses and ferns or over there a sunny hillside speckled with alpine flowers, a sphagnum bog in the hollow, and at the edge of a wood a grove of tree ferns and evergreen shrubs through which lily-flowered gloriosas twist and climb. With visions like these in our mind's eye Kåre and I and a Ugandan botanist at Makerere, Anthony Katende, set off in the estate car for Kisoro in the south-west corner of Uganda where it meets Rwanda and Zaire.

Despite a profound practical knowledge of Uganda's flora, Katende regretted that he had never been able to afford the expense of attending a British university. For six months in 1962–3 he did manage to live in Cardiff and take a short course in botanical taxonomy there – his only visit to Britain. As well as having to withstand the exceptionally severe cold of that winter he needed to extend his patience in other directions.

"I booked a room through an agency," he told me, "and when I arrived at the house in October I knocked on the door – it was pouring with rain outside. The landlady opened it, and when she saw me she gave a gasp. 'I'm sorry I'm full up,' she said. But I replied, 'Oh, you're not really. It's only because I'm black you don't want me. But I would very much like to stay. I shan't be a nuisance to you.' So she let me in."

Katende persuaded her to give him a cup of tea, and then a trial stay for a few days, and finally a room for the six months. "She was really very nice," he said, and they ended up firm friends.

Katende's experience of working with scientists in Britain and Uganda had made him realise, he told me, that the British administrators sent out to Uganda when it had been a protectorate (it was never a colony) were not first class men.

"You didn't send out your best people," he said.* Whatever truth there may be in this contentious statement, his view must have been formed in part from the differing relationships he enjoyed with these two classes of people – with administrators as a subject or subordinate, with scientists as a pupil or colleague. But though each had the advancement of Uganda's welfare as his objective the relationship differed in another way too. For Katende was dismayed by the preconceptions with which administrators presumed to direct the affairs of his country, and, worse, the prejudices they derived from an "education to rule" and brought with them when they entered the country, sustained them during their term of office there, and comforted them when they departed into retirement. In contrast the scientists with whom he had worked, though I suppose they may personally have had just as many prejudices, were explorers of the world around them, formulating questions before starting work, objectively observing the customs, societies, plants, animals, fossils, and rocks before reaching a conclusion, and drawing inferences that were presented in such a way as to be susceptible of confirmation or disproof. Between the quest for knowledge and the ambition to rule is a gulf that Katende observed with clarity.

He illustrated this outlook with the story from some years back of a young district officer sent out from Britain to administer Karamoja, a rather arid region in north-east Uganda. The soil is generally dry, hard, and rocky, so the Karimojong were accustomed to leave the bodies of the dead out for the vultures to consume. Regarding this as an insanitary and disgusting practice, the district officer issued an order that the dead must be disposed of more suitably, namely by burial. Attempts to enforce this novel procedure against the traditions of the Karimojong caused at first

* According to Curzon the greatest danger threatening British rule in India was "the racial pride and the undisciplined passions of the inferior class of Englishmen in this country."[36]

stubborn opposition and then dangerous unrest, so that in the end the district officer had to be transferred elsewhere. One up for the Karimojong.

But, as it happened, the following year I could show Katende that this kind of insensitivity to tradition and misunderstanding of what was best in a particular environment was not exclusively a British failing. The first time I visited Karamoja the men walked everywhere naked except for a small leather cloth over one shoulder. On the second occasion they were wearing shorts or trousers, a resented insult to their tradition and not particularly appropriate in that hot, dry climate.

"What's happened?" I asked Katende.

"It's a government decree. Obote got the idea that trousers are more civilised. But," he added, "they take them off when they get away from Moroto" (the capital of the district).

"It seems like the British district officer all over again?"

Katende fell to cutting up a pineapple we had bought at the roadside.

"We learnt some foolish things," he replied.

Despite having nine children of their own, his wife and he regarded it as no burden to take on a tenth, the son of one of his wife's sisters who had fallen ill. One evening they invited me out to have a meal at their home outside Kampala. Katende had borrowed a car in which he picked me up on the campus and then drove for a few miles over a rough road through the banana plantations, the usual cloud of red dust trailing behind us as we bumped along over pulverised ridges of laterite. Standing in a clearing among the trees, his house was more substantial than some and had the advantage too of a concrete floor, so that it was free of the chiggers that on an earth floor are apt to burrow into one's feet. When we had dismounted and been greeted by his wife, Katende opened the boot of the car and released from it a friend of his who had lain curled up there during the journey unknown to me until that moment. He shook himself politely and joined us in the living room, while Mrs Katende returned to the adjacent kitchen to continue cooking the meal.

We sat down at two small tables, Katende and I at one, his friend in response to a gesture from Katende at the other, and by way of aperitif Katende produced a bottle of waragi, a local drink like gin but distilled from bananas. Half-pint tumblers were set out, and knowing the strength of this liquor from previous experience I asked for an inch or so in the glass. The friend on pushing his glass forward raised a hand to indicate that he would like to have rather more, so Katende filled it half full. But noticing the impassivity of his friend's features tighten into anxiety at such a meagre helping he generously extended the horizons by filling the glass to the top. With a slow but grateful smile his friend picked up the tumbler and drank its contents to the bottom as though they had been water.

When the meal was ready two of the older children unrolled a mat on the floor and they all sat down on either side of it. After serving the adults Mrs Katende filled in turn each of a pile of bowls and passed them down the expectant ranks. We all tucked in to stewed meat on matoké (vegetable banana), sweet potato, and some kind of cabbage.

On another occasion when we were out botanising Katende and I drove over to a much smaller house of his about 100 miles from Kampala. His wife offered us milk which had been heated over a wood fire and tasted strongly, though pleasantly, of wood smoke. She poured it from a handsome teapot into china cups, and we refreshed ourselves for half an hour before driving on. Fortunately Katende was a skilled driver, because later that day I felt so drowsy over the wheel of our Landrover in the afternoon sun that I had to ask him to take over.

So this was Katende who was driving down with Kåre Lye and me to Kisoro. After driving for about 150 miles and leaving the small town of Kabale we mounted by a skein of hairpin bends to a pass at 8500 feet (2600 m) where the road passed through bamboo forest at the Kanaba Gap. The view alone was enough to arrest us at the summit, for ahead lay the majestic range of volcanoes, some extinct, some active, stretching from Muhavura in the east through Mgahinga, Sabinio, Nyiragongo, and Karisimbi westwards into the clouds. Far below us was the fertile plain of Kigezi lying in the western arm of the Rift Valley with its lakes and polka dot pattern of extinct volcanoes. Their neatly circular cones were cultivated in terraces all the way up the outside of each cone, over the top, and down into the crater within, as though the surface of the moon had been painted green and terraced. Near the summit of the pass the banks of the road and the stems of the bamboos in the forest supported a variety of unusual lichen species, one of them being restricted to the rough joints of the bamboos.

Descending another long winding road where we dodged the boulders and the ruts scoured by heavy rain in its surface, we reached the village of Kisoro below, with its renowned Travellers' Rest Hotel, small but clean and hospitable. There the news of our arrival spread rapidly into the town, so that within the hour we had been able to engage guides and porters to meet us at 0630 the next morning for an ascent of Muhavura. Collecting lichens from trees in the main street I watched the Tutsi women, many nearly 6 feet tall, swagger by with swaying hips and swinging skirts, a large basket balanced on the head, a baby in a sling on the back, the left arm supporting an older child, the right hand clasping the bowl of a long-stemmed pipe, at which they puffed while they strode along without a glance in my direction. Unconcerned and disdainful, assured, stately, and beautiful, they were queens of the human race, rulers of their secluded homes among the volcanoes of the Rift Valley.

> Quand tu va balayant l'air de ta jupe large,
> Tu fais l'effet d'un beau vaisseau qui prend le large,
> Chargé de toile, et va roulant
> Suivant un rythme doux, et paresseux, et lent.
> — BAUDELAIRE. *Le Beau Navire*

Among the men walking by were some carrying a long pole over the shoulder which swung up and down to their pace. At the end of the pole was a parcel of smouldering moss and twigs in which the draught created by the swinging motion stirred some embers to be used when they wanted to light up a fire for cooking or warmth at night. The poles were thus a kind of "pilot light" always burning and ready for use when a fire had to be kindled in the perennially damp atmosphere of those regions.

To my surprise the porters and guides we had engaged turned up on time the next morning so that we could get away at 0630, driving to the foot of Muhavura, which rose above us another 7000 feet (2100 m). Its cloud-capped cone is so undeviatingly steep that according to legend a tent cannot be pitched anywhere on it below the summit. It seemed to consist mostly of lava pebbles, so that every step upwards was followed by sliding half the distance back again, and the shrubs growing densely through them sometimes presented a further barrier to our progress. On this mountain, as on the others round the equator in East Africa, the vegetation is distinctively zoned, so that a band of forest is followed by bands of helichrysum, alchemilla, and giant heathers, senecios, and lobelias. The lobelias grow like pillars up to about 20 feet (6 m) high, bearing hundreds of flowers up the sides. Fertilisation is by small birds which perch on the lips of the bracts and plunge their beaks into the flower within for its nectar, then carrying away the pollen to their next port of call.

At about 12 000 feet (3600 m) I took the opportunity of a rest to ask my porter, called Peter, if he knew the country spread below us in a map-like panorama. With a sweep of the arm he gestured to the east, "Rwanda, good," and to the west, "Congo, not good." Having epitomised these countries in an English of greater clarity than I could have attempted in his own language he looked pensive for a moment, then rose to his feet, came over and put my rucksack down beside me, and with an intonation at once peremptory but respectful uttered the one word, "Foodie." It was time for lunch, so we all fell on the sandwiches and hard-boiled eggs the hotel had provided.*

We continued our upward slog over the lava pebbles now everywhere knee-deep in alchemilla shrubs. Yet obstructive though they were on our climb and sometimes concealing

* Whymper climbed the Matterhorn with a leg of mutton dangling from his belt.

dangerous clefts between the rocks into which a leg would slip and become stuck fast, they were also firmly enough rooted for us to pull our way up with their help.

But after pushing on to 13 000 feet (4000 m) I felt that my 52 years were a handicap to further effort if I was to spend time collecting lichens there and get down again that day. So Peter stayed with me and I waved the others on to the summit 1000 feet (300 m) above us, arranging to meet them on the way down. In this way I conserved enough energy to continue collecting lichens while making a slow descent before being joined by my companions a couple of hours later.

Coming down was not so tiring as going up owing to the reduction in altitude and so increase in oxygen, but slipping on the branches of the shrubs and sliding on the lava pebbles sometimes seemed to demand the skill of a skier rather than the preoccupied attention of a botanist looking for plants, though to fall on the springy vegetation was no hardship and in fact sometimes afforded an excuse for a rest. As we reached the foothills again I felt so tired by the effort of scrambling up and sliding down that I was reminded of some of the marches in my army days a quarter of a century before, when we would push outselves to the limits of endurance. I knew again what it was to "march automatically", a state that soldiers sometimes get into when discipline alone keeps them marching in an orderly fashion and prevents them from falling out on a bank at the wayside or even retaining much awareness of the road they are traversing. Not that I was quite so lost in automatism: I recollected rather than experienced the state, imagined that I must be near it rather than supposing I was actually slipping into it.

And then suddenly, as though it were a cry of recognition beckoning across the stillness, I heard by the track we were stumbling along the notes of a flute cleaving the air. And we came upon a young man sitting on a boulder with an end-blown flute like a large recorder to his lips, oblivious of our passing, filling the cool of the evening with his music. We paused for a few minutes to greet him and enjoy the relaxation of listening to the tune, but we could not wait for long because dusk would overtake us and darkness fall over the rough tracks that we had to follow back to our hotel. So on we went.

But for botanists the day does not end with a drink at the bar and a warm meal. By the light of butane lamps we sorted the specimens we had collected, put them in temporary packets made from old newspapers impregnated with mercuric chloride as a preservative against beetles and moulds, and labelled them with locality numbers, entering these in notebooks and adding detailed references from the maps. Only then did we allow ourselves the luxury of a sleep untroubled at that altitude by mosquitoes but periodically interrupted by the clattering of flying bush crickets or the fluttering on our faces of moths in search of a salty drink at our eyes or mouths.

Dust everywhere on the roads, dust in clouds and eddies and billows, creeping under our finger nails, coating our ears and eyelids, finally broke through the defences of the car's filters and silted up the carburettor. After a week's travelling in Kigezi among the lakes and forests below Muhavura the engine coughed and spluttered up the side of the Rift Valley to the Kanaba Gap on the way back home, but we realised we must get it cleaned if we were to travel much further, so coasting down through the hairpin bends on the other side the car managed to cough its way into Kabale.

There to our delight a garage stood among the trees by the dusty road. Better still, its owner understood engines, and in no time had got out his spanners, wrenched this way and that, and produced handfuls of dirt from the carburettor. He stripped it down, cleaned it out, reassembled it, cleaned up the aluminium cylinder head, and got the engine going again while we went off to buy some bananas. As we returned he switched off the engine and with his bare hands put a final polish on the cylinder head, running his palms over the curves to restore it to its pristine gloss, stroking the recesses with his fingers as though he were in an art gallery enjoying the feel of a piece of sculpture. Skilled mechanic though he was, the intricate lines and surfaces of the machine appealed to him as much as its working order. His gaze lingered on it as his fingers absorbed the virtue of its beauty, till we had to interrupt his aesthetic enjoyment of it and tell him we must be going on our way. With a last touch he withdrew his hands, closed the bonnet, made a small charge for his services, and waved goodbye as we drove off. "Beauty is truth, truth beauty" is what he knew. While he solved the problem the machine had posed, he enjoyed the harmony of its metallic spirit. An engineer yet an artist, skilled in his craft and living for the satisfaction he obtained from it, he would have appealed to Keats.

Back at Makerere I was packing up my specimens before returning to England the next day. Most were of species I had not seen before, but I thought the collection, labelled and annotated, might be of value to the British Museum. Kåre came up to me and said, "Why don't you make a study of Uganda lichens? Nobody else has done much on them." Yes, why shouldn't I? – But I should have to return for some more serious collecting.

"I shall be here next year," he said, "I've got a spare room in my apartment if you'd like to stay there."

So on the impulse I began to lay plans for a work that in the end occupied years of my life. For like many apparently impulsive decisions this one bypassed rational thought and offered fulfilment of a deeply felt need.

25 Muddy road to heaven

June 1970 found me back at Makerere for three weeks staying with Kåre Lye. But in a day or so he and Katende and I were off to western Uganda and the Ruwenzori range, crossing the equator a little way south of Kampala to explore the beautiful forests there. Saw mills had been established in some places because, to the sorrow of the naturalist and the destruction of their inhabitants, these enormously varied forests are an economic asset and provide valuable timber for export. Hunting for lichens as I was, I generally sought out the areas being worked in this way so that I could examine the upper branches of the felled trees, for only near the tree tops did enough sunlight penetrate to allow these plants to flourish. The edges of the forests and their glades provided the same open environment that lichens need; and, though sometimes overgrown with shrubs, including the introduced *Lantana camara*, favourite haunt of the tse-tse fly, they were often as colourful as gardens with their flowering plants, tree ferns, and butterflies. Walking along a humid track one day I found the air so thick with butterflies that I had consciously to keep my mouth shut lest I inhale one from the myriads that thronged in the sunlight. They settled all over me as I walked, fell at my feet, and fluttered into my eyes.

Staying at Mweya Lodge in western Uganda near the frontier with Zaire we drove out in our Landrover one morning and came upon the extraordinary spectacle of three leopards playing about in a grassy clearing. Obviously we remained in the car, but they were not unduly nervous of our presence, and one of them sat down by a shrub near by. Finally they all bounded away, and as the one by the shrub got up a hare he had been sitting on leaped off in the opposite direction, lucky to have been unnoticed. Though cheetahs are commonly seen by day, leopards are much shyer creatures, so I was glad to have obtained photographic evidence of the encounter for my unbelieving friends.

That evening Katende brought in some mushrooms for our supper, and on my questioning him about how certain he was that we should not all die in delirium if we ate them he explained their distinctive origin. Some species of termites have larders in the depths of their nests where they cultivate the hyphae of a certain fungus on a compost bed they prepare. This fungus species has now evolved such a specialised existence that it grows nowhere else but in the termite larders. Every so often it sends hyphae through the wall of the termite nest – a wall as hard as brick – to form a crop of fruiting bodies on the exterior. These mushrooms are thus identifiable partly from their form and colour but mainly from their growing on the wall of a termite nest, and experience has shown that they are both pleasant to taste and harmless – as we found at supper.

During the day we had been along to see the lions that live up in the trees in that part of Uganda. Normally these animals prefer a terrestrial existence, and when they need shelter they settle in shade on the ground. But here the elephants had eaten so much of the shrub vegetation that the lions had learnt to take their rest among the branches of large trees that had withstood elephant attack. When our car stalled under one of these trees with a lion lying on a branch immediately above us we had an anxious 10 minutes trying to get the engine going again without stepping out on to the ground, and it did at last with reluctance manage to produce a spark.

That afternoon we were fortunate to see a spitting cobra in action. Kåre was driving us slowly along a track when the snake reared up vertically beside us. Kåre quickly stopped and reversed so that we could obtain a better view of it, and as we drew alongside the snake it caught sight of our near headlamp and projected a stream of venom at the glass. An instinct impels it to shoot the venom at a glittering object, usually an animal's eye, and enough enters the blood circulation at least to paralyse it and probably to kill it.* Snakes are numerous in East Africa but rarely visible because they are resentful enough of disturbance to glide timidly from human intruders.

Even so, collecting plants where potentially dangerous animals are so numerous as they were then in East Africa demands reasonable caution. I used to make a noise by beating a tin or perhaps shouting for a minute or two when starting work at some locality, especially if there were outcrops of rocks where leopards or lions might lurk. When botanising near a river I was careful never to stand between the water and any hippopotamus that might be grazing near by, because if it became frightened it would probably rush to the river and attack me to clear the way. With one bite the hippo is said to be capable of severing a man's waist.

Though I have been twice warned not to botanise in certain areas without an armed guard, owing to the numerous lions there – once in central Kenya, the other time in Ghana – and in consequence kept away, men armed with rifles once accompanied Kåre and Katende and myself in north-east Uganda: we were advised to take this precaution against the possibility of an incursion from Kenya of marauding Turkana tribesmen.

Among the most dangerous animals because of their speed, weight, and aggressiveness are buffaloes. On two occasions in Uganda solitary buffaloes made a lunge towards my Landrover when I had to drive past them on rough tracks. In Kenya, where they are common in the montane forest, they seemed less aggressive, at least in that environment, but if I saw one standing in the track ahead I never drove towards it in the hope of shifting it. Once when I was driving with Katende along a track in southern Uganda we turned a corner and came up behind a herd of buffaloes blocking the way.

"What do we do now?" I asked him.

"It's all right to keep going, just drive on as though you were going through a herd of cows."

* It has been shown in man that if the eye is immediately washed out with water no permanent harm should follow.

We pushed ahead gently and after a time came out the other side.

"A herd like that is all right," he said, "because it is all females with a dominant male. It is the solitary buffaloes that are dangerous – they are males excluded from the herd."

Invaluable for his knowledge of the fauna and flora of Uganda and the history and customs of its peoples, Katende spoke English and Swahili well in addition to his native Luganda and could make himself understood in the other 17 languages of the country, which incidentally fall into separate world groups – Bantu in the southern half and Nilotic in the northern.

A different hazard came our way on another occasion when we found a herd of Ankole cattle filling the track ahead. They derive their name from a district in southern Uganda and are distinguished by their long horns – slender cones up to a metre long sticking out sideways. Driving through this herd I was on tenterhooks lest one of the beasts by no more than a sharp turn of its head might put a horn straight through the windscreen, so I was stopping and starting, pausing and rushing, and twisting this way and that till we finally got through them with the glass intact.

During this trip we also collected in the montane forest of Ruwenzori at its southern end, where steep rocky outcrops and cliffs covered with mixed semi-evergreen and bamboo forest made the terrain difficult to work over. And it was among these intricate ridges and valleys that I experienced the only real anxiety I felt when botanising in East Africa. Kåre and I were collecting specimens until the time came when in the late afternoon we felt we should return.

"Where's Katende?"

I blew the whistle I always carry when botanising in the field. We both shouted. No reply. More shouts, and then straining the ear to catch any response. Perhaps he had already gone down towards the car. We started off in that direction, finally reached it, only to find it empty. Could he have fallen in that maze of rocks and forest, be trapped in a crevice, lying unconscious at the foot of a cliff? Back we went again calling and whistling. Still no reply. Yet again we returned to the car – but it was empty. What to do next? I turned round to look up the track again – and there was Katende coming down it.

"You naughty man," I shouted at him, "where have you been?" He looked sheepish.

"I heard you calling," was all he would say. He must have noticed anyway that my feelings of relief had diluted the severity of my rebuke for his having wandered off without telling us where. But we all felt subdued by our imaginings on the way back to the lodge.

After a week in the west we drove home via Fort Portal, where on collecting lichens from some avenue trees I noticed a wild orchid growing in the branches of one of them as though it were in the forest instead of in the main street of a populous town. Pausing again to collect from some woodland just beyond the town, we were overtaken by a young man in a spotless white shirt (how did they do it, those Ugandans, living by dusty roads and served by primitive sources of water – how did they keep so spick and span?), a young clerk as I think he was, who wanted a lift. He came up to me and asked in perfect English what I was doing. I explained my interest in the lichens growing on the surrounding trees. Carefully thinking out his reply, he finally said:

"I thank you, sir, for coming to my country to do your researches."

The trust that these words implied, that what I was doing would be of value to a land so much poorer than my own, worried me then and troubles me still with a sense of obligation that I fear is beyond my power to fulfil.

Next year the same sense of obligation was imposed on me but from the opposite point of view – by rejection rather than gratitude. I was dining one evening at Makerere when a member of the teaching staff, a young lecturer, asked me what brought me to the country. When I explained my interest in Uganda's lichens, his only reply was, "I don't see what good that does the country."

I explained that they were an important feature of its vegetation. Studying them would provide a baseline from which to measure changes in the coming years – not just in lichens but in the whole complex of vegetation there. He was unconvinced. What was important to him was man and his immediate needs for food, fuel, foreign currency. In his opinion he did not differ from 95 % of the earth's inhabitants.

Is research that simply discovers something about our world a luxury for well-off people who can afford their next meal? Or should it be devoted entirely to increasing our food crops, making better clothes, beating our competitors in the world's markets, inventing more effective weapons to kill them? No doubt a balance has to be struck, and it may well be struck differently in Great Britain and Uganda, yet between the opposite poles of research are many connecting links; they are not divided by a barrier and certainly not glaring at each other in opposition. The discoveries of one often relate to the other.

But there is more to it than that. I forebore to tell my Makerere critic that I was there largely at my own expense because that would have evaded what I believe to be the point, namely that research not directed to man's immediate needs should nevertheless be of scientific or aesthetic value and so in some way be of benefit to man.* To exclude developing countries from research that is not strictly "operational" (to use a favourite wartime epithet) is to patronise them, as though Lady Bountiful were handing out apples to some ragged urchins.

Even so, as a practical man I have some sympathy with that lecturer's doubts. The question is a natural one to ask: What good is *your* research doing *my* country? A visiting research worker needs to be clear in his own mind how he would answer it, not so much that he may be able to give a confident reply if it does in fact reach the surface: rather that he may conduct and report his research in the light of it. And reporting on his studies is particularly important. Twice I was told of scientists, one European and one American, who had visited East Africa, engaged the time and help of academic and other people to travel extensively, gathered

---

* I did many times have financial help from the Royal Society and the Linnean Society, for which I am deeply grateful, but paid much the greater part of the cost out of my own pocket.

large collections of specimens (in one case a unique collection) – and published nothing. The sense of frustration and betrayal that such conduct causes is poor repayment for the trouble taken to help the visitors or the welcome they are almost invariably accorded.*

"Come on, let's have a look at Elgon." Kåre Lye and Katende and I had just come back from collecting in Karamoja, and I had another week left of my three weeks' visit in June 1970. So after ensuring that our specimens were dried, packeted, labelled, and in my case sent back to England by airmail, we gathered up sleeping bags, a tent, cooking utensils, food and water, spare petrol, and torches and set off in the Fiat eastwards towards the Kenyan border. Mt Elgon, which goes up to 14178 feet (4321 m), is a vast rounded cone, what in Scotland might be called a pap, lying on the frontier between the two countries.

As we drove through the foothills with the aid of a fairly adequate map the mountain itself remained as usual hidden under cloud. The Uganda side has a more or less perennial rainfall owing to the proximity of Lake Victoria, while the Kenya side is drier from being in the rain shadow. The road

***

* To let down developing countries like this is harmful to science as well as to the countries themselves, for it adds fuel to the flames of an incomprehending and damaging nationalism. According to Dr J E Lovelock, FRS, "None of the great journeys of exploration of the last century, such as the voyages of the *Beagle* or the *Challenger*, could now be accomplished without let or hindrance. Rightly or wrongly, research ships are often regarded by developing nations as agents of neo-colonial exploitation seeking mineral wealth on their continental shelves. In 1976 the Argentinians raised this type of resentment to a new level by firing on the *Shackleton* as she sailed near the Falkland Islands in the course of her scientific investigations. Similarly, it is now difficult for an independent observer to take equipment for atmospheric analysis into many tropical countries. Scientific investigation appears to have become nationalized; it must be done by a citizen of the country or not at all. Whether or not there is a real or historical justification for such fears of exploitation, they are undoubtedly widespread in that half of the world which lies in the tropics, and in consequence scientific investigation on a global scale is becoming increasingly difficult."[37]

became steeper and rougher as we went up into the drifting cloud which billowed and swirled about us, sometimes immersed us and obscured the way. Finally the road, rutted though it was, worsened into a complex of ditches and boulders, and with a crash we felt our undercarriage become impaled on one of these obstructions. Dismounting to survey the damage, we were quickly joined by an eager crowd of people who lifted the car off the rock on to all four wheels and pushed it into a clearing beside what, as now became evident, was a village street. We had reached Bumagabula.

After pitching our tent near the car we took a stroll up the street, where a procession of young boys playing drums insisted on drawing us into marching with them up and down the village to the accompaniment of shouts and gesticulations in time with the drums. Further up the street I fell out of the procession on noticing what proved to be a rare lichen growing over some boulders, and after collecting some of it I surveyed a remarkable scene.

Among the ruts and boulders were three circles, each of about 12 men and women, sitting on stools in a motionless torpor with tubes about 8 feet ($2\frac{1}{2}$ m) long in their mouths or clutched listlessly against their chests. The far end of each tube was dipped in a large bowl of the local beer, or pombé, standing on the ground in the middle of each circle. Every so often the owner of a tube would draw up another mouthful of beer while continuing to stare ahead with an expressionless gaze that doubtless reflected the vacancy within like the curtainless windows of an empty house. I passed from one group to the second and thence to the third, fascinated by the obliteration of all being in these men and women sitting there like old tree boles in their immobility, content in their placid hebetude, as a community composed, as individuals annihilated. While I lingered by the third circle one of its members grinned slowly up at me and thrust his tube into my hand, inviting me to take my fill from it by making a long sucking noise and pointing at the bowl. Ever eager to try something new, I had the resolution nevertheless to decline his offer.

The night was both beautiful and restless. Never have I seen so many fireflies darting in their myriads through the tropical air, their light bursting out in a flash and then dying away in a fading gleam. In the background the drums filled the darkness with their interlinked rhythms, calling and responding to each other, for we had arrived when preparations were being made for the circumcision of some boys who had reached the prescribed age, and not till dawn broke did the drums at last fall silent. As the sun rose we brewed up for breakfast and Katende after making inquiries showed us where a small lavatory stood at the edge of the village. It was a tiny thatched hut with an oval hole in the floor over a deep pit, the floor, walls, roof, and approach path all scrupulously clean. The visitor had to stoop to enter through a little wooden door.

An energetic young man claimed to be the headman of the village, and Kåre entered into negotiations with him for the guarding of the car and tent while we went up the mountain and for the provision of a guide and porters. Being accustomed to the occasional party trekking up Mt Elgon, the headman was not disposed to allow us to travel on the cheap. His rates started at the exorbitant, slid down gradually to the unreasonable, and finally reached a level, after more than an hour's bargaining, of the reluctantly acceptable. Kåre went through the whole procedure skilfully: I speak as a connoisseur of a charade that, unlike most of my countrymen, I always enjoyed. For goods in shops or fruit at the wayside, for the hire of a car or the purchase of a rug, I always entered with spirit into the great game of getting somewhere near the real price by acting, first, agreeable attention to the vendor's welcome, then astonished horror at his price, impatience at his presumption, putting on a puzzled frown as his expectation became less outrageous, but, as his price suddenly stuck, once again expressing annoyance, flouncing out of the shop, though, in response to his pursuit of me to the road outside, yet again becoming interested, then, on having another look at the goods, proposing another reduction in price till, yes, that's about it, but another 10% off – and he agrees, all smiles and gratitude at having been able to sell me something for about 50% more than his countrymen would have paid for it. So we part at the door as friends will say goodbye after watching a play at the theatre, pleasurably reliving the performance in the memory, both vendor and purchaser relaxed by the emotional relief of being convinced that he got a good bargain.

Finally, we took to the track through cultivated fields that led up to the steeper slopes of the mountain. When the forest itself came into view an hour later and we had reached the end of the patches of corn and peas, our porters suddenly dropped their loads and without a word disappeared from sight over a low hill. Our guide quickly followed them. On pursuing them we found them already lying on the ground by a hut from which beer was dispensed. Rather as a petrol station will advertise "last petrol before the motorway", so here was the last beer before the real ascent began. Few delays can be more exasperating to a botanist eager to reach good collecting ground than to be left stranded by weedy patches of vegetables while his porters and guide drink away the morning hours with successive pints of pombé. So it was with annoyed but relieved expressions that we welcomed back the guide some time later and he led us away from this den of iniquity up into the forest. But what about the porters? we asked. They will follow, he said. We trudged away with some trepidation.

Going up Mt Elgon, at least on the wet Uganda side, is a long slog over muddy tracks that runnels of water have worn into a V formation, so that every step from about 8000 feet (2400 m) upwards slides down into the furrow of the V. Should one's boot be allowed to turn this way or that as it slips down on the mud? I tried to vary it so as to spare my ankles from twisting one way all the time, but gaining height through the forest was nevertheless a wearisome dragging of one foot after the other in the squelching mud and, for several hours, pouring rain. But the porters in the end made light work of all this, and having filled themselves to their contentment with beer they put on a spurt and reached the Sasa Hut at just over 10000 feet (3090 m) as soon as we did. They put their loads down with an unconcerned air and disappeared again.

The best botanical ground proved to be slightly below

rather than above this area, and we made some good collections among the tree heathers and in open forest glades. Even the bamboos in this wet climate bore many species of lichens. The high ground in the tropics provides some of the most enchanting places on earth in which to study the vegetation, a botanical heaven where the air physically and the flora mentally are alike exhilarating. But in contrast to the tropical warmth below how cold those nights are on the mountains! I certainly found sleep came fitfully. Temperatures drop to freezing and showers of powdery or sleety snow often fall.

Bumagabula offered its familiar mixture of bustle and torpor when we returned. Our car and tent had been safely guarded, and the headman, having put our bargaining altercation in the past, was now all smiles awaiting the fee we were glad to pay for his services. Taking a last look up the village's boulder-strewn street before our departure I saw again three circles of people, like three dark chrysanthemum flowers in the street, sitting round bowls of pombé, their faces glistening in the sun that had now broken through the clouds, their bodies motionless as the rocks strewn around them, sucking on their tubes from the stagnant pools of beer, dreaming with contented indolence of...life?

26 Closing the lids

For the last few years of her life my mother lived with my brother Godfrey and his family, but in the autumn of 1970 her increasingly poor health following a fractured neck of femur the previous year led her finally to enter a residential nursing home. It was not far from where we lived, so we used to go over and visit her often. Just after Christmas Josephine and I spent half an hour with her in the evening talking about her numerous Christmas cards, for every year the numbers she received, and from whom, were topics for serious consideration. She planned to go through them in detail the next day, sort out those from friends she thought deserved a letter in reply, and arrange for the rest to be given to a charity. I moved over to kiss her goodbye, but she delayed me with a gesture and added,

"Don't kiss me, I've got a germ of some sort."

In the night at about 2 am the nursing home telephoned me to say that she had passed into a coma and would not recover. I asked whether I should come over – "No, there is no point in doing so."

When I entered her room at half past 7 in the morning, she lay just as she had died, with her left arm across her chest and her right hanging out of the bed. Her blue eyes stared at the ceiling. She always slept with her eyes open, having scared her school mates long ago by this unusual condition, as she would often relate, and she had probably passed into a coma and died with them open too. In a way she was proud of having blue eyes. They gave her a feeling of kinship with sailors watching the sea and airmen sweeping the heavens. Both her brother, who had been in the navy, and her lover, who had retired from it when she knew him, had clear blue eyes, as did her sons and her husband. "You'll find most naval officers have blue eyes," she once said to me, and she would always comment favourably on the eyes of a friend if they were blue. To her the colour signified a command of practical realities, resolution, staunchness, and honest endeavour.

On one of those dot diagrams that illustrate the frequency distribution of some characteristic, with a crowd of dots near the middle gradually thinning out towards the periphery, there is usually one far out lying in eccentric isolation. There I think to myself went my mother. Medically speaking she was about as far as could be from any statistical norm, for when she faded away so peacefully at the age of 81 she completed a life that in almost every way contradicted the advice doctors commonly give their patients.

It was in her early 20s that she picked up the habit of cigarette smoking. She added cigars in her 30s, and from middle age on smoked a pipe. For over 40 years she never contemplated a night's sleep without a couple of barbiturate tablets, and most of her days she made tolerable (for she was subject to many aches of head and body) by a steady intake of aspirin-and-codeine tablets. Partly because of the codeine she took an aperient every day, ringing the changes of senna, liquid paraffin, and cascara. All this was what might be called her basic medication. On top of it she was treated for all sorts of illnesses. They included pneumonia – not single but double pneumonia, as she liked to stress – both typhoid and paratyphoid fevers (a conjunction in which she took pride, surviving on each occasion by restricting her diet to champagne), three major abdominal operations, anaemia (many tablets and injections), and rheumatism (many more injections). Tonics, carminatives, and antidepressants were also among the potions she liberally enjoyed. Her appetite was always excellent, and despite plentiful eggs, milk, cream, and butter her figure remained trim, her arteries patent, and her blood pressure low. Once she learnt to drive at the age of 28 she went everywhere by car, even from one shop to another along Union Street and Fleet Street and the Strand in Torquay, as roadside parking was no problem in those days.

If physically she seemed to defy the fates, so she did

mentally. Wholly lacking any of that capacity for equanimity that philosophers prescribe as beneficial, she had a combative temperament – some would say cantankerous – that led her to speak frankly in circumstances when tact would have been more appropriate, so that fallen friends sometimes seemed to lie as thick as the leaves in Vallombrosa. Nor, as a crowning contradiction, did she claim to have enjoyed her life. Some of it she regretted, some detested, and in her later years she often declared her existence to be unendurable.

"I'm sick of hanging around," she would say, and then add, "it's about time I kicked the bucket."

But whatever she thought of other people she had never been anything less than a devoted mother to my brother and me. And now the blue eyes that had so often looked at me with affection lay as blank as the ceiling they stared at. I closed the lids. The end?

> Even such is tyme which takes in trust
> Our yowth, our Joyes, and all we have,
> And payes us butt with age and dust:
> Who in the darke and silent grave
> When we have wandred all our wayes
> Shutts up the storey of our dayes.
> And from which earth and grave and dust
> The Lord shall rayse me up I trust. – SIR WALTER RALEIGH
> (written on the night before his execution)

27 An ancient South

November 1971 found me heading for Uganda again, this time in an American plane from Accra, in Ghana. As we flew eastwards along the equator towards Entebbe airport a storm gathered in the knotted clouds around us, and lurid colours struck across them in patches of purple, pink, and orange. Lightning flitted about the rocking plane in which we were now all securely strapped, sudden shadows enveloped us as clouds came between us and the sinking sun, and passengers looked at their watches to see how much longer the journey was due to last.

At the same time a film was being shown. It was a drama whose human convolutions I did not clearly understand because as usual I was not wearing the headphones offered. Its most striking feature, to me at any rate, was a scene of monkeys being experimented upon in what I think must have been an academic institution. Strapped into metal chairs, they were subjected to some kind of experiment – psychological or sociological – as part of the work carried out by the human characters with their white coats, brisk movements, and professional detachment. And I wondered what the audience in the plane, who were nearly all Africans, thought about those monkeys, creatures that were a part of their daily lives. Strapped in my seat like the monkeys, watching the livid skies outside and the mechanically unfolding drama within, I felt ashamed to be part of a culture that could for the sake of amusement present scenes of animal experiments. In addition to their intention of giving entertainment they simply degraded that great western creation, science.

My trip to Uganda this time was for five weeks and formed

part of a three-month holiday which my employers, the BMA, had very kindly granted me in recognition of my having served them for 25 years on the staff of the *BMJ*.* I had arranged to rent a flat in one of the student's hostels on the Makerere campus. Kåre Lye was no longer there, having returned to Norway. But Katende was once again eager for the opportunity for more botanical exploration in the extraordinarily varied country that Uganda presents, ranging in an area about the size of England and Wales from low lakes to high mountains, dense forests to sub-deserts.

Deciding to visit Karamoja again and travel up to the north where it joins the Sudan, we found that it was more tightly controlled than formerly. A permit was needed to enter southern Karamoja to reach the capital town, Moroto, and once there we should have to obtain a second permit to enter northern Karamoja. But if there is one quality that Africa teaches the agitated, mobile European it is patience: I had learnt this lesson. Consequently to spend a whole morning in Kampala obtaining the first permit did not disconcert me. I knew it was inevitable. And the next day we took to the road in a Landrover I had hired from the university. Reaching Moroto in the evening we presented ourselves at the government rest house looking forward to washing off the dust and having a good meal.

"Sorry. No room."

"But when I telephoned yesterday you said you could put us up."

"We have had a message since then."

"What message?"

"A government minister is coming."

"But he won't need every room."

"Nobody else may stay."

We had no choice but to look for a meal and accommodation in a private house, though we were not the only people in Karamoja to feel some resentment at the comings and goings of government ministers. For several years a large painted notice at the entrance to a permanent army camp

* And I am grateful too to the then editor, Martin Ware, and my colleagues who took over my work while I was away.

down the road had displayed the message (in English): "No politician may enter this camp without the permission of the commanding officer."

After one or two refusals Katende and I were fortunate to be given a hospitable welcome by a Protestant missionary priest and teacher who was an Indian. A charming host, he gave us supper and beds, and cooked us an old-fashioned breakfast of fried egg on fried bread which he had learnt about on a visit to England he had once made.

At his house I met an Indian doctor practising in the district, and in discussing his work I asked him what was the most frequent operation he performed. "The repair of spear wounds," was his reply. And he told me that the second commonest after that was closing the hole that is made in the lower lip of Karimojong boys in infancy to accommodate a metal plug. The disadvantage of the hole is that saliva leaks through it, especially when the plug is removed, as it may be at night. In recent years the young men in particular, less influenced by tradition than their elders, had come to regard this decoration as imposing an unnecessary handicap.

The same doctor, though educated in India, had received his medical education there in the English language. From India he had come straight to Karamoja, probably at the instigation of a missionary society, but so excellent was his English that I warmly complimented him on it. He smiled in acknowledgment and said,

"But you are the first Englishman I have ever heard speaking the language."

"How do you think it sounds as I speak it?"

"You speak clearly, but your intonation is slightly different from what I thought."

Certainly I do try to speak clearly, especially when talking to people whose native language is not English – and even more especially after hearing the criticisms of a doctor at Makerere. He observed how indistinctly some of the visiting British lecturers addressed their audiences there, mumbling incoherently but sagely, he presumed, and leaving behind a sense of inadequacy in the people who had failed to grasp their message.

Calling at the government rest house the next morning to satisfy my curiosity about the minister's travel arrangements, I was not surprised to learn that neither the minister nor his entourage had arrived. The place had been empty all night.

Being a visitor I told Katende I would abide by the instruction I had received to obtain a permit for us to enter northern Karamoja. He demurred, looked impatiently at his watch, and said we would be wasting our time, but I felt bound to insist that we follow the decreed practice. So at 0830 am we presented ourselves at the district commissioner's office and, finding that official within, asked if he would kindly give us a permit. He told us to wait in the anteroom and himself withdrew to his office beyond. After waiting for 20 minutes we became hopeful of progress when a clerk came in from outside and sat at a desk in our room. We explained our presence to him and suggested he should ask the district commissioner if we might now have our permit. A few minutes later the clerk rejoined us and said that the district commissioner was busy at the moment but would see us in due course. Nobody else came or went, so we were delighted when after another 10 minutes or so the door opened and the district commissioner himself ushered us into his office. He may have been spending some time thinking how to investigate our motives for wishing to enter northern Karamoja, for he now examined them in impeccable English.

"Plant collecting? What sort of plants?"

"We are looking for plants called lichens."

"What are lichens?"

"They are like a fungus and they grow on rocks and trees."

"Do you mean the rocks and trees out there?"

"Well, yes, but more in the countryside."

"I do not think I have seen them."

"You would see them if you looked very carefully."

"How do they grow?"

"They obtain their food from the air."

278

"What is your method of travel?"

"We have a Landrover."

And so on. But at length we satisfied the requirements and received our permit. Outside I averted my eyes from Katende but could not avoid hearing his reproachful "I told you we shouldn't waste time on this."

But if any reader supposes that the measured pace of bureaucracy in Karamoja was a peculiarly Ugandan infliction he would be mistaken. I have received not merely leisurely but much more obstructive treatment from a local Department of Health and Social Security office in England when by prior appointment, which had been forgotten in the office, I sought advance information, which was refused, on my old age pension.

To have one's hand on the wheel of history is of course one of the joys – indeed compensations – of being a bureaucrat: a permit allowed or withheld, an explanation demanded, a delay imposed, a form required, an expectation aroused or moderated or erased, an agreement denied or granted. I fear the British must have taught many such lessons in East Africa before withdrawing the guiding hand. That is the dull side of the coin that bore our image. The other shines more brightly: it is the legacy of early morning tea. Wherever British rule has left its mark there the traveller, whether in hotels or rest houses or hutted camps, can rely on waking to the chinking of china, the drawing of a curtain, and the placing beside him of a delicious cup or more likely pot of tea while the early morning sun shines through the window on to his bed. This refreshment that dispels sleep and rouses the spirit of inquiry is surely one of the most civilised rituals we have bestowed on mankind.

Driving up through Kaabong towards Kidepo in the northern tip of Uganda, Katende and I were worried by having been told in Kampala that, if by any mischance we should hit a child who had run into the road, we must on no account stop. In the turmoil of any such accident the local people would immediately spear us to death. Even if the injury were problematical, we were told, we must not stop to see how severe it might be and offer treatment or compensation or even comfort. The only acceptable recompense would be our lives. In a population unaccustomed to seeing more than one or two vehicles passing through in the course of a day the children especially and the adults to some extent tended to wander unconcernedly on to the road, which is in any case only a slightly more compressed track of dusty rock or laterite than the similar material extending round their huts and beyond into the dry acacia scrub in that region. So as well as cautiously I drove nervously and slowed down to a bumpy walking pace in the neighbourhood of huts or groups of gossiping Karimojong.

Children would sometimes wave the car down so that they could sell us some bananas or perhaps a water pot made from a gourd. And though, as I mentioned above, I enjoyed the game of bargaining, I must say that my conscience did not allow me to pay less than what I thought a fair price to the children of this dry, impoverished land. In fact on several occasions I paid more than what I thought was far too low a price that some child was asking for the most delicious bananas I have ever tasted in the world.

Before going out on a trip into the country I used to visit the bank in Kampala and buy a bag of Ugandan shillings; that is, if I could obtain them, though on one occasion coins had become so scarce that I had to be content with fewer than I thought I should need. But as a payment for small services carried out for me when collecting in the field or for the purchase of fruit at the wayside I found that shillings were everywhere acceptable, and they had the merit of being harmless in contrast to that other popular currency, tobacco. Young boys would often appear from nowhere when I pushed off into the bushland or forest beyond the shambas of cultivated bananas and ask to carry my rucksack and bags of specimens. In fact I was often surprised by the arrival at my side of quizzical children or adults despite my having seen no huts near by. The boys would try collecting some lichens on their own and bring them along for me to add to the collection I was making, but the difficulty of distinguishing interesting specimens from common weeds often meant that the warm thanks I bestowed on them with the shillings were in recognition more of their good intentions than of their success. I have heard people say they would never dream of paying boys to help them in this way, regarding their presence as an intrusion rather than what at heart it is: the assertion of a territorial claim. Of course I could perfectly well carry my rucksack, but paying them to do so was simply the modern equivalent of the passage money, or hongo, that was demanded of the nineteenth century explorers when they passed through a chief's territory. "This is *our* home," the boys are thinking, "and you ought to acknowledge it by making some recompense for our letting you walk through it – and we'd also like to know *why* you are here." Naturally this is a more explicit formulation of their thoughts than what actually passes through their minds, but it would nevertheless be a great mistake to suppose that an African boy who emerges from a thatched hut with a ragged cloak over him, bare feet, and a shy demeanour is any less sharp intellectually than a European boy who lives in a house, knows how a motor car works, and watches television.

After going through Kaabong we reached country where zebras and giraffes were abundant, together with gazelles and a few elephants.

"My god!" I suddenly shouted to Katende above the grinding rumble of the Landrover's engine, "look at them all – the car's full of tse-tses." They had poured in through our open windows and were whining around us. "Shut your window." I braked to a standstill, and we both shut our windows and began hitting the flies with our maps and squashing them against the glass. I felt one beginning to thrust its proboscis into the skin of my right leg just above the ankle, and I swiped it against the floor before it had time to thrust in deeper. It is more difficult than might be supposed to kill them because they seem to be able to withstand a degree of compression that would kill any other kind of fly.

Time and again we would press one against the windscreen under a map only to see the wretch fly off when the map was lifted away. But as we flicked and pressed them their grey corpses gradually accumulated on the seats and floor, and in the end we killed over 40, though it was still unsafe to open the windows despite the sweltering heat because swarms of them were flying outside and settling on the glass. Knowing their predilection for a moving target I saw here an opportunity to measure their speed of flight. Starting the car forward again I accelerated to 20 mph (32 kph) and then slightly opened the window beside me to attract them with the scent of our sweat. They buzzed at the gap while I hit them away from it with a map. I put on a little more speed and finally found that we were doing just over 30 mph (48 kph) when we began to leave them behind.

On another occasion they were particularly troublesome when Katende and I went by motorised canoe over to one of the Sese Islands in Lake Victoria. Some care was needed on the journey itself to prevent the lake water which was vigorously splashed up from falling on our skins, owing to the dense infection of bilharzia in some places round the shore. But our troubles did not cease as we stepped ashore on the island, for the familiar whine of tse-tse flies told us we were under attack. Unlike northern Uganda, where at that time the strain of trypanosome was believed to be one that infected only animals, the strain round the great lake was known to be infective to man. In the end we decided that one area of scrub on the island was too heavily infested with tse-tse for us to investigate it further, so whatever lichens it may have held remain known only to the flies.

At Kidepo in the northern tip of Uganda, where a national park had been created and most of the larger mammals flourished, Katende and I shared a room in the guest house. In the middle of the first night there I heard him get up and lock the door leading to the veranda outside.

"What was that?" I asked still half asleep.

"It was a lion growling. I locked the door. I thought he might put his paw on the door handle." It was of the lever kind, and anyway I suppose we were rather careless not to have locked up for the night.

Limestone is extremely rare in Uganda,[38] so that we were fortunate the next day to come upon a substantial outcrop of it in northern Kidepo. Waiting for some elephants with their young to move off the track we were driving along, we then rounded a corner and saw a mass of white rocks spread over the ground. Volcanic springs bubbled among them, filling pools with hot water and ejecting eddying clouds of steam that hung over sheets of a green alga lying in the pools and growing up over the rocks. Also growing on the rocks was a lichen that I saw nowhere else in East Africa, identifiable to generic level (*Synalissa*) but not at present to species.

As we were close to the border with the Sudan I suggested we should go over and do a little botanising in that country. Relieved that we had the Landrover to carry us up a rough track to the ridge above in the burning sun, we stepped out and walked into the Sudan over a frontier which the map told us was there but to which the land itself, with its rustling grasses and stunted shrubs, its buzzing insects and cracked earth, was as indifferent as an old blind beggar to the people who pass him by. Lichens were indifferent to its charms also, for none of any note were there.

The country round there is not a paradise for plants, and for man it has proved to be a tragedy. Changes brought ruin to the fragile society of the Ik tribe, a disintegration poignantly recorded by Colin Turnbull[39], and all the sadder for being irreparable. Thereafter we collected mainly in the valleys and drove southwest through Kitgum and Gulu (since ravaged by civil war) and on to Masindi, where we stayed a night under the most inadequate mosquito netting I have ever suffered or the mosquitoes have enjoyed.

We had been travelling for a week, and now on returning to Kampala I suddenly felt so faint that I asked Katende to take the wheel. What could this be, I wondered; malaria? At any rate I recovered on the rest of the journey back until we reached Makerere, when I felt faint again. Katende said he would put the car away, so I dragged out the specimens and went up to my flat. Feeling hot and feverish I decided the most important first aid was to cool myself, so I took off my clothes with the accumulated dust in them, went into the bathroom, and turned on the cold tap, feeling that nothing would comfort me so much as a cool bath. But owing to some malaise in the plumbing, which had worked satisfactorily before I set out for the north, hot water followed by hot air and steam rushed out. So I hastily turned that off and tried the hot tap – only to evoke a gurgle and spurt, and then silence. Frustrated by the bath I turned to the window, pushed my bed under it, and flopped down in the cool air that was fortunately billowing through it. At the same time thinking I might be dehydrated despite the evening beers after a week of being dried up in the sun, I drank two bottles of Fanta, a drink whose ready availability on the campus contrasted with my distaste for it. Happily my treatment was successful. In an hour or so I felt much restored, and on thinking again about the diagnosis I came to the conclusion my condition was nothing more than simple heat exhaustion. By the next day I was perfectly fit again.

Southwards again with Katende, this time in a van that he owned privately: it was a Honda, a small vehicle with a two-cylinder 250 cc engine under the floor. We planned to take it over the hairpins up to the Kanaba Gap and down the other side to Kisoro for another look at the Bufumbira volcanoes whose eastern sentinel is Muhavura. Exploring the rich forests just south of the equator on the way, we stopped for a night at a small hotel in Masaka.

The next morning as we were leaving the town on our way to Mbarara, which is about 80 miles away, two soldiers in uniform sprang into the middle of the road and stopped us. I was driving, and as they approached the cabin I noticed that, though drunk, they were not armed.

"Mbarara," one of them said.

Katende looked worried as I glanced in his direction. He was all too familiar with the conduct of the army, drunk or sober. Uganda's tensely controlled smile under Obote had now given way to the suspicious frown of Amin's rule. "We don't seem to have much choice," I said as the soldiers glared at us, and while one stood in front of the van the other climbed into the back, to be closely followed by his comrade. We drove off wondering whether they intended to attack us on a quiet stretch of the road and hijack the vehicle, for if a dispute came to unarmed combat I fear youth was on their side. Suddenly I remembered that my rucksack in the back contained the sheath knife with which I collected specimens. Would they start rummaging through my belongings, find the knife, and be tempted to use it on us? In a quarter of an hour we came to a group of houses with a shop or two by the road, so, thinking to myself, "This is the place," I stopped the car in full view of some people by the road, walked round to the back, pointed to my head and the sun to indicate that I wanted to get out my hat, and gestured towards the rucksack. One of the soldiers handed it to me and I rapidly bore it round to the driving cabin, got my hat out, and stuffed the rucksack down beside me in the cabin. "I think they'll be all right," I said to Katende, as they seemed now to be fairly subdued under the benign influence of beer. And so it proved. They became ever more somnolent till we approached Mbarara, when they started tapping on our shoulders through a window in the cabin. We had reached their barracks.

"Thank you, good." They were all smiles now, gathering their kit together and making themselves ready to rejoin their unit. Had their absence in fact been noticed? I wondered. The last we saw of them was two slightly dazed soldiers lurching up the concrete road to their barracks, and as we revved up the engine one of them pulled a clean shirt from out of his camouflaged battle smock and waved goodbye as though with a flag. He had got it out of my rucksack.

Driving the Honda up to the Kanaba Gap was not too difficult. Despite its miniature engine and being "over-bodied" it tackled hills with vigour. But descending to Kisoro the other side was sometimes tricky. Rain had washed great troughs and gutters in the road, and every so often the camber took an alarming slope round a corner. But in the end we reached Kisoro before nightfall.

Once again a guide and two porters were readily engaged for the next morning at 0630, and we sat down to our meal with anticipation. Unfortunately the meat in the stew was so tough – the remains of a once very energetic animal – that I had to hand most of it to an enormous dog that accompanied us in the dining room, a prototype Hound of the Baskervilles and much taller than our table over whose cloth his jaws hung ravenously. He made short work of the chunks of leather I picked off my plate for him.

This time on Muhavura I was content not to go higher than about 12 000 feet (3700 m) because I wanted to move westwards towards Mgahinga and do some collecting there, so we took a slightly different course and collected more in the forest. On the way back rain fell steadily to add chill to our aching legs, and as I looked at the cloud-covered slopes, grey and sunless, with their lustreless vegetation, the rain dripping down over my glasses, I thought: Why the hell am I doing this?

> Wandering lost upon the mountains of our choice,
> Again and again we sigh for an ancient South,
> For the warm nude ages of instinctive poise,
> For the taste of joy in the innocent mouth. – W H AUDEN.
> *A Sonnet Sequence*

Yet, as an insensitive remark made by a friend at first hurts us and then fades away into the distance of time, so this moment of self-pity quickly died away and my mind regained its equanimity. More, a burst of joy flooded through me as the sun reappeared and we reached a higher concentration of oxygen in the air at about 8000 feet (2400 m). How glorious that place then seemed as the warmth of an "ancient South" enveloped us! I felt in harmony with mountains and skies so grand that the human spirit was, for the time being at any rate, drawn out of the tired old body and had flown up to enjoy the freedom of the clouds condensing and drifting over the summits.

In these outlying places travellers from Europe were not commonly seen. As we came down into the foothills at 7000 feet (2100 m) a little boy ran up to me and took my hand. He smiled doubtfully to me and said something.

"You are the first white man he has seen," said Katende. This surprised me: he must have led a remote life in those mountains.

On another occasion when collecting in northwest Uganda I became an object not so much of interest as amusement. Katende and I were walking along the side of a village towards a large rock outcrop that had some beautiful lichens growing on it. As we passed by some huts in the trees a woman called out to her neighbour "Mzungu" – a white foreigner – and they both shrieked out peals of laughter, their shoulders shaking with mirth at anything so incongruous as my appearance and presence in that out of the way place. Katende regarded their behaviour as uncouth and hurried on so that we should be spared any further innocent ridicule.

It was the last journey I had time for. "I wanted you to see that part of the country," said Katende; "now you've seen all the places I thought you ought to see." He seemed thoughtful, perhaps regretting it was past. And perhaps also preoccupied with the future. For the present, December 1971, there was unrest in the air.

Anyway, it was time for me to move on to Kenya so as to allow about five weeks for collecting there, a country in which so far I had spent only a few days. So I had far to go if I was to discover its lichen riches. I moved out of my flat on the campus into the International Hotel in Kampala, formerly the Apolo Hotel after Apolo Milton Obote but renamed in deference to Amin. From there I spent a day packing up my collections and dispatching them by air to England (all arrived safely).

In the evening I invited Katende and his wife to dinner at

the hotel. It was a cheerful meal so far as it could be, poised on the cliff of a parting that might be for a long time, perhaps for ever. The beer was good, and the two double waragis with which Katende and I concluded it even better. Reminiscing over our journeys he took another sip of the waragi and said,

"Do you remember the school children at Kabale?"

"Yes, they gave us a charming welcome."

We had stopped near a school playground so that we could collect lichens growing on trees there, when about 20 little school girls led along by their teacher uttered a soft treble ululation to us. "They are greeting you," Katende had said. In their neat blouses and blue skirts they had tripped their way across the playground into the school, white teeth twinkling in black faces, black arms swinging against white blouses, swaying gently across the grass like a row of flowers in the breeze.

The memory faded and we gazed round the half-deserted restaurant.

"Well, goodbye, Katende and Mrs."

"Goodbye, Dougal, goodbye."

The next day, Christmas Day, I flew eastwards again along the equator – to Nairobi. Later in the year the subterranean terror of Amin's regime began bursting through the surface like a crop of ulcers, and Uganda gradually slid into civil war.

28 Mountain and lake

On Christmas Day 1971 I had a belated lunch alone in the dining room of the Boulevard Hotel in Nairobi after its other visitors had gone out. Despite the incongruity of turkey and plum pudding so near the equator, its late service specially for me was an encouraging sign of the good will with which I was being received as an unbooked guest. During the afternoon I gave myself a holiday and went for a tour through the national park in a minibus to see the cheetahs and giraffes and zebras and lions and all the rest of those wonderful mammals of the African savanna, already depleted in my day, now tragically struggling to avoid extinction. But in the evening I had to think seriously: where should I start to explore this vast country, and how should I set about it?

Being an amateur, I had no formal contacts with members of the scientific establishments out there, no fellowship as a postgraduate student, no letter from one professor to another to press my claims, and no botanical institution in my own country to which I could refer an inquirer. But I had previously prepared for my lack of status by making the acquaintance of two men who were to be of great help. The first was Andrew Hicks, FRCS, an Englishman who had emigrated to Nairobi after serving in the RAMC in the war and became established as one of the leading surgeons out there. Josephine and I had met him in his capacity as honorary secretary of the BMA when we visited Nairobi for a few days in 1969. From him I was now to receive the warmest hospitality at his house during my botanical visits to the country, as also did my future colleague, Dr Hildur Krog of Oslo. It was through Andrew that I solved the problem of how to get started on my search.

My second fortunate contact was Mr Jan B Gillett, a professional botanist working at the East African Herbarium in Nairobi, who had an intimate knowledge of the country. Here too luck favoured me, for by chance I had met a brother of his at Bill Hoffenberg's house soon after Bill and his family had left South Africa and settled in England. From this meeting I learnt that Jan Gillett was to visit London later in the year, so when he came over I met him at lunch armed with a map. He then gave me an invaluable piece of information in pointing out how the east winds sweep westwards from the Indian Ocean across Kenya, bathing the hills in their path with moisture and, near their summits, with frequent cloud. Thus to pick out on the map the ridges and hills in the line of this moisture was to identify on their east-facing aspect good ground on which to look for lichens. Furthermore, when I did finally reach Nairobi he introduced me to the herbarium staff and its director, Miss Christine Kabuye, a Ugandan botanist, and they allowed me to use the drying facilities for the specimens I was beginning to collect. For a couple of days also they were able to spare a Landrover with driver and a botanical assistant, and by travelling to a few places by road or track, including the southern summit of the Ngong Hills, I began quickly to get the feel of the place and to learn what sort of problems to expect.

"Would you like to go to a party tomorrow evening?" Andrew Hicks offered to drive me over to it if I liked. "I'd recommend it: you'd see one of the real old houses built in about 1900. And you might meet someone there who could be of help to you."

As he had said, the house was built of wood and had a covered veranda along one side giving access to several rooms. The planks creaked as we walked over them, and the greyish brown tint of the exposed walls contrasted attractively with the reddish brown of the shadier interior. Among the guests clutching their glasses I noticed that in contrast to gatherings of this kind in South Africa the men and women mixed freely in conversation, and perhaps in contrast to parties in Britain, were eager not merely to talk but to unfold their hearts to a stranger as I was, to respond with animation to questions about life out there, to regret as some did the passing of the good old days, to hint at some anxiety about the future, and, several at least, to express disappointment at what they felt to be a betrayal by the home country as their status had passed with puzzling imperceptibility from pioneer to shop-soiled reject.

"The British government encouraged us to come out, you know," an elderly woman said to me, casting her recollection back to the 1920s, "my husband...later we were tea planters in Tanganyika, on the slopes of Kilimanjaro. It went quite well...we enjoyed it anyway...no money, though, really...they called us pioneers in those days...we're retired now, no option."

> Some could not bear nor break the young and mourn for
> The wounded myths that once made nations good,
> Some lost a world they never understood,
> Some saw too clearly all that man was born for. – W H AUDEN.
> *A Sonnet Sequence*

I thought of this conversation when some six years later I was up near Gilgil on my own trying to find a farm that I knew from a previous visit had some walls bearing interesting lichens. Among the rough tracks I lost my way, and seeing a stone house that I thought (though mistakenly) might be the one I sought, I went up the drive to meet its owner. He emerged from the shade of the porch as I approached it and asked me what I wanted. I told him I had made a mistake, I saw this now, it was not the place where I had hoped to find lichens. He shuffled some welcoming steps towards me and held out his hand. Tall and burly, with a thin stubble of grey beard, and the lined, tanned skin of many years in that dry climate, he glanced at me uneasily with faded watery eyes. A visitor was a novelty in his loneliness.

"Yes, I've been here many years, long before the war, I'm on my own now – a free man," he added with an attempt at irony, and he looked round sadly at the weeds engulfing the remains of a garden and now clambering at the walls of the house. "I've got nothing left here."

"Why don't you clear out?"

"I can't get anything for this place – and if I could I shouldn't be allowed to take any money out."

"You're stuck here then?"

"Yes, there's no way out. Of course I should have gone years ago – just left it all. But I never had anywhere else to go to. I'll stay here now, see it out, no choice..."

He grunted in appreciation as I said goodbye.

No option, no choice: history had gradually cut away the tracks for some of these people, and when they finally chose what was left they found it was a blind alley ending in a back yard full of weeds. Today the great majority of Europeans in Kenya have their eyes on the future, the future of the country as well as themselves. They are physicians and surgeons, agricultural scientists, biochemists, geologists, zoologists, botanists, and many others with a training that can be put to the advantage of the country and a skill whose exercise can bring the craftsman's contentment to their own lives.

Nor is it only science that has brought benefit to Kenya in recent years. That other product of human curiosity, tourism, offers even more in the short term, at least till the last elephant sinks to its knees in the dust before a poacher's rifle. So I was not surprised to find that another woman who spoke to me at the Nairobi party should tell me she was a tourist guide. Here seemed an opportunity for me.

"Let me get you another drink," I suggested, foreseeing a fount of useful information on the country. "You sound like an American," I added.

"That's right. I work for a tourist company. I'm a kind of guide, taking people on special trips to see the animals and birds."

"But do you know about animals and so on?"

She looked at me with composure. The cool expression of her brown eyes with their humorous wrinkles, her pale complexion and curly brown hair, her determined bearing – all seemed to signify someone accustomed to making her way through the world, to getting around seeing places without bothering people and without being beholden to anyone except her clients.

"Oh yes, I know enough for the tourists. My husband

works for a zoo in California. It was through his work that I first came to Africa – it was West Africa, I know it quite well, and now I've come over to East Africa. I want to see more of it."

"Perhaps we could team up."

"Have you got a car?"

"Yes, haven't you?"

"I don't drive."

Surprised to meet an American who could not drive, I said that I had been wondering while talking to her whether we could explore some of the Rift Valley territory where I wanted to collect lichens while she inspected the country round there to see whether it would appeal to her tourists. We complemented each other in our requirements with lucky precision, I needing a companion, she a driver, so we arranged to meet the next day for a trip out in the car I had now hired. This gave me the key that unlocked the door to all my botanical exploration of the country.

"By the way," I asked, "what's your name?"

"Linda Baldwin."

Linda was the ideal companion for the journeys I now undertook up to 100 miles or so in different directions round Nairobi. We would go out for the day with a picnic lunch, and when I parked the car and went off to explore the surrounding woodland or rocks she would stay in the vicinity, guard it, and do crossword puzzles, of which she was a devotee. Among the places I visited in this way was one of the most interesting sites for lichens in all East Africa. Lying near the village of Kibwezi between Nairobi and Mombasa, it consists of an old lava flow where, among the mounds of naked lava, a variety of shrubs and trees flourish: both they and the rocks supported a unique treasure house of lichens. Jan Gillett originally suggested it to me as worth studying because of its unusual geological structure and rich flowering-plant flora, for under the heaped-up masses of lava water lies permanently, providing moisture at the roots of the plants and also in the overlying air trapped in the shelter of the vegetation. As a result of several subsequent visits with my colleague Dr Krog, who joined me later, three species of lichens new to science were recorded there in addition to several others that were not seen elsewhere.

With Linda's help simply as a passenger and map reader while I did the driving I came to understand the nature of travel in Kenya, which presented different problems from those I encountered in Uganda. The distances in Kenya were much greater, much of the land was more arid, the roads though generally of better quality were relatively unpopulated, while the traffic, though sparse away from the towns, was usually more frequent than in Uganda. To get the feel of the maps was also important – how much detail were they likely to show, and how accurately. In the small and unreliable cars which were all that my limited means allowed me to hire the long distances in the hot sun were tiring to drive over (none of the cars was air conditioned like those one finds in the USA), and near the towns I was often passed in a cloud of dust by a Mercedes full of politicians or a minibus full of tourists. But everywhere the inspiring scenery, and especially the mountains and lakes of the Rift Valley or the dappled forest glades, drew away the curtain of fatigue and discovered to my lasting delight a landscape which had the assurance and grandeur of a Bach cantata, a vision that remains as clearly imprinted on my mind to this day as, for example, in adjacent galleries of my memory, the Turner seascapes at the National and Tate Galleries or the El Grecos from the Prado that I saw 50 years ago in Geneva during the Spanish civil war: some of their individual details I may have forgotten, but their impact as a whole caused permanent changes of course in the river of my life.

After some days of collecting lichens in this way I decided the time had come to find out what was growing high up on Mt Kenya. Confidence in the reliability of my car had waned; neither the steering nor the gearbox seemed likely to sustain life for much longer. So I returned it to the car hire firm and booked a journey to Naro Moru, which lies at the foot of the mountain, by Peugeot taxi. These vehicles were licensed to take passengers over long distances, and with my rucksack and sleeping bag I set off from Nairobi in one of them after breakfast, sitting with two other passengers on the back seat – making nine all told instead of the eight for which this taxi was licensed. Consequently as we left Nairobi, and on passing through inhabited areas on the way, one of us in turn had to crouch on the floor so that only eight passengers would be apparent to any policemen around. In this way we had an untroubled journey, and I was dropped off within walking distance of the Naro Moru Hotel, about 100 miles north of Nairobi.

Here the proprietors lent me some thicker boots than the suede pair I normally wore and arranged for a Kikuyu guide and porter to accompany me up the mountain from a 7 am start on the morrow.

Of all the hotels I have ever stayed in I think the Naro Moru is one of the few of which I could say that I loved visiting it, and of those few it remains pre-eminent. Its setting in sunlit glades beside the River Naro Moru that flows by the lawn invites the visitor to rest in a Garden of Eden where the air is balmy by day and cool in the evening, though the place is only a few miles from the equator. From its terrace the peak of Mt Kenya is visible. From its bar in the evening brandy and ginger ale warmed the blood when the cold air was sliding down from the mountain. The dining room provided excellent meals and the showers water that flowed pleasantly hot. The guests were generally from many nations – Australian, American, French, German, Italian during the several visits I made to the hotel – but all had something in common, whether a love of spacious mountain scenery, a devotion to the natural history of the region, or a professional concern in its geology or biology.

From here I set off the next morning in a Landrover with the guide and porter so that we could drive up the track to 8000 feet (2400 m) and walk from there up through the forest to the alpine moorland above. On this first journey to the mountain I did no collecting on the way up to Mackinder's Camp at just under 14000 feet (4100 m), because I wanted to reach the high ground as early as possible to collect examples of the species peculiar to it while the weather, always unpredictable, was suitable. At about 12 000 feet (3600 m) I paused to take some aspirin for a headache that was due partly to the altitude, partly to a poor night's rest. Having arranged this visit without much notice I had to persuade the hotel, already fully booked, to find room for me, and I could only feel grateful that they agreed to give me a makeshift bed on a sofa.

Arriving at the camp in the afternoon I dumped my kit, had a mug of warm tea, and began collecting lichens. A hot stew under the stars in the evening revived me, and then night fell and I crept under my tent while the temperature dropped sharply as the sky darkened over us.

Soon the wind was beating at the tent and driving snow and hail against it. While the canvas flaps and sides crackled in the snowstorm I burrowed into my sleeping bag but could do no more than doze fitfully. After a few hours I realised I should have to get out and relieve my bladder despite the hostility of the storm but with a feeling of satisfaction that at least my kidneys must be working efficiently, since renal failure is apt to be one of the first symptoms of that fatal mountain disease, acute pulmonary oedema. Mt Kenya had a bad reputation for being particularly liable to induce this disease because several people had died of it at high altitude in the previous year or two. Still, at that moment it was not the oxygen tension so much as the bladder tension that worried me most, for I quailed at the prospect of venturing into the storm and having snow blowing down my neck, to say the least of it. So I conceived a plan with a plastic bag. Blowing it up like a balloon to test that it was impermeable, I passed urine into it with a sense of relief mingled with self-congratulation and prepared to take it outside so that I could cast its contents away behind a boulder there – only to be struck with dismay on finding that my test had yielded a false positive result: the plastic was permeable and was already leaking on to my sleeping bag. So as well as venturing outside to dispose of the remainder I had to mop up inside. I suppose that to seasoned mountaineers these problems are much more readily soluble with a minimum of sense and experience, but for myself all I can say is that for the rest of the night I remained sleepless in comfort rather than discomfort, though owing to a deterioration in the weather the cold was intense till the sun rose over a hot breakfast that my porter brought me.

Though I had intended to stay there for two days, the weather became so unsettled that I was driven to leave after only a day's collecting. A belt of thick cloud had settled on the mountain at about 11000 feet (3300 m), concealing the lower slopes and on them, 1000 feet below, a gap in the trees that we had to identify in order to find the track down through the forest. My guide paused before the cloud, silhouetted darkly against it as he stood on a boulder peering ahead as far as he could see, which was only about 50 yards; then with a nod he started downhill again. This part of the mountain led on to the so-called vertical bog, a long, steeply sloping boggy incline. It presents a wearisome obstacle to the climber on the way up dragging his feet out of one squelching hole after another. On the way down it gave us a slippery, and with its pitfalls between grass tussocks, treacherous slide through the cloud. Yet after an hour of traversing these almost featureless slopes the upper edge of the forest became visible with, there, right in front of us the gap in the trees leading to the track we needed. It was really admirable navigation.

Knowing that there was much more to be found on the high moorland above the forest I went up again a couple of days later to about 12000 feet (3600 m). On this occasion a porter was not available, and feeling confident that I could now find my way about on that part of the mountain I did something I invariably advise other people not to do – I went alone. No harm came of it, but enthusiasm outran discretion in a manner I would have criticised in anyone else.

It was a beautiful clear day. This was lucky for me: the weather can change quickly and dramatically on that mountain, but on that day it favoured me with a settled aspect. I was in the realm of the tree senecios and lobelias. Far below I could see the upper margin of the forest and still had in sight the all-important gap in the trees from where the track in the forest went down. In the vast expanse of the

297

mountainside where great outcrops of rock jutted from the boggy moorland and the boulders were clothed with lichen, I was suddenly startled to hear a shout. A thousand feet above me a Kikuyu had appeared waving his arms and calling in an agitated manner. I moved up towards him as he ran down to me calling. As he came up he said, "There is a man ill."

"Where is he?"

"High up there. They are trying to bring him down."

"Shall I come and help?"

"No. Go down. Get help. He is heavy."

So I ran and slithered down over the moorland, reached the gap in the trees, and then went on as fast as I could to the forest ranger's station at 8000 feet (2400 m), where I knew there was a radio transmitter that could be used in such emergencies as this. At last I reached the station and puffed out my message, which the ranger radioed down to the hotel. By then it was too late to go back up the mountain, so I waited for a Landrover that was expected at the station and persuaded its driver, in the kindness of his heart but against the forestry service's regulations, to give me a lift down to Naro Moru. We passed the rescue team with its stretchers and oxygen going up the mountain track in a Landrover as we drove down through the lower forest. I asked if as a medical man I could be of any service to them, but they said no, they knew all the first aid drill, the most important thing being to get him down quickly – I would only impede them.

In fact first aid was not needed. The man had died high up on the mountain, and a few hours later they brought in his body. He was a heavily built German in his 50s. But age alone is no drawback on mountains: it used to be said out there that it was the fit young climbers who were the more likely to succumb to acute pulmonary oedema than the older and less impetuous people like me scrambling about with a bottle of aspirin to hand. And anyway – was it acute pulmonary oedema that he died of? It was the diagnosis assumed at the time because he was at high altitude, became breathless, and passed into a coma. Yet he might simply have had some kind

298

of heart attack such as lies in wait for any of us. But that particular mountain's reputation was such that no one doubted its evil spirit had struck again.

Next day after drying my specimens as much as possible in the sun during the morning I caught another long-distance Peugeot taxi back to Nairobi. This time I sat just behind the driver and was able to watch with fascinated anxiety the speedometer needle creep up to 85 mph (136 kph) as we sped through torrential rain. The road lay out in a straight ribbon ahead, visible every so often through the windscreen wipers sweeping at double speed through the cascade. In the distance another car came into view racing towards us. Our driver chose this moment to put his right elbow on the steering wheel in order to control it while extracting cigarettes and matches from a trouser pocket and using both his hands to light up. With a whoosh through the rain torrents the two cars passed, and our driver exhaled the cigarette smoke with satisfaction.

Back in Nairobi I found Linda Baldwin in the throes of an exciting plan. It was to visit Lake Rudolf up in the north, where Kenya joins Ethiopia. This lake about 130 miles long by 20 to 30 miles wide lies in the Rift Valley and is surrounded by arid country that is largely desert. The country between the lake and Uganda 100 miles to its west is occupied by the Turkana tribe, those dreaded marauders in preparation for whom I had travelled with an armed guard in Uganda when collecting on Mt Moroto. But a cattle raider who does not stop at murder on one side of a frontier is a peaceable pastoralist who shows off his metal bracelets on the other side. So when Linda asked me if I would like to go too I jumped at the opportunity of seeing whether any lichens were growing up there.

Linda also had a special reason for wanting to see the lake. Recently a camp had been established on its west side as a tourist attraction, but few tour operators knew of its existence yet, and fewer still had visited it to find out whether it was an attractive place to include in their itineraries. Linda wanted to examine its suitability for her clients and with this in mind had arranged to charter a small plane to fly us up to an airstrip there. She was to be accompanied by her sister, who had flown over from the USA, and the seat she offered me was going at half price. So on a clear January morning we set off for Lake Rudolf and arrived at Ferguson's Gulf half way up the west side early in the afternoon.

The Turkana were living in round thatched huts like bee skips along the shore of the lake, in whose waters they found their staple food, the abundant perch and tilapia, as delicious as they were enormous. Along the shore all was desert, but further to the west I noticed shrubs and some palm trees. Many of the children were naked except for a few bracelets, and the adults wore as little as modesty would permit. All were of an intense, almost bluish black, well nourished, and showing the scars of vaccination against smallpox.

As we had some time in the afternoon for a bit of exploration of the gulf, we decided to hire a dinghy with an outboard motor in the charge of a Turkana tribesman and go over to an attractive creek across the bay. There was vegetation which I thought might be worth investigating. But these are the sort of places where no journey goes quite according to plan. About a mile out in the bay a turmoil of splashing and grinding round our propeller told us that we had fouled some object. It proved to be a Turkana fishing net, and it stopped our motor dead. Our boatman removed the net easily enough, but nothing he or any of us could do would start the motor into life. Time and again we pulled the cord with varying degrees of choke or none: to no avail. Finally we hailed a passing boat of Turkana fishermen, but they went on oblivious of our pleas and aloofly content that people who damaged a fishing net were now paying for their carelessness. Left alone in the bay, but with the shore easily visible only a mile away, we waved and shouted and hallooed and whistled to the people we could see walking about on it. But the distance was just too great. They remained maddeningly wrapped up in their own affairs, deaf and blind to our signals. Linda and her sister gallantly took off their white blouses and waved them in a last attempt to catch the attention of the people walking unconcerned on the shore, sometimes even appearing to gesture in our direction, sometimes pausing in their business, yet ever ignorant of our presence, so near and yet so far.

"They've seen us at last," cried one of my companions, "somebody waved." But they hadn't.

"Look – he heard that whistle – did you see that?" But nobody had heard anything.

Several times one or other of our party believed they had detected a response from the shore to our appeals for help, convinced that some casual movement showed our signals had at last been observed, that help would soon be on the way. And for a moment my memory brought before my mind as I sat in the boat a vision of unshaved, camouflaged soldiers standing in slit trenches dug in the sandy soil at Arnhem. Then a rumour had gone round that salvation was at hand because the rumble of tanks had been heard of the Second Army fighting its way up through Holland to relieve us. The observation was as mistaken then as it quickly proved to be on Lake Rudolf. And often reflecting on incidents of this kind I have realised that one of the most difficult things in life – though it is generally dismissed without a thought as one of the most naturally and easily accomplished – is to make an exact observation. Into everything we do some hope enters – else why should we do it? Even that mythical creature the dispassionate scientist makes his collection, examines his specimen, conducts his experiment, interprets his results with some degree of hope, some slight expectation in mind that he will prove or disprove something, will take a step however small from the arena of knowledge into the darkness beyond. And if making an exact observation requires us to be as alert in every faculty as we can rouse ourselves to be, how much more intense must our concentration be if we are to make an unbiased judgment. Perhaps it is in this kind of striving that we can speak of exercising free will.

Within an hour the sun would set, and here we were marooned in a lake reputed to harbour 20000 crocodiles. So far I had not seen here any of these creatures slowly drifting like logs with their eyes and nostrils just above the surface of the water. But as by now it was clear we should not be rescued I examined the boat itself to see what sort of propulsion we might give it. It contained no oars – something we should have checked before setting out. The seats looked promising though. I found they were bolted on to brackets in the fibre glass hull of the dinghy. One of my faithful travelling companions was a pocket knife that included a variety of implements besides the blades, among them a small screw-driver. With this I unscrewed two of the boat's three seats, handed one seat to Linda, and took the other myself. Using them as makeshift oars, we paddled the dinghy on an erratic course back to base. As oarsmen we certainly lacked the cohesion of a university boat race crew, but by the end of our journey in a temperature of over 100 °F (38 °C) in the sun we felt as delighted and looked as bedraggled as Oxford or Cambridge do on passing the winning post.

Lake Rudolf has three islands spaced along its length, North, Central, and South. Our base was opposite Central Island, so next day we hired a larger boat to take us over to inspect it. At first a good landing place was difficult to identify, but at last we scrambled ashore, struggled up a hill of volcanic dust into which at each step we sank half way up to the knees, and at the top found ourselves on the rim of a crater looking down at a lake within it. The far side of the crater was broken down to form a gap leading to the shore of the island, and it was doubtless this aperture that had allowed the numerous crocodiles we could see in the island's lake gain access to it from Lake Rudolf. Inert in the warm water of the crater lake, the crocodiles would have had to return to the large lake for their food.

The starkness of the scenery in its aridity, its angularity, its sharp contrast between the desert and the lake silent in the clear air and the burning sun, forced on the Turkana inhabiting that region a life that had to be almost entirely devoted to winning the necessities of food and shelter for themselves and their cattle. In contrast was the magnificence of their personal adornment. Massive ropes of coloured beads swathed their necks like scarves, a dozen or more metal bracelets were fastened round arms and legs in a kind of flexible armour, both men and women had decorative rings dangling from their ear lobes, and some of the women had metal plugs in the lower lip. Nearly all of both sexes had scarified patterns on their bodies, and many of the men had their hair elaborately dressed with coloured clays. Beside them I must admit to looking a rather wan creature, and the only one of my few possessions they expressed any interest in was my wrist watch, which they offered to barter off me. Several of the men in fact wore wrist watches, though perhaps more as a decoration than as a measure of the time through which their lives passed in a rhythm that the sun delineated more effectually.

The journey back to Nairobi ended with one of those incidents that come out of the nightmares of pilots' lives to stop their hearts in the daytime. As we were coming down to land another light plane passed immediately below and touched down on the landing strip just ahead of us. Though startled by this intrusion, our pilot kept his nerve admirably. He pulled out of the descent, zoomed upwards, and circled the airport again before bringing us down to a less congested landing.

29 A long way

Space, like time, engenders forgetfulness; but it does so by setting us bodily free from our surroundings and giving us back our primitive, unattached state. Yes, it can even, in the twinkling of an eye, make something like a vagabond of the pedant and Philistine. Time, we say, is Lethe; but change of air is a similar draught, and, if it works less thoroughly, does so more quickly. – THOMAS MANN. *The Magic Mountain*

While time heals our wounds and allows the seething surface to ebb into placidity, so space draws us out of the shadows cast in narrow streets. It impels us, as though a ghostly herald had appeared, to gaze intently beyond the files of papers to the foothills, the slopes, the summit of a distant mountain and to watch the clouds drifting across its peak. Many botanists must have felt a sense of release when travelling through great landscapes. And it is one of the virtues of lichens that they grow with the greatest luxuriance and diversity in the places farthest away from human interference with nature, whether it is the smoke that factories pour into the air or the chemicals that farmers spray over the ground. It is on the far mountains and unfrequented coasts that they flourish, in such woodland as has so far escaped being felled and replanted every few generations, and on old walls and posts and bridges abandoned to the wind and rain. In beautiful contrast to many other parts of the continent, East Africa still has unpolluted regions as well as large areas where, though man is very much the dominant species, he has not yet become so technologically destructive as he has almost everywhere in Europe.

My travels in Uganda and now my first steps in Kenya had shown me that a diverse lichen flora was waiting to be studied systematically, and I had mentally drawn up a plan to report on the species found in Uganda. Now in Kenya, having returned from Lake Rudolf, I was planning the next move and at the same time awaiting the arrival from Ethiopia of a Norwegian lady, Dr (now Professor) Hildur Krog, who was in charge of the lichens at the Botanical Museum of Oslo University. She had been staying for three weeks with a former student, who was a missionary in Addis Ababa, and having made a collection in the uplands was keen to extend her studies to the little-known lichen flora of Kenya.

Her joining with me in these researches transformed them in two different ways. First, it soon became evident that the lichens of Kenya, Uganda, southern Ethiopia, and northern Tanzania formed a floristic unity that shaded off at its boundaries into very different assemblages of plants. So we decided that for me to follow my first plan of limiting my systematic study to Uganda would result in too fragmentary a survey of the flora, even though the vast area we now proposed to cover would take the investigation into an entirely different order of complexity. Secondly, the relatively superficial study I had proposed for the production of a manual to help botanists visiting Uganda as well as the African and expatriate staff at Makerere was replaced by the ambition to provide a thorough revision, by means of anatomical and chemical studies, of most of the genera we should come across. While I was accustomed to preparing microtome sections myself and testing the specimens for their chemical inclusions by the crystallisation methods originally devised by the Japanese botanist Asahina, Dr Krog was and is an expert in the use of thin-layer chromatography. No serious study of lichen taxonomy can now be undertaken without the use of this method of chemical analysis.

So in a moment of exhilaration born of those spacious landscapes, whose grandeur swept us into an undertaking that matched its reckless horizons, we committed ourselves to a study covering a tropical region nearly 1000 miles north to south and the same east to west and centred on the equator. It was, moreover, the first attempt to study by modern scientific methods a diverse lichen flora in the tropics. I believe I can claim our persistence matched our rashness, for

over the next 17 years we jointly published 30 papers on the
work and finally drew it all together in a book published
by the British Museum (Natural History)[40], to which
incidentally I donated all my collections.

My problems in exploring the botanically attractive parts
of Kenya were now solved in that Hildur Krog was an
experienced traveller, as I knew, and likely to be, as she
proved, a stalwart colleague in difficult situations. A feature
of her character especially congenial to my plans was that she
had the drive needed to fill every minute of our journeys with
attention to our studies, whether dragging ourselves up
through the rarefied air of the mountains or dripping with
sweat in the tropical humidity of the mangroves by the Indian
Ocean.

In the planning of this project as an extension of my
Uganda studies I had circumscribed it by one important
restriction, which had philosophical rather than purely
technical reasons and so is perhaps worth setting out. Lichens
can be divided into those that form a crust or powdery film
on the rock or bark they grow on, so called microlichens, and
those that have a somewhat leaf-like structure or form
branched shrubs or long beard-like plants, the macrolichens.
The division is botanically arbitrary but in practice con-
venient. Though my studies of lichens over the previous 15
years had been on the microlichens, mainly those of the
British Isles, I had decided to restrict my African studies to
the macrolichens. The reason is that over the world as a
whole more is known about the genera and species of
macrolichens than of microlichens. Thus a study of the
macrolichens of East Africa would provide a body of
knowledge that could be fitted into a world context much
more completely than if the study had included microlichens
also. For, if it had included the latter, the macrolichens would
in the lifetime available have been more superficially studied
and their relationships in the world flora have remained more
speculative, while the microlichens, though we should have

learnt something about them in that region, could not have been satisfactorily related to those described from other parts of the world. My desire was to increase our understanding not only of their nature individually and their place in East Africa but of the distribution of those species throughout the world.

While the thrill of discovery, whether of what was previously unrecorded in a region or of what was hitherto unknown to science, beckons to every field naturalist and adds a lively spring to his steps, the desire to understand the harmony that I sense in the universe and to discern the aesthetically and logically true relations between things has equally animated me. What is this in itself? is one question. What is its place in the universe? stands beside it. So having set these limits and made my collections in Uganda in accordance with them, I was pleased to find that when Hildur Krog joined me in Kenya she agreed with them.

When hiring a car in Kenya I always took the precaution of driving it out on the first day for a relatively short distance before embarking on a long trip. In about 20 to 50 miles I hoped to find its peculiarities and faults – and is any hired car without them? On one of these preliminary excursions in a Landrover I drove with Linda Baldwin and Hildur Krog out to Ol Doinyo Sapuk, a hill to the north-east of Nairobi rising to about 7000 feet (2100 m) and looking in profile like a cone that had been pushed sideways. On our way back through Thika and then Ruiru a wild clattering suddenly broke out from the engine and a cloud of steam rose from it. On coming to a halt and lifting the bonnet I saw a hole torn in the radiator by a piece of the cooling fan, whose fins had disintegrated and shot off centrifugally. Several Kikuyu were at the roadside, and one of them who came over and peered under the bonnet beside me acted a good deal more promptly. Picking up a small branch from the ground he hacked it to a point with a knife and rammed it into the hole. The cure was dramatic. The steam subsided, hot water ceased to flow out of the radiator, and so effective was the plug in the wound that we reached Nairobi half an hour later with at least some water in circulation.

Luck was often with us on these trips. Later I procured an even more decrepit Landrover to drive from Nairobi down to Mombasa to enable Hildur and me to collect specimens at the coast. After stopping to collect on the lava flow at Kibwezi with its wonderful variety of species we turned in for the night at Mtito Andei, about 150 miles from Nairobi and leaving another 150 miles to cover the next day to Mombasa. But when I came to start the car in the morning nothing would induce its battery to produce sufficient spark to get the engine going. Wondering what to do next, I noticed at that moment an official of the East African Automobile Association drive his own van off the road up to the petrol pump. He proved to be as well equipped as he was helpful. With a jump lead from his battery we soon got started. The problem was now to keep going over the long hot road down to the coast, for if the engine stopped we should not get it started again. Pounding along in the sun, we seemed to be sweeping along before the wind, skiing down the slopes of time – when we came to an unforeseen obstruction. A long stretch of roadworks lay ahead of us controlled by traffic lights. And, just as we approached, they changed from green to red. All we could do was halt and keep the engine running despite the sun beating on it. The thermometer crept up and up. I opened the bonnet to let air circulate more freely, and for a time the thermometer seemed to rise more slowly. But just as the minute hand of a watch moves on inexorably even though its movement second by second is imperceptible, so the thermometer needle, delusively immobile, edged upwards. Still the minutes ticked by, for the roadworks were being carried out over several miles, and the needle just touched – I had to admit it – just touched boiling point, when the lights changed to green. Slamming down the bonnet I jumped in, started off, and got into top gear as soon as possible.

We just made Mombasa – but only just. In the middle of the town the car came finally and incurably to a halt on a roundabout. Yet our luck held. Beside the roundabout was a garage. We pushed the car into it and were delighted to find they had a battery they could sell us, though it needed to be filled with acid and then charged up before it was working.

Down on the coast we explored the mangroves, those swampy margins where land meets sea and shrubs have evolved special adaptations enabling them to live in brackish, waterlogged mud, one of the most striking being the aerial roots that project up in the air like a myriad greyish brown snakes and worms. In the glistening mud fiddler crabs scuttled in and out of their burrows, one claw much larger than the other, together with giant snails, shrimp-like crustacea, and a plethora of insects. In the drier, sandy parts of the mangrove the shrubs supported many unusual species of lichens characteristic of the tropical coast.

In the rank and humid air the sweat dripped from us all day, so that on returning to the hotel one evening depleted of fluid and salt we immediately ordered and as quickly drank a pint of iced lime juice each – and then drank another after that, one of those drinks whose unfading memory is a part of friendship.* Looking for further fluid we sat on the terrace among the hotel guests and ordered tea. Our fellow guests were on package holidays from various European countries, drinking their tea in groups at the outdoor tables after a day's bathing or sightseeing. While they too recruited their energy, an African woman appeared, smartly dressed in the uniform of the Salvation Army as we see it in Europe, navy blue with red trimmings and old fashioned bonnet, and passed from table to table with her collecting tin. All she encountered were circles of blank, pink faces, moist in the humidity, staring into nothing, drugged by indifference, reminding me of the people I had seen in Bumagabula sitting like so many statues round their bowls of pombé. Sometimes the guests at a table shifted this way and that for a few moments as she

---

* Just as the memory of a smell when recalled may vividly evoke an experience long past, so may a particular drink, for me at least, conjure up the sight of a friend with whom I enjoyed it: a mixture of brandy and champagne brings to mind my fellow officers of the 1st Airborne Reconnaissance Squadron; a long lager, vodka, and soda water my ebullient host in Ghana, Professor Richard Haines; a dry Martini cocktail my colleague Hildur Krog, who makes them incomparably.

approached, as though a passing breeze were chilling them. Then they resolutely stirred their tea or gazed out to the distant line of sea in the bay. Embarrassed on behalf of our European culture as much as glad to be able to contribute to a thoroughly admirable charity, Hildur and I went over to her, lest she should be discouraged from coming to our part of the terrace, and put some coins in her tin. We felt apologetic rather than generous.

Unusual though the mangrove was with its richness of specifically tropical species, our favourite collecting grounds were the montane forests on Mt Kenya and the Aberdare range. Here the trees form mansions, palaces, cathedrals of vegetation, with their roof of leafy branches catching the sunlight in a green or golden lustre, allowing shafts to filter through and lie in a mosaic on the shrubs and mossy banks below, or filled with low cloud drifting through them, misting the bark with a film in whose moisture the lichens flourish, while on the boles and lower branches they hang like coloured rags or spread out to form leafy plates over the mosses. From the upper branches grey or straw-coloured species of *Usnea* dangle their beaded curtains from the twigs, many of them hanging a metre or two metres long, hardly stirring in the quiet reaches of the forest or swaying gently while their tips release drops of rain during a shower. Among the tree heathers above the denser forest, more light penetrates their wiry foliage to fall on the gnarled trunks 10 to 20 feet high, encouraging by its illumination a growth of lichens so profuse that they largely conceal the bark in places and form tufts among the mossy boulders on the ground. In the open glades may be seen colonies of orchids (*Disa* species), and among the heathers or high up on the moorland *Gladiolus watsonioides* lights up the crevices among the cliffs with its spikes of brilliant scarlet flowers above clumps of sword-like leaves.

In 1974 we visited similar country in Tanzania when

staying for a week with Dr D Vesey-Fitzgerald.* His house must be one of the most beautifully situated in the world. It stands alone on a knoll. From its north side we looked on to Kilimanjaro, over which, as the sun rises, the snow-capped summit and belts of cloud become pink and green and yellow until finally the day at first veils and then illumines the vast volcanic cone against the sky. To the south-west of the house our eyes fell on another mountain, closer and in its different configuration as majestic, likewise conical but with one side blown away in an old volcanic eruption to expose the further walls of the crater. This was Mt Meru. The sunset catches it in sheets of gold that change to deep orange as the shadows lengthen across the cliffs round the crater, marking the rocks with a transient fiery margin and in a moment suddenly plunging it all into dusky shadow against the paler sky beyond, the mountain then darkening to a black rocky mass against the stars.

Through the forest slopes of Mt Meru Vesey drove us one day with his African assistants up into the crater, past trees with stags' horn ferns in their branches and further up through glades where the Usneas again hung in the air and draped the trees with their pale curtains. At 9000 feet (3000 m) we found growing on the bole of a large tropical species of *Prunus* a lichen that proved to have an unusual history (*Catapyrenium psoromoides*). The species was first described from England in 1831, having been found on two trees, an elm and an ash, in Sussex. Thereafter it was not seen in Britain again and was dropped from the lichen flora for this country, being regarded as a fungus, though it was reported from a few localities on the European continent. Thus Mt Meru was far from its previously known haunts. But since we reported its presence there[41] it has been identified again in Britain after an interval of about 150 years. Such are the vistas the field naturalist enjoys.

* To our great sorrow he died of a heart attack a few weeks later.

311

East Africa is not a placid region. The high mountains spread on either side of the equator, with their exhilarating air and snowy peaks, the sharply walled valleys and their lakes filled with flamingoes, the rich forests and desiccated hillsides, the contrasts of flamboyance and aridity, scarlet and brown, squelching swamps and seedpods whistling in the wind, are a fit setting for the Masai and Turkana people rattling with iron bracelets and brass rings and ropes of coloured beads, the Kikuyu with their push and drive, the Luo with their pride and skill in rural crafts, and many smaller tribes who are joining the larger and drifting to the towns in white shirts and pressed trousers. And at the same time, however stressed and strained the relations between man and man, the pressure of mankind on the finest assemblage of mammals the world has ever seen is overwhelming.

The mammals of the African savanna represent one of the most remarkable of evolution's triumphs. But they face extinction. Threatened by poachers killing them for their meat and skins and picking over their carcases for tusks and horns, they yield also to man's irresistible competition for their habitats, his ever more pressing claims on their land for his ranching of cattle and cultivation of crops. The conflict that has already largely destroyed wild life in Europe and the USA is being carried into the heart of Africa. Many Africans, politicians among them, are aware of the nature of this tragedy. But it is doubtful whether they have either the will or the power to prevent its culmination any more than British politicians and citizens have been able or even attempted to conserve our moors, woods, and downs, our native and migrant animals and plants, to retain any semblance of the richness of species once known in our forests and – what may surprise the general reader – the sphagnum bogs where multitudinous complexes of plants and animals have been living since the last ice age melted away.

With its variety of peoples far greater in range biologically than anything we know in Europe, the African continent is one of the most difficult places on earth to understand in its linguistic complexity, technical backwardness, and cultural heterogeneity. And, just as in Europe and the USA, the university students in African countries sometimes boil over with impatience at the inertia of their elders, with enthusiasm for wielding power themselves, and with the belief, not entirely false, that their energy will turn the world slightly faster towards the dawn.

One morning when Hildur and I were in Nairobi posting our letters home from the main post office we suddenly found ourselves surrounded by stampeding young men running up the street and barging everyone out of the way. We squeezed ourselves against the wall of the post office, which was solidly stone-built and had small buttresses that gave some protection against the trampling throng, but no sooner had we withdrawn into these niches than the police drove up in armoured cars and began firing plastic bullets into the students immediately in front of us. It was time to take cover, so we pushed through the mêlée into the post office, as did students, shoppers, and anyone else who happened to be in the line of fire. Some of the students tried a spirited defence by ramming the doors shut against an incursion of police who had by now dismounted and were forcing an entry into the building. But this tussle was quickly brought to an end by the police outside throwing canisters of CS gas through the open windows. The pandemonium changed its note as the brownish-grey vapour spread through the crowd, blinding us instantly. Forcing one pair of eyelids open with my right hand I saw that they had failed to close the doors, for beams of light were coming through the gap. By this time the crowd was entirely blinded by the spasm this gas induces in the eyelids – it is impossible to open them by voluntary effort – and people were pushing this way and that till they collided with someone else like so many paramoecium swimming about on a microscope slide. Gripping my colleague's arm with one hand and holding one eye open with the other I started towards the beam of light which was all I could see of the doorway through my torrents of tears, and we zigzagged through the disorientated students and shoppers to the outside again, darting through the crowds round to the back of the building before we dared to take a deep breath of the less polluted air there. In a few moments we could see through our tears, though the glands continued to gush a volume of fluid I would never have believed possible.

"Let's restore our spirits with some coffee," I suggested, breaking into a trot to get away from the gas that still hung around in the street.

"Surely we shouldn't run," said Hildur, "that might make them suspicious of us." So we settled down to a brisk walk towards our favourite cafe, the Sunflower, a few streets away. In half an hour we felt perfectly fit again. Our tears had ceased, and the repulsive metallic taste of the gas had cleared from our palates. In the upshot I was left with a certain admiration for a gas as effectual as it was harmless in preventing an outbreak of violence that might, even if inadvertently, have caused serious injuries to people caught up in the stampede.

As in Kenya, so in Nigeria, the conflict between educated and uneducated is sharp. Josephine and I were in Ibadan in 1971. Coloured lights hung from tree to tree by the dining table in our host's garden on the outskirts of the town. They glowed in the warm, heavy darkness over the party as we sat around talking about Nigeria and Britain. Our Yoruba host, a teacher in the medical college there, together with his wife had invited some of his colleagues and their wives to meet us. All these Nigerians had doctorates from British universities – Oxford, Cambridge, Edinburgh, London. Apart from the glow of colour over the table and some lighted windows in the house nearby, we were surrounded by a dark moonless sky against which the trees were blackly silhouetted. Other houses stood away behind trees in their own grounds, and beyond them lay miles of streets and endless houses, huts, and shanties – Ibadan, a million souls, "the largest village in Africa," our host called it.

They were talking, all of them, eagerly as though they had if not something new to say at least a new audience to say it to, something they wanted us to understand about the identity of their aims with ours despite a disparity in our, not so much lives, as habitats which explained why their sense of accomplishment fell short of what they hoped for.

"It's got worse at night," one of the professors remarked, and his wife added, "Mmm, I don't go out then."

"In the car of course, might have to go out – and then get back home."

"We have to guard our house at night, you know," – one of my fellow guests turned to me – "even at home. People break in, take everything, and they would attack you in bed. I employ a night watchman."

"So do I here," said our host.

"But what about a guard dog?" said one. They were on to a favourite topic of conversation. "He won't run away – he'll attack. A watchman is liable to run away or hide."

"No, they've got wise to the dogs. They put out poisoned meat. It knocks the dog out."

"Watchmen get drunk."

"You have to get a good one. And hope he stays."

The darkness wrapped us up in its warmth. Under the night-blue sky with its bracelet of fairy lights their white eyes looked at us in friendly confidence. Then our host turned to me and paused to find the phrase he sought, his features under a dim orange light expressing at once perplexity, sadness, and amusement –

"You see, we are aliens in our own country."

Africa is a continent where chaos is at a higher level than some other places. In speaking of chaos I am not disparaging Africa, because I mean simply that human order is a less pervasive governor of its technical equipment, its lands and rivers, its infecting organisms than we are accustomed to in Europe. Its moorlands are not meadows, its downlands not ploughed up, its swamps not drained. Roads are often destroyed by storms and washed away, or flooded with water and debris, telephones demand patience as well as electric current to bridge the gaps, cars collapse at the wayside, documents are mislaid, appointments overlooked, addresses unknown, meetings cancelled: all familiar enough in Europe, just more so in Africa.

The disorder is relative. It is also refreshing. The human spirit enjoys being able to pause for a moment on the road to the creation of order out of disorder. There is no question here of actually preferring chaos – the natural state of children and the rebellious prerogative of adolescents. Maturity is the creation of order; so is science and so is art. Sometimes the old order is broken in the process of creation, but the object of the iconoclasm is to prepare for the creation of new order. For the universe which we seek to understand by rational inquiry or aesthetic intuition is found at every step to be ordered, even if events within the order are unpredictable except in terms of probability. To scrutinise a table of random numbers such as statisticians need to use is to recognise that nothing like this occurs in nature, except perhaps at subatomic level.

But surely, you might say, the grains of sand on a beach – are they not thrown down at random? No. As I walk along the beach at Exmouth in South Devon, with the sunlight glittering low over the bay in winter, the patterns they form show me that each of them has been borne from some spot on the sea bed, theoretically calculable and actually so if one considers for example the pebbles on the Chesil Bank in Dorset or Auchmithie beach in Angus, and deposited at some spot below the sea walls in accordance with their weight and shape and the strength of the wave and wind that bore them, so that every grain of the "ribbed sea-sand" conforms to a natural order.

The object of taxonomy is not merely to classify organisms for convenience of reference but chiefly to delineate their natural relationships to each other, their "genetic propinquity" to use Gaylord Simpson's words, so that the order in nature, the pattern of life, is gradually revealed. Through the exploration of nature and examination of samples of it by a variety of techniques, through comparison with what is known and obedience to an internationally agreed body of rules, the taxonomist tries to elucidate the distinction between

316

organisms so that the ones he includes within a set are more closely related to each other genetically than they are to the organisms he excludes from that set. Thus an ever more exact understanding of the order in the universe is reached. And it is the hunt for the genetic pattern – which may be no more than a debatable presumption in the absence of direct knowledge of genetic action in a group of organisms – it is this hunt that is at the heart of the taxonomist's zest for his occupation.

Just as a lover may take no heed of some traits that irk him in his beloved simply because he has allotted her to that role, so does a taxonomist see in an individual plant or animal the features of the species to which he is assigning it despite his discounting the presence or absence of particularities he has observed in some other members of the species. And this generality of understanding, whether reached through the affections or the intellect, is achieved too by the artist who appeals through his vision to our imagination.* Thus there is a point where love, truth, and beauty meet.

Exciting though it is to examine a specimen, to section it, stain it, study it under the microscope, test it chemically – and the mere performance of such techniques, fiddling with slides and chemicals and microscopes, has always given me a kind of pleasure that I suppose a craftsman feels in, for example, making a piece of furniture – yet the search for it in the wild and the discovery of something new, unknown, and mystifying, the voyage of exploration itself, takes the naturalist into the very heart of life. I have sometimes heard the phrase, "There is nothing new left to explore". This may be superficially true in a geographical sense, but biologically it is so false that I am often perplexed at the number of people who are so lacking in curiosity as to travel near or far without equipping themselves to see anything afresh or learn anything new on their journey.

The relative disorder in East Africa extended to knowledge of its lichens, which are a prominent constituent of the

---

* "Shakespeare is above all writers, at least above all modern writers, the poet of nature.... In the writings of other poets a character is too often an individual; in those of Shakespeare it is commonly a species." – SAMUEL JOHNSON[42]

vegetation in the damper regions there: many of the species were little known and some previously undescribed. Over the years from 1974, when we published the first of our joint papers, Hildur Krog and I brought at least some taxonomic order to this fragment of the African scene. But our work can only be a first approximation. Specialists will come along and bring a more precise understanding of these plants, edge their steps a little further up the curve of knowledge, a curve that in time to come will flatten out but never reach the limit of finality.

The excitement of hunting in unexplored localities, and finding previously undescribed species or discovering another link in the pattern of nature, are among the joys of the naturalist's life, and to Hildur when she joined me as partner in our studies I owe their intensification. To sustain any human partnership necessitates attentive effort, implies a will to succeed, draws upon such qualities as patience and discernment, and floats most buoyantly in the stream of a common purpose. Hildur warned me early on that colleagues told her the project would falter and probably fail: scientific collaboration more often than not ends in discord. No doubt the faults in my character sometimes divided us, for I am conscious of being apt to push my plans along heedlessly, of sometimes being stubborn and aloof, of holding mutually contradictory opinions, of lacking the ambition thought proper to a professional man, of following unorthodox faiths, of enjoying the beauty as much as the logic of a mathematical formula, and like that garage mechanic in Kabale of admiring the lines of an engine as much as its output. And no doubt there are many more failings of which I am not so conscious but which can irritate a colleague. Yet it is a sign of our dedication to the project, and doubtless also of my colleague's patience, that we brought it 17 years later, not to completion, for that cannot be an appropriate end of a scientific study, but at least to a recognisable conclusion.[40]

Now that the battered old boat has reached the sea I am grateful for the many friends I picked up on the way, but at the same time hear in my pulse the beat of that mysterious phrase with which James Joyce concluded *Finnegans Wake*:

a way a lone a last a loved a long the

PART 7

30 Harmony with nature

Though I am old with wandering
Through hollow lands and hilly lands,
I will find out where she has gone,
And kiss her lips and take her hands;
And walk among long dappled grass,
And pluck till time and times are done
The silver apples of the moon,
The golden apples of the sun. – W B YEATS. *The Song
of Wandering Aengus.*

One afternoon when I was a boy of 15 I sat by a stretch of the
River Dart flowing smoothly down from the slopes of
Dartmoor, broadening out into a peat-stained pool, and
tumbling over some granite boulders. In the still summer air
I watched the reflections from its surface. On the far bank
was an oak tree whose trunk and branches formed a
motionless image in the moving water. On the river's
buoyant film an occasional bubble drifted by, or a dead twig
fallen from among the green leaves, or a tuft of moss from the
bank upstream. However swiftly or slowly the river ran past
my attentive gaze, the image of the tree, lying before me
unchanging and calm in the ceaseless flow of the water,
seemed to suggest that in the rush of daily life were
reflections, sometimes disturbed and disrupted by the
turbulent falls, sometimes arrestingly clear in the pools –
reflections of ideals that had the quality of permanence.

But while I speculated on the possible existence of eternal
values in the perpetual flux, I also derived comfort from the
thought that as well as permanence there might be stability.
And on recalling in later years that experience and the hopes
it implanted in me, I felt these had been fulfilled, as the

branches of the oak tree stretched their shelter over the river, in the happy home I have been fortunate enough to enjoy since Josephine and I were at last able to settle down after five years of wartime separation. Now for 47 years my loving wife and witty companion, she has exercised a patience that she has rarely allowed to be ruffled by my restless preoccupations, and shown a sympathy for my divagations that has evoked in me, I hope, a response to which I attach especial value in family relationships, and that is kindness. Underpinning as she has done the foundations of my adult life, or rather two lives, medical and botanical, she has provided an exact contrast to the days of my youth, when my emotions were so torn among the discords of my home that I was 35 before I suddenly realised, with a shock of surprise at recognising what I was doing, that I could look back on them with equanimity. And our three daughters have been, at least to me, a continuing education at a university from which I have not yet graduated.

The sight of the happy home that fired my longing when I was invited out to tea with the maths master at my prep school left an unfading vision which, at the time so unfamiliar as to seem beyond attainment, now in recollection appears rather as a premonition of what I strove for and was fortunate enough to attain. And it was more than a premonition of what good fortune might bring: for I felt the impulse it gave me of what could realistically be attempted.

But like many people I puzzle over the nature, the existence even, of this "I" of which I speak. What "I" was attempting anything? The genes with which I was born recognisably interacted with the home and schools in which they were set when a core of self began to be differentiated among the growing network of impressions, feelings, thoughts, memories, and hopes. Are we any more than the onion from which Peer Gynt peeled away layer after layer?

What an incredible number of layers!
Don't we get to the heart of it soon?
No, I'm damned if we do. Right down to the centre
there's nothing but layers – smaller and smaller...
Nature is witty! – IBSEN. *Peer Gynt*, Act 5

Can it be true that a search down through the layers of our being finally reaches – nothing? Does that mixture we think of as our self have no more freedom to make a decision than a plum pudding taken from its basin has to emit steam? I have often shared the thought that worried Boswell[43] –

After the ladies went away, we got into conversation on human liberty and GOD's prescience. Sir William and Mr Nairne could not give up the latter, yet maintained the former: for if it is *certainly foreknown* that I am to be at the play tomorrow, then it is certain I am to be there; and if it is *certain* I am to be there, then I cannot have a liberty either to be there or not. This is the subject which most of all has perplexed and distressed me at different periods of my life...I was quite sober today. But the abstruse question saddened me.*

Yet there is in most of us a sense of creation at times, a moment when we experience a flash of understanding, discover something hitherto unknown or set it in a wider context, make an image that no one has carved before, take a step along a convergent series leading to but never reaching the rainbow's end. The genes that we share with our parents and with so many people, and with our more distant relations and their relations and so on right through to the whole of mankind and beyond, with all of life in fact – these genes make of the individual person a small wave puffed up by the wind sweeping over a great sea of life, a wave that rises to a crest, turns over, and sinks back again into the groundswell of the genetic ocean. What is this wind? I do not believe it is simply a random conjunction of chemicals, for though the concept of randomness is useful when we come to study the results of a multiplicity of causes, I do not see any action in the universe (from atomic level upwards) taking place at random.

We see two components in the world: matter, which is running down to simplicity, and life, which is building up to complexity. Both exist under the reign of causation, but the essential feature of life, however simple the organism we examine, is what at its highest level, man, we describe as creativity or free will. These are two aspects of the same

* No wonder Boswell recorded earlier that year: "I indulged in old hock and became very drunk." (Diary entry for 22 July 1774.)

property of life. Though of course we cannot attribute to an amoeba what in man we call free will, I believe the groundwork for that attribute lies in any organism – and even in simpler organisms than the amoeba, such as those that lack a distinct nucleus, the so-called prokaryotes. It imbues all life.

That there is some sort of self in the middle we all seem to recognise, but on looking over the decisions I have made I see in each of them mainly other components – the influence of my genetic inheritance, the influence of relations and friends, the influence of those multitudinous events we call chance. Deliberate choice in the consciousness of all possible alternatives is an ideal we may strive to attain, but it must of necessity elude us. Rather we are like a potter I watched at work years ago in one of the Torquay potteries. He had his pots on a table in front of him. They had been fired once to the "biscuit" stage and now, cool, they awaited the green glaze he was to put on them. He picked one up, dipped it quickly but not completely in the bucket of liquid glaze, stood it back on the table, and allowed the glaze to run down the sides from the top towards the base, making a pattern determined partly by the viscosity of the glaze, partly by the texture of the pot's surface, partly by his skill in giving little tips and turns to the pot on the table – and partly by chance. In the end chance played a large part in determining the flow of waves and streaks and blobs of glaze on the pot's rough sides. What he started with, the pot and the glaze, what he contended with, the chance flow, what he concluded with, his craftsman's skill – these seem to show me on reflecting about my life how I too tried to turn it this way or that, to make choice more deliberate, chance less decisive. Between conscious skill and casual indolence the potter's judgment, alert or fatigued, attentive or distracted, varied from pot to pot.

Thus, at least in its ideals, our garden by no means stops at merely creating and arranging beautiful spots, but aims to be natural, in order to give peace and rest, and to be a fitting abode in which the soul can wander and find nourishment. – J HARADA[44]

These words perhaps find their fullest expression in the Saihoji garden in Kyoto. Simple in design, it is a small, irregular lake containing some rocks and islands surrounded by trees over a floor of mossy hummocks, lit up by the fresh green of the maple leaves in spring and their fiery scarlets and yellows in autumn. The moss carpet is said to have inspired an evocative poem* in one who wandered round its lake, returned to his desk, but left no trace of his name:

> The nightclothes lie in a heap.
> The tea grows cold in the cups.
> In your eyes is the dew
> From mosses under the maples.

In its woodland glade where it catches the sky in the mirror of its lake through the trees this garden, seemingly so natural is, rather, an intricate work of art, not nature itself but a place where an ideal of a universally harmonious nature comes close to being realised. Even to the Western visitor unable to enter into the devotional framework of those Buddhists who see it as a sacred place it offers a glimpse of eternity, a grove where his dearest wish as he gazes over the moss down to the water is for time to stand still.

> O temps, suspends ton vol! et vous, heures propices,
>   Suspendez votre cours!
> Laissez-nous savourer les rapides délices
>   Des plus beaux de nos jours!
>
> Assez de malheureux ici-bas vous implorent:
>   Coulez, coulez pour eux;
> Prenez avec leurs jours les soins qui les devorent;
>   Oubliez les heureux. – A DE LAMARTINE. *Le Lac.*

---

* Four-line Japanese verse; translator's name uncertain.

Just as it is not the peaks of the mountains but their middle slopes where their fauna and flora are generally most richly diverse and abundant, so on looking back over my life have I found that to be true also of the way I have taken. A certain diffidence that by worldly standards must be counted a failing, and more positively a desire to explore the intellectual and aesthetic riches the world offers us, have combined to mitigate the promptings of ambition and impelled me to decline promotion in both war and peace, in the army and in my job. I have found my greatest satisfaction in the middle slopes rather than among the rocky peaks, with their fine view but absence of life. Now in stepping into a garden I look, not for blooms that win a prize at the local show or a rarity proudly tended in the shelter of a wall, but for a cessation of the flow of time, the entry to a golden age.

Though many gardens made today must from economic necessity offer little more than herbaceous borders and "island beds" filled from garden centres, with areas for the children to play, the dog to run, and the washing to hang, the crowds who visit such parks as Stourhead, Rousham, Blenheim, and West Wycombe are evidence of the attraction the eighteenth century's humane spirit still holds for us. That spirit is the peace and harmony these great creations can transmit from nature to man through art. And the harmony between man and nature that a garden may compose must surely leave a trace that alters the pattern of our lives and induces the resonance of a similar concord between us all. Love and friendship are thus fostered.

Yet the time comes when the flowers are over. The petals turn brown, hang limp, and blow away. We look at the scene with a touch of regret; summer is on the wane. But, while we turn away from the fading, the lily in contrast attains fruition as its pods swell with embryo progeny, split open, and disperse the seeds over the earth.

> If one looks for Tao, there is nothing solid to see;
> If one listens for it, there is nothing loud enough to hear.
> Yet if one uses it, it is inexhaustible. – *Tao Te Ching*, Chapter 35

References

The authors and titles of poems quoted are given in the text and not included in this list. The quotations from the *Tao Te Ching* are from the translation by Arthur Waley: *The Way and its Power*. London: Allen and Unwin, 1934.

1 Johnson S. *An account of the life of Mr Richard Savage*. Oxford: Clarendon Press, 1971.
2 Anonymous. *Reading without tears*. London: Longmans, Green, 1904.
3 Wells H G, Wells G P, Huxley J. *The science of life*. London: Cassell, 1931.
4 Nibs (Nisbet H). *Experiences of a jungle-wallah*. St Albans: Fisher, Knight, 1935.
5 Sitwell O. *Left hand right hand!* (5 vols.) London: Macmillan, 1945–50.
6 Nisbet U. *Spread no wings*. London: Fortune Press, undated.
7 Quennell P. *Baudelaire and the symbolists*. London: Chatto and Windus, 1929.
8 Baudelaire C. In: Le Dantec Y-G, ed. *Oeuvres: Le peintre de la vie moderne*. Vol 2. Paris: La Pleiade (NRF), 1938: 324–63.
9 Starkie E. *Arthur Rimbaud*. London: Faber and Faber, 1938.
10 Churchill W S. Quoted by Balfour J. *Not too correct an aureole*. London: M Russell, 1983.
11 Bloom A. *The closing of the American mind*. New York: Simon and Schuster, 1987.
12 Bonnard G A, ed. *Edward Gibbon: memoirs of my life*. London: Nelson, 1966: 103.
13 Bennet E A. *What Jung really said*. London: Macdonald, 1968.
14 Boswell J. In: Brady F, Pottle F A, eds. *Boswell in search of a wife*. London: Heinemann, 1957.
15 Anonymous. *Memoranda on medical diseases in tropical and sub-tropical areas*. London: HMSO, 1941.
16 Swinscow T D V. Some suicide statistics. *Br Med J* 1951; i: 1417–23.
17 Swinscow D. The holy grail: qui on en servoit? *Folklore* 1944; 55: 29–41.

18 Churchill W S. *The second world war.* Vol 4. London: Cassell, 1951: 740.

19 Alanbrooke, Field Marshal Lord. Diary quoted in: Bryant A. *The turn of the tide, 1939–1943.* London: Collins, 1957: 639.

20 For several details in this paragraph I have relied on: Fairley J. *Remember Arnhem.* Aldershot: Pegasus Journal, 1978.

21 Swinscow T D V. *Statistics at square one.* London: British Medical Association, 1976.

22 Anonymous. The gold-headed cane. (Editorial.) *Br Med J* 1956; i: 791–3.

23 Brain R. The gold-headed cane. *Br Med J* 1956; I: 857–8.

24 British Medical Association. Proceedings of Council. *Br Med J* 1956; i (suppl): 277.

25 British Medical Association. Annual Representative Meeting. *Br Med J* 1956; ii (suppl): 14.

26 Troubridge, Lady. *The book of etiquette.* Vol 2. Place unstated: Associated Book Buyers' Company, 1926: 143. (This work is a neglected masterpiece and wonderful light reading.)

27 Rose F. Record in: *South-Eastern Naturalist and Antiquary* 1952; 57: xix.

28 Johnson S. Rambler No. 5. In: Bate W J, Strauss A B, eds. *The Rambler.* New Haven and London: Yale University Press, 1969: 25–30.

29 Swinscow T D V. A bryophyte flora of Hertfordshire. *Trans Br Bryol Soc* 1959; 3: 509–57.

30 Jung C G. Commentary on "The secret of the golden flower." Trans. Baynes C F (revised). In: *Psychology and the east.* London: Ark, 1978.

31 Swinscow T D V. The amateur in lichenology. (Editorial.) *International Lichenological Newsletter* 1980; 13: 1–3.

32 Hoffenberg R. Non-white doctors in South Africa. *Br Med J* 1962; i: 1202–3.

33 Huxley L. *Life and letters of Sir Joseph Dalton Hooker, OM, GCSI.* Vol 2. London: Murray, 1918: 25.

34 Huxley L. *Life and letters of Sir Joseph Dalton Hooker, OM, GCSI.* Vol 2. London: Murray, 1918: 442.

35 Swinscow T D V. Friedrich Welwitsch, 1806–72. *Biol J Linn Soc* 1972; 4: 269–89.

36 Rose K. *Curzon: a most superior person.* London: Macmillan, 1969: 343.

37 Lovelock J E. *Gaia: a new look at life on earth.* Oxford: Oxford University Press, 1987: 138.

38 Thomas H B, Scott R. *Uganda.* Oxford: Oxford University Press, 1935: 55.

39 Turnbull C M. *The mountain people.* London: Cape, 1972.

40 Swinscow T D V, Krog H. *Macrolichens of East Africa.* London: British Museum (Natural History), 1988.

41 Swinscow T D V, Krog H. The genus *Dermatocarpon* in East Africa with an overlooked species in Britain. *Lichenologist* 1975; 7: 148–54.
42 Johnson S. Preface to the plays of William Shakespeare. In: Greene D, ed. *Samuel Johnson*. Oxford: Oxford University Press, 1984: 421.
43 Boswell J. In: Ryskamp C, Pottle F A, eds. *Boswell: the ominous years*. London: Heinemann, 1963: 46.
44 Harada J. *The gardens of Japan*. London: The Studio, 1928: 39.

Index

Earle, Josephine   75, 88 *see also*
    Swinscow
Eliot, T S, quoted   236
Epsom, move to   39, 42

Family Doctor   158
Ferguson's Gulf   300
Ferns   209
1st Airborne Reconnaissance Squadron
    107
First Army headquarters   91
Fish caught at Looe   15
Flack, Harvey   136, 155, 156, 162
Fort Portal   265
Fraser, Major Hugh   98

Gamage's catalogue   32
Germany, holiday in   64
Gibbon, quoted   70
Gillett, Jan B   290, 293
Gold-headed cane   166
Gordon, Richard   163
Gough, Major C F H   107, 110
Gregg E A   168
Grey-Turner, Elston   136

Haig, Sir Douglas (later Earl Haig)
    4, 11, 13, 61
Harada J, quoted   324
Health magazine   156
Hext, skill with cucumbers   19
Hicks, Andrew   289
Hill, Austin Bradford   154
Hoffenberg, Raymond   239, 290
Holy Grail   86, 93
Hopkins, Gerard Manley, quoted
    205
Horner, Gerald   131, 134, 136
Hughes, Gordon   68
Huxley, Julian   37

Ibadan   314
Ibsen, quoted   322

James, Peter   227, 229
Japanese gardens   325
Johnson, Peter   76, 77

Johnson, Samuel, quoted   211
Journal committee of BMA   129, 159
Joyce, James, quoted   318

Kaabong   279
Kabale   259
Kabuye, Christine   290
Kanaba Gap   255
Karamoja   253, 276
Katende, Anthony   230, 252, 264, 267,
    269, 276, 287
Katende, Mrs   254, 287
Keats, quoted   67
Kelly College   34, 42
Keswick, Edith   8, 9
Kibwezi   293, 308
Kidepo   282
Kirstenbosch   245
Kisoro   256, 286
Knebworth   139, 189
Kreisler, Fritz   209
Krog, Hildur   289, 294, 305, 307, 313,
    318
Kyoto   325

Lake Rudolf   299, 300
Lamartine, Alphonse de, quoted   325
Lambert, Gillian   228
Lancet   129, 135
Lecky W E H   150
Lichenologist   227
Lichens   221, 224
Liston R P   151, 159, 160
Liverpool School of Tropical Medicine
    88
Looe, living at   15
Lovelock J E, quoted   267
Lye, Kåre   251, 261, 267, 269

Mackinder's Camp   295
Makerere University (College)   249
Mann, Thomas, quoted   304
Manum, S   251
Masaka   284
May (Cox)   189
Mbarara   284
Medwar P B   217
Medical Association of South Africa
    240

332